RELIGIOUS AND SOCIAL REVOLUTION IN ANCIENT INDIA

Encyclopaedic History of India Series

RELIGIOUS AND SOCIAL REVOLUTION IN ANCIENT INDIA

Dr. Mahesh Vikram Singh
Professor, Deptt. of History
Mahatma Gandhi Kashi Vidyapeeth
Varanasi (UP)

Dr. Brij Bhushan Shrivastava
Head of Deptt., Ancient History, Archeology & Culture
SMMTPG College, Ballia (UP)

CENTRUM PRESS
NEW DELHI-110002 (INDIA)

CENTRUM PRESS

H.O.: 4360/4, Ansari Road, Daryaganj,
New Delhi-110002 (India)
Tel: 23278000, 23261597, 23255577, 23286875

B.O.: No. 1015, Ist Main Road, BSK IIIrd Stage,
IIIrd Phase, IIIrd Block, Bangalore-560085 (INDIA)
Tel: 080-41723429

Email: centrumpress@gmail.com
Visit us at: www.centrumpress.com

Religious and Social Revolution in Ancient India

First Edition, 2011

ISBN 978-93-80836-57-7

PRINTED IN INDIA

Printed at Mehra Offset Press, Delhi

प्रो. विपिन चंद्रा
अध्यक्ष
Prof. Bipan Chandra
Chairman

नेशनल बुक ट्रस्ट, इंडिया
नेहरू भवन
5 इंस्टीट्यूशनल एरिया, फेज़-II, वसंत कुंज, नई दिल्ली-110 070
फोन/ Phone: 011-26121880 फैक्स/ Fax: 011-26121883

NATIONAL BOOK TRUST, INDIA
Nehru Bhawan
5 Institutional Area, Phase II, Vasant Kunj, New Delhi-110 070
ई-मेल / E-mail: chairman@nbtindia.org.in
वेबसाइट / Website: www.nbtindia.org.in

FOREWORD

The term 'history' is derived from the Greek word 'historia' that means knowledge acquired through investigation. Obviously, this knowledge can be correct if the method of investigation is objective and not vitiated by any kind of bias. In other words, if the study of human past is comprehensive and obtained through scientific inquiry, it can provide perspective on the present day problems and help one plan for the future.

A true historian has to identify the sources that can be most useful in a given context. Documents, coins, archaeology, anthropology, geography, travel accounts, oral traditions, mythology and so on can be useful but they can be used only after their veracity is tested and they are critically examined. They should be checked and counter-checked.

Over the centuries, one finds the study and writing of history vitiated by biases. There are numerous instances in which historical data have been distorted to support or oppose certain preconceived ideas and purposes. Strictly speaking such history is just like fiction to accord with preconceived notions and serve some ulterior purposes.

The study of the past has never been static. Conclusions go on changing because of the discovery of new materials and tools of investigation. To give a concrete example, the carbon 14 or radiocarbon dating test has revolutionized the study of civilizations and settlements, especially of prehistoric times, for which written documents, coins, etc. are seldom available. This method has enabled historians to determine more accurately than before the time period of a particular civilization or settlement. This method was discovered only 70 years ago by American scientists.

In our country, excavations brought to light the Indus Valley Civilization and its various features, hitherto unknown. Similarly, no complete text of Kautilya's Arthashastra was available before it was discovered by Shamasastry, the chief of the Mysore Government Oriental Library in the first decade of the last century. Likewise, people's knowledge of the history of the Buddhist period got extended after excavations at Sarnath and the ruins of the Asokan period at Patna. In the future, if the Harappan inscriptions are deciphered, our knowledge of the Indus Valley Civilization will increase enormously. All these instances underline the fact that our knowledge of history is never static and its frontiers go on extending.

In the light of what has been said above the encyclopedic history is going to be of great help to students interested in Indian history. It is comprehensive and as far as possible free from biases. It includes the latest materials, and objective conclusions.

Prof . Bipan Chandra
Professor Emeritus, JNU
Chairman, National Book Trust, India

Contents

Preface (*viii*)

1. Buddhism, Jainism and other Religious Ideas 1
2. Jainism 15
3. Jain Doctrines of Relativity 77
4. Karma Theory 115
5. Origins of Guru-Shishya Parampara 147
6. Jain Texts 167
7. Other Heterodox Ideas 185
8. Period of Mahajanpadas 203

Bibliography 285

Index 293

Preface

The people of India have had a continuous civilization since 2500 B.C., when the inhabitants of the Indus River valley developed an urban culture based on commerce and sustained by agricultural trade. This civilization declined around 1500 B.C., probably due to ecological changes. During the second millennium B.C., pastoral, Aryan-speaking tribes migrated from the northwest into the subcontinent. As they settled in the middle Ganges River valley, they adapted to antecedent cultures.

The political map of ancient and medieval India was made up of myriad kingdoms with fluctuating boundaries. In the 4th and 5th centuries A.D., northern India was unified under the Gupta Dynasty. During this period, known as India's Golden Age, Hindu culture and political administration reached new heights. Islam spread across the Indian subcontinent over a period of 500 years. In the 10th and 11th centuries, Turks and Afghans invaded India and established sultanates in Delhi. In the early 16th century, descendants of Genghis Khan swept across the Khyber Pass and established the Mughal (Mogul) Dynasty, which lasted for 200 years. From the 11th to the 15th centuries, southern India was dominated by Hindu Chola and Vijayanagar Dynasties. During this time, the two systems—the prevailing Hindu and Muslim—mingled, leaving lasting cultural influences on each other.

The first British outpost in South Asia was established in 1619 at Surat on the northwestern coast. Later in the century, the East India Company opened permanent trading stations at Madras, Bombay, and Calcutta, each under the protection of native rulers. The British expanded their influence from these footholds until, by the 1850s, they controlled most of present-day India, Pakistan, and Bangladesh. In 1857, a rebellion in north India led by mutinous Indian soldiers caused the British Parliament to transfer all political power from the East India Company to the Crown. Great Britain began administering most of India directly while controlling the rest through treaties with local rulers.

In the late 1800s, the first steps were taken toward self-government in British India with the appointment of Indian councillors to advise the British viceroy and the establishment of provincial councils with Indian members; the British subsequently widened participation in legislative councils. Beginning in 1920, Indian leader Mohandas K. Gandhi transformed the Indian National Congress political party into a mass movement to campaign against British colonial rule.

—Authors

1

Buddhism, Jainism and other Religious Ideas

The sixth century B.C. was an important stage in Indian history as far as the development of new religions is concerned. In this period, we notice a growing opposition to the ritualistic orthodox ideas of the Brahmanas. This ultimately led to the emergence of many heterodox religious movements. Among these Buddhism and Jainism developed into well organised popular religions.

Firstly it is important to explain the factors that were responsible for the emergence and growth of heterodox ideas. Then it interesting to know how Buddha and Mahavira tried to find a solution in their own ways to end human suffering. Since the causes for the emergence of the two religions are common in nature, there is some similarity in the principles adopted by these religions. However, they differ completely on some of the basic principles.

The other heterodox religious ideas which were current during the sixth century B.C. have also been dealt with.

Rise of New Religious Ideas

The new religious ideas during this period emerged out of the prevailing social, economic and religious conditions. Let us examine some of the basic reasons which contributed to their emergence:

i) The Vedic religious practices had become cumbersome, and in the context of the new society of the period had become in many cases meaningless ceremonies. Sacrifices and rituals increased and became more elaborate and expensive. With the breakup of communities, the participation in these practices also became restricted and as such irrelevant to many sections in the society.

ii) Growing importance of sacrifices and rituals established the domination of the Brahmanas in the society. They acted both as priests and teachers and through their monopoly of performing sacred religious rites, they claimed the highest position in the society which was now divided into four vamas.

iii) Contemporary economic and political developments, on the other hand, helped the emergence of new social groups which acquired considerable economic power. You have seen that merchants living in cities or even rich agricultural householders possessed considerable wealth. Similarly, the Kshatriyas, whether in the monarchies or in the gana-samghas, came to wield much more political power than before. These social groups were opposed to the social positions defined for them by the Brahrnanas on the basis of their heredity. As Buddhism and Jainism did not give much importance to the notion of birth for social status, they attracted the Vaisyas to their folds.

Similarly, the Kshatriyas i.e. the ruling class were also unhappy with Brahmanical domination. Briefly put, it was basically the discontent generated hy the dominant position of the Brahmanas in the society, which contributed to the social support behind the new religious ideas. It is worth remembering that both Buddha and Mahavira came from Kshatriya class but in their search for answers to the pressing problems of society they went beyond boundaries set by their birth. Further, when we try to find out how their ideas were received by their contemporaries, we notice that they had a range of people responding to them: Kings, big merchants, rich householders, Brahmans and even courtesans. They all represented the new society which was emerging in the sixth century B.C. and Buddha and Mahavira, and other thinkers of those times, in their own ways, responded to the problems of a new social order. The Vedic ritualistic practices had ceased to be of much relevance to this new social order.

Buddha and Mahavira, were by no means, the first to criticise the existing religious beliefs. Many religious preachers before them, like Kapila, Makkali Gosala, Ajita Kesakambalin and Pakuda Kachchayana had already highlighted the evils of the Vedic religions. They also developed new ideas on life and God. New philosophies were also being preached. iiowever, it was Buddha and Mahavira, who provided an alternative religious order. This was the background which helped the emergence and establishment of new religious orders in the sixth century B.C. Among these Buddhism and Jainism were most popular and well organised. We will now discuss the origin and development of Buddhism and Jainism separately.

To hundreds of millions outside the country, India is simply the land of the Buddha. Buddhism, and not any political system or material export, still remains for all time the most important discovery of India for the great majority of Asian people. The art and architecture of Burma, Thailand, Korea, Japan, and China, and hence world art, would be much poorer without Buddhist motifs developed under Indian influence. The Buddhist scriptures constitute by far the greater part of classical Mongol and Tibetan literature. The entire state machinery of Tibet consisted till 1959 of a few Buddhist monasteries and their nominees.

The people of Ceylon, Burma, Thailand, and Indo-China not only follow the Buddhist creed (as they understand it), but regard that religion as the prime civilising influence at the dawn of their various histories. The powerful and indispensable role of Buddhist monasteries in the economic development of China, especially of the hinterland during the fifth and sixth centuries A.D., has only recently been realised.

Countless pilgrims from many distant countries braved and still suffer the rigours of deserts, high snow-clad mountains, and typhoon-swept ocean to visit Indian sites connected with incidents in the Buddha's life. The westward spread of the religion was even more marked in its day than that to the east. The gigantic 60-metrehigh statues of the Buddha carved out of the living rock at Baraian (Afghanistan) would by themselves be sufficient testimony. Innumerable ruined stupas (relic monuments) in central Asia bear further witness. The religion not only influenced Manichaeanism but must earlier have helped in the formation of Christianity.

The scholars who wrote die Dead Sea scrolls, though good Jews, show peculiarities that appear to be of Buddhist origin. Their practice of living in a monastery almost on top of a necropolis would be repulsive to Judaism, though quite agreeable to Buddhists. The 'Teacher of Righteousness' mentioned in the documents of this (probably Essene) Palestinian foundation bears the precise title of the Buddha. It is not, therefore, surprising that the Sermon on the Mount should sound more familiar to Buddhists than to the followers of the Old Testament who first heard it preached. Some of the Christ's miracles such as walking on the water were current much earlier in literature about the life of the Buddha. For that matter, the Christian saint's legend that goes under the title 'Barlaam and Josaphat' is a direct adaptation of the Buddha's life-story.

The Barmecides, an important ministerial family under the Abbasid Caliph Harun al-Rashid of Baghdad (immortalised in the Arabian Nights) were once the hereditary abbots (paramaka) of the Buddhist monastery of Naobehar. As new converts to Islam, they came under suspicion of retaining some heretical doctrines from their old religion. This extraordinary diffusion has two striking but mutually inconsistent features. The dissemination outside India was without force of arms or corresponding growth of Indian political influence. The name of Asoka (Sanskrit, Asoka) is venerated far beyond his own country because he was the great Buddhist emperor, not for any conquest or other manifestation of power. The Kushanas did rule parts of central Asia and India together; but they also patronised, besides Buddhism, several other Indian cults and gods such as Siva, whose worship nevertheless did not travel far. Beginning with Min-ti of the Han dynasty, a long line of Chinese emperors went out of their way to invite Buddhist missionaries. Yet, in the very land of its origin, Buddhism vanished but for traces on the northeastern fringe of India.

This complete internal eclipse unaccountably runs contrary to the external success. Even today educated Indians would generally be aghast or indignant if told that Buddhism-which they regard as a passing aberration-was their country's outstanding contribution to world culture. The 1500 years of the full cycle of the rise, spread, and decline of Buddhism saw India change over from semi-pastoral tribal life to the first absolute monarchies and then to feudalism.

The varying roles played at different stages by this religion inside the country of its origin must therefore occupy a central place in any serious treatment of Indian civilisation. At the same time we must try to explain the dual and puzzling development of the doctrine within and outside the country. The sixth century B.C. produced the philosophy of Confucius in China and the sweeping reforms of Zoroaster in Iran. In the middle of the Gangetic basin there were many entirely new teachers of whom the Buddha was only one, not the most popular in his own day. The rival doctrines are known mostly through biased reports in hostile religious documents. However, Jainism still survives in India, and traces its origins to founders before the Buddha. The Ajivikas are known from Mysore inscriptions to have survived as late as the fourteenth century A.D.

The main proponents of these two sects, Mahavira (though the Jain claim a long line of earlier Tirthamkaras of whom Parsva might be historical) and Makkhali Gosala respectively, were two of the numerous contemporaries of the Buddha who taught in much the same places. The Buddha himself took over and extended the teaching of two elder contemporaries, Alara of an Aryan Kalaraa tribe, and Uddaka, son of Rama. Therefore, Buddhism cannot be treated solely as a personal achievement of its unquestionably great founder nor was its decline due to the imperfections of humanity. Obviously, the simultaneous rise of so many sects of considerable appeal and prominence in one narrow region implies some social need that older doctrines could not satisfy.

This need can be analysed by looking for the factors common to all the new lines of teachers, and inspection of the new classes of disciples. If it were a matter of simple continuity and gradual evolution, the new religions should have arisen on the Indus with its ruined memories of a great civilisation, or in the north-west which had been. and remained the centre of Vedic culture for centuries, or in Kuru-land which was the locus of the Mahabharata story and a suitable place for the morality with which the great epic is overloaded, or at Mathura from which a new and powerful cult of Krishna as all-god was eventually to spread. Why did the newest and in some cultural respects rather backward lands of the east take the lead in the most advanced forms of religion?

The existence of new classes in the Gangetic basin of the sixth century is undeniable. The free peasants and farmers were one. The neo-Vedic pastoral class of vaisyas within the tribe was replaced by agriculturists for whom the tribe had ceased to exist. Traders had become so wealthy that the most important person in an eastern town was generally the sreshthi. The term, not known earlier, is derived from the word for Superior', or 'pre-eminent'. The sreshthi was actually a financier or banker, sometimes the head of a trade guild. Even absolute, despotic kings treated these sreshthis with respect, though they had no direct voice in politics. However, the prime indicator for the new class is the changed significance of the word gahapati (Sanskrit, grihapati)', literally 'lord of the house', equivalent hereafter to the Roman paterfamilias. It had meant the host and principal sacrificer at any considerable but not royal sacrifice in Vedic and Brahmana literature.

Now, for the first time, it came to mean the head of a large patriarchal household of any caste who commanded respect primarily because of his wealth, whether gained by trade, manufacture, or farming; but no longer wealth measured simply in cattle. The gahapati, as the executive member of the new propertied class, could do what he liked with the riches at his disposal, though obliged to support members of the household and bound by the inheritance laws of his kinship group; but he was no longer bound by tribal regulations. The new class position was obscured for a while by formal ties of caste and kinship, which became progressively lighter. Even the word gotra ('cowpen') used earlier to denote the exogamous clan unit would hereafter mean also the gahapati's large patriarchal family, though the older meaning of gotra was never lost like the older meaning of grihapati. Both agriculturists and traders suffered from the constant warfare which was regularly preceded by Vedic yajna fire sacrifice.

The trader had to be on good terms with people beyond the territory of his tribe and state; but he also needed safe trade routes, free from robbers. A part of this demand could be satisfied only by the growth of a 'universal monarchy', a single state that would end petty warfare and police the entire countryside. But trade always extended beyond political frontiers.

The existence of free, tenant or land-owning peasants (kassaka, karshaka), necessarily implied by the existence of gahapati and shresthi, is clear from the texts. As explained, large-scale slave labour was not available. Food-gatherers were too few, rarely inclined to perform the hard, regular labour of a farm. They were drawn into food production mostly when their lands were cleared by others; in feudal and modern times, by famine.

(This last led to the formation of 'slave' castes like the Haris, out of aboriginals who had contracted away their freedom for bare but regular subsistence; their labour, known to the last generation, was inefficient and unproductive.) The real peasantry had to derive in the main from more advanced 'Aryan' tribesmen, who had begun to clear land on their own, in small groups not always in touch with most of the tribe. The only incentive they had to produce any surplus came from trade in that surplus. This in turn was possible only if there were no clan obligation to share the surplus food, if cattle were not owned in common, arid the plots were not subject to redistribution by tribal councils-in a word, private property in farm animals, in land and its produce.

The Punjab remained conservative in this respect; tribal life continued much as before, with nearly the same type of chieftain-king as in the Brakmattas. Yajurvedic kingship was a powerful deterrent to unlimited agrarian production by individual households, and an insupportable burden for the peasantry. Peace and lower taxes were essential. Cattle and other animals were requisitioned in increasing number for the yajna without payment. This is shown by Pali stories of royal fire-sacrifices. The strain upon regular agriculture was intolerable. Only a few brahmin priests (such as those to whom the sixthcentury monarchs like Pasenadi and Bimbisara gave away whole villages) gained permanently. Thus, it is natural that all the new sects denied flatly the validity of any ritual, especially of Vedic ritual. This included brahmin teachers, as, for example, Purana Kassapa and Samjaya, son of Belatthi.

Regular human sacrifices had gone out of brahmin fashion by the time of the Satapatha Brahmana, in spite of the human victims listed in the Yajurveda. Sporadic human sacrifice did continue, being considered necessary to make impregnable such strong points as bastions and city gates and to prevent dams from being swept away by flood waters. The victim had to be buried in the foundations of the new construction in such cases. But these exceptional sacrifices were very rare, frowned upon, and never conducted according to Vedic rites. The horse sacrifice was also rather rare. None is, in fact, definitely recorded for the Gangetic basin till a brief and futile revival in the second century.

The main Vedic sacrifice was of cattle, natural in a predominantly pastoral society. How completely the sixthcentury reform drove this, too, out of fashion is seen by the absolute Hindu tabu upon cattle-killing and beef-eating which is still in force, though now senseless, uneconomic, and cruel to the cattle in a land short of pasturage. A modern orthodox Hindu would place beef-eating on the same level as cannibalism, whereas Vedic brahmins had fattened upon a steady diet of sacrificed beef. The Satapatha Brahmana gives ritual arguments in a famous passage why the flesh of cow and cart-ox (anaduh; nothing is said about the bull) should not be eaten. The whole passage ends in a blunt and now embarrassing statement by the leading brahmin party of Yajnavalkya: "That may very well be; but as long as (it puts) flesh on (my) body, I shall continue to eat it." When the Upanishads were added to supplement the various Brahmanas, no direct acknowledgement was made of any change; but the contents of brahmin books became entirely different. The yajna was now cited primarily for some mystical philosophy with generally fantastic interpretation, not for its original blood-and-guts performance.

The Upanishadic brahmins, who had once finished their studies near or to the west of the Indus, now went even to eastern kshatriyas like Asvapati Kaikeya and Pravahana Jaivali to learn the 'inner significance' of the sacrifice. There appeared a new concept, Brahma, an undefined divine essence whereof the attainment is superior to all other human endeavour. For the rest, the questions dealt with by the Upanishads are just those which the other sixth-century Gangetic philosophers treated: What is the nature of the soul, if there is a soul? What happens to man alter death? What is the supreme good for man? No reference was made to Buddhism or any other anti-brahmin religious sect. This has led many to believe that the oldest Upanishads must all precede Buddhism. The mention of a past king 'Ajatasatru of Kasi' in the Upanishad attached to the Satapatha Brahmana shows that this cannot always be true, for that king was the Buddha's younger contemporary. The nascent doctrines were 'in the air' of the sixth century.

Two quotations suffice to prove the economic basis of the tabu on beefeating. Archaic verses ascribed to the Buddha read, "Cattle are our friends, just like patents and other relatives, for cultivation depends upon them. They give food, strength, freshness of complexion and happiness. Knowing this, brahmins of old did not kill cattle" (Sutta-nipata, 295-6). There was no question of beef-eating as a sin in the earlier days of the ban. Mao Tse-tung's Report of March 1927 on the peasant uprising in Hunan says, "Draught-oxen are a treasure to the peasants.

As it is practically a religious tenet that "Those who slaughter cattle in this life will themselves become cattle in the next, draught oxen must never be killed. Before coming to power, the peasants had no means of stopping the slaughter of cattle except the religious tabu. Since the rise of the Peasant. Associations, they have extended their jurisdiction even over cattle and have prohibited their slaughter in the cities. Of the six beef shops in the county town of Hsiangtan, five are now closed and the remaining one sells only the beef of sick or disabled cattle. Cattle slaughter is prohibited throughout the county of Hengshan. A peasant whose cow stumbled and broke a leg had to consult the Peasant Association before he dared kill it...". That the Chinese peasant did not use the cow's milk, butter, cheese or curds presumably accounts for the difference between his position and that of the Indian peasant.

The exact parallel to the development of a universal monarchy would have been a single exclusive religion with a strict unitary ritual. I his was impossible for the society in question without an immense use of force. The limitless Gangetic forest could have sheltered those for whom a separate common ritual was an indispensable common bond, as ritual observances remain even now in India. The new eastern teachers rose above all ritual and broke the strongest tabu by eating cooked food from the hands of another caste however low, or even leftovers of soiled food. What the last means is difficult to explain to anyone who does not know that most Indians would rather go hungry, and many have preferred death by starvation to eating soiled food or that prepared by a person of lower caste.

The leaders of the various innovating sects and their monkish followers (not the lay believers) gained their livelihood mostly by alms. This was at base a reversion to food-gathering. Many continued to prefer a life of solitude in the jungle. They killed nothing and obtained what food they required from vegetation. Only salt was acceptable from human hands to these extreme ascetics. Celibacy and abstinence from holding property made the new teachers much more economic than greedy fire priests in an acquisitive society.

The Yajurvedic and later brahmins hoped for rich gifts in unlimited quantity and actually claimed to have received them from legendary ancient kings: numberless elephants, cattle, chariots, beautiful slave women, and many pieces of gold. The sharp impression made even upon brahmin practices by the new asceticism was indelible; poverty and penance remained high ideals ever afterwards. The Upanishads, too, tell of a famished brahmin accepting soiled food from a low-caste elephant driver. Another such brahmin spied upon a chant-and-dance for food by dog-totem tribesmen. The yajna was ended for the easterners in all but theory; the brahmin of the future would eventually agree to serve all castes as priests and to adapt new worships to old forms in order to gain his livelihood-paying lip service to the Vedas all the while.

The Middle Way

The roots of the main schools of later Indian philosophy can clearly be discerned in the sixth century B.C. Ajita, nicknamed 'with the hair blanket" (Kesakambali), preached a thoroughgoing materialist doctrine: good deeds and charity gained a man nothing in the end. His body dissolved into the primary elements at death, no matter what he had or had not done. Nothing remained. Good and evil, charity and compassion were all irrelevant to a man's fate. The Lokayata school from which the brutally practical theories of Magadhan statecraft were to develop seems to have taken a great deal from this Ajita, though the outstanding name in Indian materialism is of Carvaka, whose original teachings are lost. Pakudha Katyayana added three more to the list of primary indestructible elements (which were normally taken as earth, water, air, and light): namely, happiness, sorrow, and life. These, too, could be neither created nor destroyed. The sword stroke that seemed to end life was a mere passage of metal between molecules of flesh and bone, with no power over man. This could be the origin of the Vaiseshika school of later times. Purana of the Kassapa brahmin gotra may have laid the foundations of Samkhya doctrine in regarding the soul as distinct from the body, unaffected by anything that happened to the body.

His immediate following later merged into that of Makkhali Gosala, a teacher who believed that the soul had to pass through a vast, immutable cycle of foreordained rebirths, regardless of any action by the particular body to which it was attached in each birth. The Jain Mahavira followed the four rules ascribed to his predecessor Parsva: Taking no life (ahimsa), taking no property from others, possessing no property of one's own, and truthfulness. To these he added a fifth, celibacy. Though a kshatriya of high Licchavi tribal birth, Mahavira reached his ultimate state of knowledge by the severest penance and constant meditation. He abandoned even the three sheet-like togas allowed for a monk by Parsva, to go stark naked. His followers would not drink water without straining and filtering it, lest some life be destroyed thereby. A careless step might kill some insect.

The in-breath must also be filtered through a piece of cloth, not for hygiene but to save any life floating in the air. Castigating one's own flesh by long hours in the hot sun and the rain was not only a Jain fashion but also the practice of many other teachers and sects of the day. Gosala also went naked, but drank and practised orgiastic sexual rites which doubtless originated in contemporary primitive fertility cults.

Even so did later Tantric rites originate, but they were not always put into practice, being more often sublimated through mystical interpretation and symbolic innocuous substitution. It should never be forgotten that there always existed a marginal population to whom sorcery, fertility rites and secret tribal cults seemed essential. People who felt dissatisfied with official 'civilised' religion continued to learn and adopt these secret rites through the ages down to Muslim times and even later, in the belief that they thereby achieved some special powers or at least a short cut to perfection. Gosala's actions were regarded as obscene self-indulgence in his own day, but the reports are of hostile origin.

Tribal medicine-man's rites left other marks upon ascetic life in the form of punishing observances: total abstinence from food and water for incredible periods, control of breath, maintaining excessively contorted bodily postures-all these and many other senseless exercises were supposed to confer extraordinary powers. It was thought that true adepts could become invisible or fly through the air at will. Later yoga practices and physical poses developed from this. Yoga within limits is a good system of exercise in a hot climate for people who do not live by muscular exertion and hard physical labour. The most that one can attain by it is some measure of control over normally involuntary functions of the body, and good health; but no supernatural powers. Buddhism stood between the two extremes: unrestrained individualistic self-indulgence and equally individualistic but preposterous ascetic punishment of the body. Hence its steady rise, and its name "The Middle Way".

The core of Buddhism is the Noble (arya) Eightfold Path. The first of the eight steps is proper vision: this world is filled with sorrow generated by uncontrolled desire, greed, cupidity and self-seeking on the part of mankind. The quenching of this desire is the path to peace for all; the eightfold path is the way that leads to this end. So much for the first step, proper vision.

The second step is proper aims: not to increase one's wealth and power at the expense of others, not to be lost in the enjoyment of the senses and in luxury; to love others in full measure and to increase the happiness of others-this is proper design. Third step, proper speech: lies, calumny, vituperation, useless chatter, and such misuse of the tongue spoils the organisation of society. Quarrels arise that may lead to violence and killing. Therefore, correct speech must be truthful, conducive to mutual friendship, endearing, and measured. Fourth step, proper action: taking life, theft, adultery and such other actions of the body would lead to great disasters in society. Therefore it is necessary to abstain from killing, stealing, fornication; and to do such positive deeds as will lead to the benefit of other people. Fifth step, proper livelihood: no man should make his living by means that harm society, e.g. by the sale of liquor, dealing in animals for butchery, etc. Pure and honest methods alone should be followed. Sixth step, correct mental exercise: not to let evil thoughts enter the mind, to remove evil thoughts already in the mind, to generate good thoughts actively in the mind, and to carry to fulfilment the good thoughts that are already within the mind.

This sort of active mental self-discipline is the sixth of the eight steps. Seventh step, correct awareness: to be ever conscious that the body is made of unclean substances, to examine constantly the sensations of pleasure and pain in the body, to examine one's own mind, to meditate upon the evils that come from bonds of the flesh and attachments of the mind; and to meditate upon ways for the removal of these evils. Eighth step, proper meditation: this is a carefully worked out mental training in concentration. Briefly, it is to Buddhism what 'gymnastics' was to the Greek body.

Clearly, this was the most social of religions; the applications of its various steps are carefully developed and expounded in a long series of discourses ascribed to the Buddha. There were regulations specially meant for the monk, such as celibacy, which were not binding upon the lay follower. The Buddhist monastic Order was organised and conducted its meetings precisely on the lines of the tribal sabha assembly. The total number of monks in the Buddhist Samgha (Order) could not have exceeded 500 during the Teacher's lifetime, nor is there any credible record of their having all gathered together at any one time till after his death.

The rules of the Order which form a special vinaya (discipline) section of the Buddhist Canon are all ascribed to die Buddha himself in order to lend them his authority; but they are obviously of later origin for the most part, though formulated not long after his death. During his lifetime, and even long afterwards, any group of six or more almsmen could, if so minded, frame their own special rules and follow their own separate discipline without interference by the rest of the Order, provided, of course, they respected the main doctrine.

The monk was permitted no property beyond a begging-bowl, a water-pot, at most three pieces of plain, unembroidered, patternless cloth (preferably pieced together from rags) for wear; oil-jug, razor, needle and thread, and a staff. The more delicate were allowed plain sandals. Though he might beg his food in a village or town, the one daily meal of leftover scraps (mixed together to minimise any pleasure of taste) had to be eaten before noon. Nor could the almsman stay in a householder's dwelling even for a single night (later altered to permit three nights or less).

His residence had to be outside the settlement, in a grove, cave (originally, natural cave), under a tree, or by a corpse-enclosure into which dead bodies were thrown to be eaten by birds and animals, or sometimes cremated. These were just the places where the most gruesome primitive rites were practised, including cannibalism for the attainment of magic powers. The monk was enjoined not to let the terrifying sights move him, but to overcome all such perils by his own firm determination. For the three or four months of the rains the residence had to be in some one place. Otherwise, he must travel on foot (never by chariot, elephant, horse, cart, or packanimal) to preach to the people.

The early monks, like the Buddha himself, were expert food-gatherers, as is evident from their recorded arguments about begging soiled food from other human beings; long trips through the wilderness did not trouble them. Generally they would accompany caravans, but even then pass the night outside the camp. The Buddhist monk was forbidden labour for profit and for agriculture, having to live on alms or by gathering food in the forest without the taking of life; only thus would he be free to concentrate upon his social dudes, the obligation to lead all to the proper Way. His own salvation was freedom from the cycle of rebirth, nirvana, a mysterious ideal never fully explained.

The Buddha would refuse to answer questions as to the existence or non-existence of a soul. However, the doctrine of rebirth and transmigration (no matter what part of personality was reborn) seemed natural to contemporary society. The Vedas and Upanishads did not have this. Though it was only one step from the primitive conception of return of the departed individual to an animal totem, the step was of the utmost importance. Primitive reversion to one specific totem was obligator)', independent of the individual's will.

Buddhist transmigration depended upon karma, the man's action throughout his life. Karma as merit would correspond not only to a store of acquired money or harvested grain, but would also come to fruition at the proper time as a seed bore fruit or a loan matured. Every living creature could perform some karma which would raise it after death to rebirth in a suitable body; a better body if the karma were good, a mean and vile one, say of an insect or animal, if the karma were evil. Even the gods were subject to karma. Indra himself might fall from his particular heaven after the course of his previous karma was fully run; an ordinary man could be reborn in the world of the gods, even as an Indra, to enjoy a life of heavenly pleasure for aeons-but not for ever.

The Buddha and the truly enlightened monks were released from the otherwise endless chain of births, death, and rebirth. The eightfold path and the Middle Way, a pure life of no possessions and no worldly attachment, dispassionate and compassionate, devoted to helping mankind discover the right trail through the maze of conflicting personal desires, would achieve ultimate liberation for the best of the bhikshu almsmen.

2

Jainism

Jainism is an ancient dharmic religion from India that prescribes a path of non-violence for all forms of living beings in this world. Its philosophy and practice relies mainly on self-effort in progressing the soul on the spiritual ladder to divine consciousness. Any soul which has conquered its own inner enemies and achieved the state of supreme being is called *jina* (Conqueror or Victor). Jainism is often referred to as *Jain Dharma* or *Shraman Dharma* or the religion of Nirgantha by ancient texts. Jainism was revived by a lineage of 24 enlightened ascetics called tirthankaras culminating with Parshva (9th century BCE) and Mahavira (6th century BCE). In the modern world, it is a small but influential religious minority with as many as 4.9 million followers in India, and successful growing immigrant communities in North America, Western Europe, the Far East, Australia and elsewhere. Jainism is divided into Digambaras and Swetambaras.

Jains have sustained the ancient *Shraman* or ascetic religion and have significantly influenced other religious, ethical, political and economic spheres in India. Jains have an ancient tradition of scholarship and have the highest degree of literacy in India; Jain libraries are the oldest in the country.

Principles and Beliefs

Jainism regards every living soul as potentially divine. When the soul sheds its karmic bonds completely, it attains divine consciousness. It prescribes a path of non-violence to progress the soul to this ultimate goal.

A *Jain* is a follower of *Jinas* ("conquerors"). Jinas are spiritually advanced human beings who rediscover the *dharma*, become fully liberated and teach the spiritual path to benefit all living beings. Practicing Jains follow the teachings of 24 special jinas who are known as *Tirthankaras* "('ford-makers", or "those who have discovered and shown the way to salvation"). Tradition states that the 24th, and most recent, *Tirthankar* is Shri Mahavir, lived from 599 to 527 BC. The 23rd Tirthankar, Shri Parsva, lived from 872 to 772 BC.

Jainism encourages spiritual development through reliance on and cultivation of one's own personal wisdom and self-control. The goal of Jainism is to realize the soul's true nature. "Samyak darshan gyan charitrani moksha margah", meaning "true/right perception, knowledge and conduct" (known as the triple gems of Jainism) provides the path for attaining liberation (moksha) from samsara (the universal cycle of birth and death). Moksha is attained by liberation from all karma. Those who have attained moksha are called *siddha* (liberated souls), and those who are attached to the world through their karma are called *samsarin* (mundane souls). Every soul has to follow the path, as described by the Jinas (and revived by Tirthankaras), to attain the ultimate liberation.

Jaina tradition identifies Rishabh Bhagwan (also known as Adhinath) as the First Tirthankar of this declining (avasarpini) time cycle (kalachakra). The first Tirthankar, Rushabhdev/ Adhinath, appeared prior to the Indus Valley Civilization. The swastika symbol and naked statues resembling Jain monks, which archaeologists have found among the remains of the Indus Valley Civilization, tend to support this claim.

Jains hold that the Universe and Dharma are eternal, without beginning or end. However, the universe undergoes processes of cyclical change. The universe consists of living beings ("Jîva") and non-living beings. The samsarin (worldly) soul incarnates in various life forms during its journey over time. Human, sub-human (animal, insect, plant, etc.), super-human (deity or devas), and hell-being are the four macro forms of the samsari souls. All worldly relations of one's Jiva with other Jiva and Ajiva (non-living beings) are based on the accumulation of karma and its conscious thoughts, speech and actions carried out in its current form.

The main Jain prayer (*Namokar Mantra*) therefore salutes the five special categories of souls that have attained divine consciousness or are on their way to achieving it, to emulate and follow these paths to salvation.

Another major characteristic of Jain belief is the emphasis on the consequences of not only physical but also mental behaviours.

Jain practices are derived from the above fundamentals. For example, the principle of non-violence seeks to minimize karmas which may limit the capabilities of the soul. Jainism views every soul as worthy of respect because it has the potential to become Siddha (Param-atma-"highest soul"). Because all living beings possess a soul, great care and awareness is essential in one's actions in the incarnate world. Jainism emphasizes the equality of all life, advocating harmlessness towards all, whether these be creatures great or small. This policy extends even to microscopic organisms. Jainism acknowledges that every person has different capabilities and capacities and therefore assigns different duties for ascetics and householders. The "great vows" (mahavrata) are prescribed for monks and "limited vows" (anuvrata) are prescribed for householders.

There are five basic ethical principles (vows) prescribed. The degree to which these principles must be practiced is different for renunciant and householder.

Thus:

- Non-violence (Ahinsa)-to cause no harm to living beings.
- Truth (Satya)-to always speak the truth in a harmless manner.
- Non-stealing (Asteya)-to not take anything that is not willingly given.
- Celibacy (Brahmacarya)-to not indulge in sensual pleasures.
- Non-possession (Aparigraha)-to detach from people, places, and material things.

Ahimsa, "Non-violence", is sometimes interpreted as not killing, but the concept goes far beyond that. It includes not harming or insulting other living beings, either directly, or indirectly through others. There can be even no room for thought to injure others, and no speech that influences others to inflict harm. It also includes respecting the views of others (non-absolutism and acceptance of multiple views).

Satya, "truthfulness", is also to be practiced by all people. Given that non-violence has priority, all other principles yield to it, whenever there is a conflict. For example, if speaking truth will lead to violence, it is perfectly ethical to be silent. Thiruvalluvar in his Tamil classic devotes an entire chapter clarifying the definition of 'truthfulness'.

Asteya, "non-stealing", is the strict adherence to one's own possessions, without desire to take another's. One should remain satisfied by whatever is earned through honest labour. Any attempt to squeeze others and/or exploit the weak is considered theft.

Some of the guidelines for this principle are:

- Always give people fair value for labour or product.
- Never take things which are not offered.
- Never take things that are placed, dropped or forgotten by others
- Never purchase cheaper things if the price is the result of improper method (e.g. pyramid scheme, illegal business, stolen goods, etc.).

Brahmacarya, "monastic celibacy", is the complete abstinence from sex, which is only incumbent upon monastics. Householders practice monogamy as a way to uphold brahmacarya in spirit.

Aparigraha, "non-possession", is the renunciation of property and wealth, before initiation into monkhood, without entertaining thoughts of the things renounced. This is done so one understands how to detach oneself from things and possessions, including home and family, so one may reach *moksa*. For householders, non-possession is owning without attachment, because the notion of possession is illusory. The reality of life is that change is constant; thus, objects owned by someone today will be property of someone else in future days. The householder is encouraged to discharge his or her duties to related people and objects as a trustee, without excessive attachment.

Main Points:

- Every living being has a soul.
- Every soul is potentially divine, with innate qualities of infinite knowledge, perception, power, and bliss (masked by its karmas).

- Therefore, regard every living being as yourself, harming no one and be kind to all living beings.
- Every soul is born as a celestial, human, sub-human or hellish being according to its own karmas.
- Every soul is the architect of its own life, here or hereafter.
- When a soul is freed from karmas, it becomes free and attain divine consciousness, experiencing infinite knowledge, perception, power, and bliss.
- Right View, Right Knowledge and Right Conduct (triple gems of Jainism) provide the way to this realization. There is no supreme divine creator, owner, preserver or destroyer. The universe is self-regulated and every soul has the potential to achieve divine consciousness (siddha) through its own efforts.
- Navakar Mantra is the fundamental prayer in Jainism and can be recited at any time of the day. Praying by reciting this mantra, the devotee bows with respect to liberated souls still in human form (Arihantas), fully liberated souls (Siddhas), spiritual leaders (Acharyas), teachers (Upadyayas) and all the monks. By saluting them, Jains receive inspiration from them for the right path of true bliss and total freedom from the karma of their soul. In this main prayer, Jains do not ask for any favours or material benefits. This mantra serves as a simple gesture of deep respect towards beings who are more spiritually advanced. The mantra also reminds followers of the ultimate goal, nirvana or moksha.
- To be in Soul Consciousness rather than body consciousness is the foundation of right View, the condition of right Knowledge and the kernel of right Conduct. It leads to a state of being unattached to worldy things and therefore being nonjudgemental and Non-violent which includes compassion and forgiveness in thoughts, words and actions toward all living beings and respecting views of others (Non-absolutism).
- Jainism stresses on the importance of controlling the senses, as they can drag you far away true nature of the soul into being increasingly addicted to the material world leading into the tunnel of darkeness, ignorance, love, hate and

violence (Led by the fear of losing what we are attached to)

- Limit possessions and lead a pure life that is useful to yourself and others. Owning an object by itself is not possessiveness; however attachment to an object is. Non-possessiveness is the balancing of needs and desires while staying detached from our possessions.
- Enjoy the company of the holy and better qualified, be merciful to those afflicted and tolerate the perversely inclined.
- Four things are difficult for a soul to attain: 1. human birth, 2. knowledge of the law, 3. faith in the law, and 4. practicing the right path.
- It is important not to waste human life in evil ways. Rather, strive to rise on the ladder of spiritual evolution.
- The goal of Jainism is liberation of the soul from the negative effects of unenlightened thoughts, speech and action. This goal is achieved through clearance of karmic obstructions by following the triple gems of Jainism.
- Jains mainly worship idols of Jinas, Arihants and Tirthankars, who have conquered the inner passions and attained divine consciousness. Jainism acknowledges the existence of powerful heavenly souls (Yaksha and Yakshini) that look after the well beings of Thirthankarars. Usually, they are found in pair around the idols of Jinas as male (yaksha) and female (yakshini) guardian deities. Even though they have supernatural powers, they are also wandering through the cycles of births and deaths just like most other souls. Over time, people started worshiping these deities as well.

Tirthankaras

In Jainism, a Tirthankar: "Fordmaker"; also Tirthankara or Jina) is a human being who achieves enlightenment (perfect knowledge) through asceticism and who then becomes a role-model teacher for those seeking spiritual guidance. A Tirthankar is a special sort of arhat, a person who has totally conquered base sensibilities such as anger, pride, deceit, or desire.

A Tirthankar is so called because he is the founder of a "Tirth" (literally, 'ford'), a Jain community which acts as a "ford" across the "river of human misery".

Overview

After achieving enlightenment, a Tirthankar shows others the path to enlightenment. The Tirthankar's religious teachings form the Jain canons. The inner knowledge of all Tirthankars is perfect and identical in every respect, for the teachings of one Tirthankar do not contradict those of another. However, the degree of elaboration varies according to the spiritual advancement and purity of humans during that period. The higher the spiritual advancement and purity of mind, the lower the elaboration required.

At the end of his human life-span, a Tirthankar achieves liberation, ending the cycle of infinite births and deaths.

Jainism posits that time has no beginning or end. It moves like the wheel of a cart. There have been an infinite number of time cycles before our present era and there will be an infinite number of time cycles after this age. The beginning of the twenty first century is approximately 2,530 years into the fifth era of the present half cycle.

Twenty four Tirthankars are born in each half cycle of time (that is forty eight in each full cycle), in this part of the universe. In the current (descending) half cycle of time, the first Tirthankar Rishabh Dev, lived billions of years ago and attained liberation ('moksh' or 'nirvan') towards the end of the third era. The 24th and last Tirthankar was Mahavir Swami (599-527 BC), whose existence is a historically accepted fact. Digambaras believe that all twenty four Tirthankars were men but Svetambaras believe that the 19th Tirthankar, Mallinath, was a woman.

The next Tirthankar in our part of the universe will be born at the beginning of the third era of the next (ascending) half cycle of time, in approximately 81,500 years.

As Tirthankars direct us to enlightenment, their statues are worshipped in Jain temples by Jains aspiring to achieve enlightenment. Tirthankars are not God or gods. Jainism does not believe in the existence of God in the sense of a creator, but in gods as beings, superior to humans but, nevertheless, not fully enlightened.

Particular Tirthankars

Depictions of the Tirthankaras in various forms, including images and statues, are always represented as seated with their legs crossed in front, the toes of one foot resting close upon the knee of the other, and the right hand lying over the left in the lap. Only two are represented differently: that of Parsvanatha, the twenty-third, who has snake-hoods over him, and Suparsva, the seventh, whom the Digambarashas depict with a smaller group of snake-hoods.

Digambara representations are quite nude, while those of the Svetambaras are clothed and decorated with crowns and ornaments. They are further distinguished from one another in representations by their attendant Yakshas and Yakshinis, as well as by their associated chihnas (cognizances) carved on the cushions of their thrones.

All but two of the Jains are ascribed to the Ikshvaku family (or Kula or Kul, which in Sanskrit means "heart community" or "intentional/chosen community/family"). Munisuvrata, the twentieth, and Neminatha, the twenty-second, were of the Harivamsa race.

All but Rishabha received diksha (consecration) and jnana (complete enlightenment) at their native places. Rishabha became a Kevalin at Purimatala, Nemi at Girnar, and Mahavira at the Rijupaluka river. Twenty Tirthankaras died or obtained moksha (deliverance in bliss) on Sameta Sikhara. However Rishabha, the first, achieved nirvana on the Kailasa Mountain of the Himalayas; Vasupujya died at Champapuri in north Bengal; Neminatha on Mount Girnar; and Mahavira, the last, at Pavapur.

Twenty-one of the Tirthakaras are said to have attained Moksha in the Kayotsarga posture; Rishabha, Nemi; and Mahavira on the padmasana (lotus throne).

Rishabha (Jain Tirthankar)

In Jainism, Rishabh Dev or Adinatha (other names used: Richabh, Richabhanth, Rushabh, Rushabhdev, Adinath or Adishwar or Kesariyaji; Sanskrit *[cabha* meaning "best, most excellent") was the first of the 24 Tirthankara. He belonged to the House of Ikshwaku, which was also known as the "House of the Sun".

According to Jain beliefs, Rishabha was the first Tirthankar of the present age (*Avasarpini*). Because of this, he had the name of Adinath-the original lord. He became a Siddha, a liberated soul which has destroyed all of its karma.

Life

Rishabha was born to King Nabhi Raja and Queen Marudevi at Ayodhya in the Ikshvaku clan. According to Jain beliefs, Rishabh existed before civilization developed. He taught people agriculture, tending of animals, cooking, and more. He had one hundred and one sons.

His eldest son-Bharat-was a chakravarti king-the conqueror of the known world. In the later part of his life he retired to become a monk and attained moksha. Because he became a siddha, he is occasionally worshipped. According to Jain beliefs, India was named Bharata-varsha or Bharata after him.

His second son was Bahubali, whose statue stands at Shravanabelagola, Karnataka as well as at Karkala. Marudevi mother of Adinath was the first person to achieve moksha-even before Rishabh himself. Rishabh's grandson Marichi's soul later became Mahavira. He attained 'Kevalgnan' or infinite knowledge at Palitana and attained liberation (Moksha) at Ashtapad mountain in Himalayas.

References in Hinduism

Rishabha is mentioned in the Hindu text of the Bhagavata Purana as an avatar of Vishnu. He is mentioned in all the Vaishnava/ Shaiva Puraoas, as well as in some other texts.

According to the Bhagavata, he was born to show the people of this world the path of salvation. It was he who advised the people to follow the path of eternal bliss, instead of indulging in a life of worldly pleasures and enjoyment. He is the founder and promoter of sramanic culture. In the depth study of the vedas and puranas, which contain numerous references to Rishabha.

Historicity of Rishabha and Links with Indus Valley Civilization

Modern scholars believe that Rishabha was a historical person, based on archeological and literary evidence. P. C. Roychoudary puts the date of Rishabha at the end of the Stone Age and the beginning of the Agriculture age. Contemporary historians like Ramprasad Chandra, Vilas Sangave, Heinrich Zimmer, John Marshall, Thomas McEvilley and Mircea Eliade are of the opinion that there exists some link between Rishabha and Indus valley civilization. Terracotta seals and other evidence unearthed at the ancient cities of Harrapa and Mohenjo Daro provide a link between Rishabha and Indus Valley Civilisation.

In his *Indus Valley Civilisation and Hindu Culture,* P.R. Deshmukh says that the first Jain Tirthankara belonged to Indus Valley Civilisation. Ram Prasad Chanda, who supervised Indus Valley Civilisation excavations, states in his article Mohen-jo-Daro: Sindh 5000 Years Ago in Modern Review (August, 1932) that, "Not only the seated deities on some of the Indus seals are in Yoga posture and bear witness to the prevalence of Yoga in the Indus Valley Civilisation in that remote age, the standing deities on the seals also show Kayotsarga (a standing or sitting posture of meditation) position.

The Kayotsarga posture is peculiarly Jain. It is a posture not of sitting but of standing. In the Adi Purana Book XV III, the Kayotsarga posture is described in connection with the penance of Rsabha, also known as Vrsabha."

Christopher Key Chappel, quoting many scholars, provides the following evidences connecting Rsabha with Indus Valley civilisation:

1. Seal 420, unearthed at Mohenjodaro portrays a person with 3 or possibly 4 faces. Jain iconography frequently depicts its tirtahnkaras with four faces, symbolizing their missionary activities in all four directions.
2. Another seal depicts seven persons in upright position with arms somewhat hanging somewhat stiffly and held slightly away from the sides of the body which McEvilley correlates with the Jaina Kayatsarga pose, the posture in which the very first Tirthankara, Rshabha, is said to have entered kevala. While this can be interpreted in may ways, Richard Lannoy however does see Jaina influences on this seal : "That of a nude man represented as a repeat-motif in a rigidly upright position, legs slightly apart, arms held parallel to the sides of his body, which recurs as a Jaina tirthankara, repeated row upon row.

3. Depictions of a bull appear repeatedly in the artifacts of the Indus Valley, Lannoy, McEvilly, and Padmanabh Jaini all have suggested that the abundant use of the bull image in the Indus Valley civilization indicates a link with Rsabha, the first of the twenty four Tirthankaras, whose companion animal is the bull.

Description in Jain Texts:

- Name: Bhagwan Rishabhdeva
- Symbol: Bull
- Father: Nabhi Raja
- Mother: Matha Marudevi
- Clan Name: Ikshvaku
- Source of Descent: Sarvarthsiddha
- Date of Descent: Ashad krishna paksha 4 (as Indian calendar)
- Place of Birth: Vinita
- Date of Birth: Chaitra Krishna
- Place of Enlightenment: Purimtal
- Date of Diksha: Chaitra Krishna Paksha 8
- Date of Enlightenment: Falgun Krishna Paksha 11
- Place of Nirvana: Ashtapad Mount
- Date of Nirvana: Magh Krishna Paksha
- Period of Practices: 1,000 Years
- Life-span: 592.704 Quintillion Years
- Chief Disciple (Gandadhar): Pundarik
- Number of Disciples (Ganadhar):
- Number of Ascetics: Thousand
- Head of Female Ascetics: Brahmi
- Number of Female Ascetics:3 Lac
- Male Laity :3.5 Lac
- Female Laity: 5.54 Lac
- Body Colour: Golden
- God of Organisation: Goumukh
- Goddess of Organisation: Chakreshwari Devi.

According to the Jain measurement of cosmic time one cycle of time has two divisions. These two divisions, ascending time-cycle there is a gradual improvement in physical and mental conditions, including physical strength, health, happiness and simplicity, of beings as well as climatic and life supporting conditions. During the descending time-cycle there is a gradual deterioration in these conditions.

The Age of the Twins

During the first three Aras of the current descending cycle man was completely dependent on nature for all his needs. The wish-fulfilling trees provided all that he needed. Man was simple, peaceful and contented in attitude. The environment was absolutely unpolluted. Water was tasteful, cold, and sweet. Even the sand was sweet as sugar. The air was healthy and exhilarating. The grains and fruits were nutritious and filing. A simple meal of little quantity of fruit and water lasted for days. Filled stomach and satisfied desires acted as antidote to irritation and reduced disputes and other sinful activities. The whole animal kingdom lived in harmony with the nature.

With the passage of time gradual changes occurred and around the end of the third Ara the yield from the Kalpa-vrikshas reduced. The alround deterioration in conditions spelled the beginning of quarrels and disputes. To guard against these disputes and to live in peace and harmony, man formed groups and the Kulkar system was evolved.

A number of people collected to form a 'Kula' (family) and the head of the group was called 'Kulkar'. It was the duty of the 'Kulkar' to remove discord and establish order. Nabhiraja was the seventh and the last in the line of Kulkars. His wife was Marudeva. This epoch of Kulkar system was known as the epoch of twins (Yugalia). A human couple used to give birth to a twin-one male and one female. This twin would become husband and wife on reaching adulthood. The twins used to lead a happy and contented life and died a natural death together.

To consume what was available was the way of life. As such this period was also known as Bhog-Bhumi-Kaal or the era of free consumption. Up to the time of Kulkar Nabhiraja man lived in this land of abundance.

Birth of Rishabhdev

It was during the last part of the third Ara of the current descending cycle of time that the great and pious soul that was to become Rishabhdev descended into the womb of Marudeva on the fourth day of the dark half of the month of Ashadh during the night. In the ancient Jain scriptures it is mentioned that during many previous births, the soul that was to be Rishabhdev had done prolonged spiritual practices. As a result of high degree of purity of thoughts and attitude as well as penance, meditation, charity and benevolent deeds it had earned highly pious Karmas.

In his incarnation as Dhanna, the caravan leader, he had offered alms and services to ascetics and others. As doctor Jivanand he had taken ample care of ailing masses as well as ascetics. As king Vajranabh he had supported poor and desolate masses. After many years of public service Vajranabh renounced the world and became an ascetic. As a result of unprecedented spiritual practices, including religious studies, penance, tolerance, and meditation, he earned Tirthankarnam-and-gotra-karma. These pious deeds of earlier births resulted in his taking birth as Rishabhdev.

When this pious soul was conceived, mother Marudeva dreamt of fourteen auspicious things.

The *First* thing she saw in her dream was that a beautiful and large white bull was entering her mouth.

The other things she saw in her dream are as follows:

1. A giant elephant having four tusks,
2. A lion,
3. Goddess Laxmi seated on a lotus,
4. A garland of flowers,
5. The full moon resplendent in the sky,
6. The scintillating sun,
7. A fluttering flag,
8. A golden urn,
9. A pond full of lotus flowers,
10. A sea of milk,
11. A space vehicle of gods,
12. A heap of gems,

13. Smokeless fire.

Nabhiraja was an experienced and scholarly person. When he heard about these dreams from Maudeva, he said, "Devi! You will give birth to a highly endowed soul who will show the path of peace and happiness to this world"

Birth Celebrations

On the eighth day of the dark half of the month of Chaitra, around midnight, healthy Marudeva gave birth to twins. This pious birth influenced the surroundings. The sky became filled with a soothing glow, the wind became fragrant and the whole atmosphere became impregnated with unprecedented joy that was hard to describe.

From all around came the fifty six goddesses of directions. They circumambulated the Tirthankar's mother and bowed before her. They also sang in praise of the child that was to become Tirthankar and then proceeded to perform post-birth cleaning rituals.

At that instant the king of gods of the Saudharm dimension, Saudharmendra Shakra, also came to know that the first Tirthankar has taken birth. He arrived with his large retinue of gods and, bowed before the mother,

"O great mother! I, Saudharmendra Shakra, bow before you and offer my salutations."

After the salutations the mother was put to sleep. Saudharmendra created five look alike bodies of himself. With one body he carefully lifted the baby in his hands. With the second body he took an umbrella in his hands and stationed the body behind the baby. With the third and fourth bodies he took whisks and stationed these bodies on both sides of the baby. With the fifth body he lifted his divine weapon, Vajra, and stationed himself ahead of the baby as a body guard. In this formation the king of gods airlifted the baby to Meru mountain. There, all gods, including their 64 kings with their consorts, ceremoniously performed the post-birth anointing rituals. This ceremony, popularly known as Janma-kalyanak, of a Tirthankar, is unparalleled in this world.

Giving the Name

Next morning Nabhiraja organized the birth celebrations. He

invited his friends and relatives to a feast and announced, "As there is a sign of a bull on the thigh of the new born, and Marudeva first of all saw a bull in her great dreams, we name this child as 'Rishabh Kumar'." His twin will be known as "Sumangala".

The Beginning of the Ikshvaku Clan

When Rishabh Kumar was one year old, Saudharmendra came to Kulkar Nabhi for formalizing the family name. He carried a sugar-cane in his hand Baby Rishabh was sitting in his fathers lap. When he saw the sugar-cane he eagerly extended his tiny hands to grab it. Saudharmendra gave the sugar-cane to the baby and seeing his affinity for sugar-cane (Ikshu) he formally named the family as Ikshvaku.

Marriage

Rishabh Kumar was married to a girl named Sunanda whose twin died in an accident. This was the beginning of the marriage system. He was also married to his twin Sumangala in a ceremony that was arranged by the gods. Prince Rishabh led a happy married life. In due course Sumangala gave birth to Bharat, Brahmi and ninety eight other sons. Sunanda had also given birth to Bahubali and Sundari.

Evolution of Crafts and Trades

Prince Rishabh was a highly endowed, farsighted and industrious individual. He had a profound insight into the human psychology. Looking at the needs the times and society he evolved numerous arts, crafts and trades and taught them to people with right aptitude and physical and mental capacities. To some he taught farming and to others the trade of agricultural produce. He invented the alphabets, language, and the numbers along with the tools for writing. For self defense he evolved martial arts and taught these to individuals with strong physique. He also established systems of social security and penal codes. Pottery, architecture, music, dance, and many other arts and crafts that enriched the human society in the fields of knowledge, arts, entertainment, administration, etc. are said to be his contributions.

Then one day, on the request of the people's representatives. Nabhiraja nominated Rishabh to become the first king of this age. He arranged for an elaborate coronation ceremony and handed over the reigns of the state to Rishabh Kumar. The ceremony was attended by all members of the family, large number of twins, and gods. The gods created a golden throne and anointed Rishabh with the water collected from various pilgrimage centres. They attired him in divine dress and ornaments and formally put the crown on his head. The twins humbly poured water on his feet from the cups made of lotus leaves. Rishabh became the first king of this era. The king of gods ordered Kuber, the god of wealth, to construct a suitable city. This beautiful city was named Vinita; later on it became popularly known as Ayodhya.

Preaching the Path of Renunciation

For many years Rishabhdev continued to rule his people and open new frontiers of knowledge. During the reign of his father the population was organized into random groups only. Rishabhdev reorganized them according to their virtues, activities and professions, and broadly divided the society into three groups. Trading community was known as Vaishya, martial community was known as Kshtriya and all other people indulging in a variety of services were known as Shudra. Till his times the Brahman group was not formed. After a long span of time (6.3 million Purva) he started losing interest in mundane things and activities, and drifting toward detachment. He felt that he should transfer all his responsibilities to his sons and proceed towards liberation through spiritual practices. He also desired to reach the state of omniscience and consequently show the path of disciplined life and spiritual practices. His concept was that indulgence in mundane things does not give happiness. It gives only an illusion of happiness. True happiness is derived out of freedom from mundane indulgences.

Following the stream of his thoughts Rishabhdev divided the area of his rule between his one hundred sons. Bharat was given the state of Ayodhya and Bahubali that of Takshashila. Getting free of the responsibilities of the state, Rishabhdev decided to take Diksha (the formal initiation into the ascetic way). At that time the gods from the edge of the universe (the Lokantikdev) arrived and requested, "O savior of the human race! Your desire to show the path of renunciation to the mankind is admirable, kindly proceed soon to the task of propagating Dharma."

After one year of meritorious charity, Rishabhdev sat in the palanquin named Sudarshan and arrived in the Siddharth-vana garden. it was the eighth day of the dark half of the month of chaitra when, under an Ashok tree, Rishabhdev abandoned all his apparels and ornaments. He started pulling out his long strands of hair. After four fistfuls, when he was pulling out the fifth fistful of hair Indra said, "Sire! This strand of hair on the crown of your head and hanging down over you shoulders looks attractive. Kindly leave it as it is.".Rishabhdev agreed. Due to this bunch of hair he got he popular name-Keshariya ji (one with hair). The king of gods collected the hair pulled out by Rishabhdev in a divine cloth and immersed them in the divine ocean of milk.

Following the example of Rishabhdev many of his subordinate rulers as well as common people got inspired to embrace the ascetic way of life. It is mentioned in scriptures that with Rishabhdev four thousand others also took Diksha.

The First Charity

After becoming an ascetic, Rishabhdev took the vow of total silence and started wandering accompanied by other ascetics. When, after his penance, he went out to beg for food, he did not get anything to eat. The common people of that age were ignorant about the practice of giving food as alms. They did not even appreciate the need to do so. Whenever Rishabhdev approached them, they offered him respect and valuable gifts as they would to a king. Rishabhdev would then proceed ahead without accepting anything. As time passed the accompanying ascetics conferred among themselves and decided to eat fruits and vegetables naturally available. They slowly drifted away from Rishabhdev and the true ascetic way of life. After one entire year of wandering from place to place and doing harsh spiritual practices without touching any food or water Rishabhdev decided to beg food once again. He came to Hastinapur town.

Bahubali's son, Somprabh, was the king of Hastinapur. His son Shreyans Kumar saw a dream during night that Suvarnagiri, the golden mountain had turned black and he had brought it back its golden color by washing it with pitchers full of milk. He narrated his dream to his father and friends, but no one could interpret its significance.

Shreyans Kumar was sitting in the balcony of his palace and brooding over the dream he saw last night. All of a sudden he heard the noise caused by happy masses who had seen Rishabhdev entering the town. Thousands of citizens of Hastinapur rushed toward Rishabhdev with gifts. Rishabhdev did not even look at these things and continued his graceful walk in the direction of the palace.

When Shreyans saw approaching Rishabhdev, he rushed to welcome his great grandfather. After bowing down at the great ascetics feet when Shreyans looked at Rishabhdev's face he could not shift his gaze. He went into a state of meditative thoughts and suddenly he acquired Jati-smaran Jnan, the knowledge that opens up memories of the past births. In his past birth Shreyans was the charioteer of king Vajranabh (the past incarnation of Rishabhdev). This knowledge also made him aware of the duties of laity toward Shramans. He realized that Bhagavan Rishabhdev had been wandering around without food or water due to the prevailing ignorance of the people regarding ascetic norms.

With due reverence he requested Rishabhdev, "Prabhu! I am honored by your presence. I have just received 108 pitchers full of fresh sugar-cane juice that are pure and suitable for you in all respects. Kindly accept the juice and break your fast." Rishabhdev extended his cupped palms and Shreyans poured the sugar-cane juice from a pitcher. Rishabhdev broke his fast and the skies reverberated with the sound of divine drums and divine applaud, "Hail the alms giving!" The gods also showered gems, flowers and perfumes.

This was the beginning of the tradition of religious charity and alms giving. In memory of this incident, the third day of the bright half of the month of Vaishakh is celebrated as Akshay Tritiya festival. The Jains specifically celebrate it as the breakfast day after the penance of Varshi Tap (one meal and fast on alternate days for one year).

Omniscience and Nirvana

For one thousand years *Bhagavan* Rishabhdev continued his harsh spiritual practices completely ignoring his body and other mundane activities. On the eleventh day of the dark half of the month of Phalgun he was meditating under a banyan tree in the Shakatmukh garden outside Purimtal town, close to Ayodhya. Around forenoon he transcended to the purest higher state of meditation. The intensity of his practice caused the shedding of the knowledge and perception obscuring Karmas as well as the illusory Karmas. As a result, he attained omniscience, the purest and enlightened state of soul. Rishabhdev became a Jina.

When Rishabhdev attained omniscience the whole world was filled with a soothing glow for a moment. Numerous gods descended from heavens to pay their respects to the Tirthankar. They also created the Samavasaran, the divine pavilion. King Bharat also proceeded toward the divine assembly riding an elephant and taking along his grandmother Marudeva. Apprehensive about the hardships of the ascetic life of her son, Marudeva was relieved when she beheld the scintillating face of Rishabhdev sitting in the divine assembly surrounded by happy and dazzling gods. The vision of her son perched on the spiritual pinnacle triggered the flow of spontaneous joy in the heart of Marudeva. This mundane joy slowly turned into the ultimate bliss and she acquired omniscience. Coincidentally, at the same moment she completed her age and became liberated soul (Siddha). Bhagawan Rishabhdev made the announcement Marudeva had become a Siddha.

In his first discourse Rishabhdev detailed the trilogy of right conduct. Knowing about the significance of life as a human being and importance of a dutiful life, thousands of people including Rishabhsen, the eldest son of Emperor Bharat, and five thousands of people including Rishabhsen, the eldest son of Emperor Bharat, and five thousand other members of royal family embraced the acetic way of life. Thousand of other persons accepted the Shravak Dharm (the religious way for laity). As he founded the four pronged religious ford at the beginning of the present era, Bhagavan Rishabhdev became popularly known as Adinath, the first Tirthankar.

The first disciple of Bhagavan Rishabhdev was Rishabhsen. He became the first chief disciple. He was also known as Pundarik.

Liberation

For a long time Bhagavan Rishabhdev continued to propagate his religion having the five great vows as its central theme. When he realized that all his remaining Karmas are approaching their end he proceeded to the Ashtapad mountain. On the thirteenth day of the dark half of the month of Magh, a little before noon time, Rishabhdev, along with ten thousand other ascetics, was observing a six day fast without water. He was sitting in the meditation in the Paryanka pose. When the moon entered the Abhijit lunar mansion he got nirvana and got liberated from all sorrows.

The king of gods, Saudharmendra, Emperor Bharat, numerous gods and men gathered and celebrated the auspicious event of Bhagavan Rishabhdev's Nirvana.

Famous temples dedicated to Rishabha:

- Adishwar Temple, Ranakpur, Rajasthan
- Adishwar temple, Palitana, Gujarat
- Adinath Mandir, Bibrod, Ratlam, M.P.
- Adinath Temple, Nahta Chowk, Bikaner, Rajasthan
- Adinath *derasar*, Vataman, Gujarat
- Adinath temple, Khajuraho, MP
- Adinath temple, Ayodhya, UP
- Adinath temple, Chand-Khedi, Near Kota, Rajasthan
- Adinath at Rishabhdeo or Rikhabdeo near Udaipur, Rajasthan
- Adinath Bhagvan Temple, Mahrauli, Delhi
- Bhagawan Adinath Temple, Hirehattihole, Karnataka
- Adinath Bhagvan Temple, Ponnur Hill, Tamilnadu
- Adinath Temple in Ranila, Rohtak, Haryana
- Adishwar Temple, Walkeshwar, Mumbai, Maharashtra
- Adinath Jain Temple, Santhu Bagra (Marwar), Jalore
- Shri Aadishwar Dada Jain Mandir, Jawahar Chowk, Durg, Chhattisgarh.

Famous Hymns dedicated to Rishabha:

- Bhaktamara Stotra.

Archaeology: Notable Pratimas of Rishabha:

- Pre-Kushana Mathura sculpture
- Kushana images from Mathura
- Bronze from Chausa hoard, 1st cent CE
- Bronze from Akota hoard, 6th cent CE
- Monumental figure at Bavangaja, Badvani, 10th cent.

Ajitnath

Ajitnatha was the second Jain Tirthankar of the present age (Avasarpini). According to Jain beliefs, he became a siddha, a liberated soul which has destroyed all of its karma. The soul that became Bhagavan Ajitnath, in its earlier incarnation, was the great king Vimalvahan of Susima city in Mahavideh area. He led a pious life in spite of the available princely grandeur. At an appropriate time, he became an ascetic under Arindam Suri.

Ajitnatha was born to King Jitashatru Raja and Queen Vijaya at Ayodhya in the Ikshvaku clan.

Birth of Bhagvan Ajitnath

Queen Vijaya Devi saw fourteen auspicious dreams. Vaijayanti, the wife of king Jitshatru's younger brother, Sumitra, also saw the same fourteen dreams. This was a queer coincidence. When the augurs were consulted they advised that Vijaya Devi would give birth to a Tirthankar and Vaijayanti to a Chakravarti (Emperor).

During the queen's pregnancy, the influence of king Jitshatru was enhanced to such an extant that even the enemy kingdoms sought and negotiated friendly treaties with him. It became a common practice to say, "King Jitshatru is invincible (Ajit)."

The queen gave birth to a son on the eighth day of the bright half of the month of Magh. Inspired by the popular lore, the king named the new born as the Ajit. The same night Vaijayanti also gave birth to a son who was named Sagar. Then both the princes came of age they were married. Time passed with the fusion of happiness.

When king Jitshatru became old and wanted to devote the last part his life to spiritual pursuits, he called his younger brother and asked him to take over the throne. Sumitra had no desire for the kingdom; he, too, wanted to become an ascetic. Both the princes were called and offered the kingdom. Ajit Kumar was a naturally detached person since childhood, and so he too declined. At last prince Sagar ascended the throne.

Ajit Kumar became an ascetic in his youth and went into remote and dense forests for his meditation and penance. His personality and the intensity of his lofty practices cast a pacifying influence all around. Natural enemies in the animal kingdom, like the lion and cow, wolf and deer, snake and mongoose used to come and sit around him peacefully. After a twelve year period of deep meditation and other spiritual practices Ajit Kumar attained omniscience on the eleventh day of the bright half of the month of Paush. The gods created the divine pavilion and Bhagawan Ajitnath gave his eloquent and magnetic discourses. Thousands of people accepted the path of renunciation.

King Sagar, during this period, conquered the six continents and became Chakravartin. King Meghvahan and Vidyadhar Bhim, the ruler of the island of Rakshasas (demons), were the illustrious contemporaries of Emperor Sagar. Once they went to a discourse of Bhagavan Ajitnath. There, Vidyadhar Bhim was drawn towards spiritual life. He became so detached that he gave his kingdom including the famous cities of Lanka and Patal Lanka to king Meghvahan. He also gave all his knowledge and miraculous powers to Meghvahan. He also gave a divine necklace of nine large and shining beads. Meghvahan was the first king of the Rakshas clan in which the famous king Ravana was born.

Death of Sagar's Sixty Thousand Sons

Emperor Sagar had thousands of queens and sixty thousand sons. Eldest among them was Janhu Kumar. Once all the princes went for an outing. When they arrived at the base of Astapad hills, they dug up large ditches and canals. In their youthful abandon they flooded these canals with the water of river Ganges. This flash flood inundated the houses and villages of the lower gods known as Nag Kumars. The king of these gods, Jwalanprbh came and tried to stop them in vain. The unruly princes were intoxicated with the regal power. At last Jwalanprabh lost his temper and turned all the sixty thousand princes to ashes.

This sudden death of all his sons was a traumatic experience for Emperor Sagar. He handed over the empire to his eldest grandson, Bhagirath, and took Diksha from Bhagavan Ajitnath.

When his last moments were approaching, Bhagavan Ajitnath went Sammetshikhar. With one thousand other ascetics, he commenced his final meditation. He attained Nirvana on the fifth day of the bright half of the month of Chaitra.

Ajitnath as a Historical Figure

The 2nd Jain Tirthankar Ajitanatha,was born in Ayodhya. The Yajurveda mentions the name of Ajitanatha, but the meaning is not clear. His younger brother, according to Jain traditions, was Sagara who became the second Chakravarti. He is known from the traditions of both Hinduism and Jainism as found in their respective Hindu scriptures Puranas.

- From the Hindu source, he is known to have many sons. One of them was Bhagiratha who brought the river Gangas.
- From the Jain account, it is clear that Sagara in his last days adopted the life of asceticism from Ajitanath and retired from the worldly life. Ajitanatha seems to be as real a person as Sagara.

Sambhavanath

Sambhavanath was the third Jain Tirthankar of the present age (Avasarpini). According to Jain beliefs, he became a siddha, a liberated soul which has destroyed all of its karma. Sambhavnath was born to King Jitari Raja and Queen Saina Rani at Sravasthi in the Ikshvaku clan. His birth date was the fourteenth day of the Margshrsha shukla month of the Indian calendar.

Previous Births

A long time after the Nirvana of Bhagavan Ajitnath, the city of Kshempuri in the Airavat area of Mahavideh was ruled by king Vipulvahan. He was a soft hearted and compassionate ruler who loved and cared for his subjects. Once when there was a devastating draught and the population was deprived even of a few drops of water, the king opened his grain yards for the public, his kitchen for the monks and ascetics and his treasury for the import of food grains. He instructed the caretaker of his personal kitchen that the doors of his kitchen should be open to all and sundry. All guests should be given priority over himself. Whatever little is left should be served to him. If nothing is left he would be contented with the pleasure of serving his guests. During the drought there were many occasions when the king remained unfed and thirsty.

As a result of this sublime feeling of compassion, Vipulvahan acquired unique purity of soul and earned the Trithankrnam-and-gotra-karma. Although, after the drought normalcy returned, the torture of the living world by the nature left a mark on Vipulvahan's psyche. One day while he was standing on the roof top he witnessed dense rain clouds being scattered by wind. A feeling of intense detachment grew in him. He handed over his kingdom to his son and took Diksha from Svayamprabh Suri. After completing his age he reincarnated in the Anat dimension of gods.

Life as Tirthankara

From the Anat dimension, the being that was Vipulvahan descended into the womb of queen Sena Devi, wife of king Jitari of Shravasti. While this being was still in the mother's womb there were sufficient rains and abundant crop. One day when the king and queen were happily watching the lush green vegetation all around, from their roof top, the king said, "My dear! This time even the waste-land is filled with grain crop. It seems that all this that is impossible, has been made possible (Sambhav) due to the auspicious influence of the pious soul you carry in your womb. We shall call our son-Sambhav."

On the fourteenth day of the bright half of the month of Margshrish, the queen gave birth to a healthy son and he was ceremoniously named Sambhav Kumar. The little prince grew up in royal comfort but he hardly ever took more than cursory interest in the luxurious life style. At the appropriate age Sambhav Kumar was married and crowned. After a long and peaceful reign he became an ascetic on the fifteenth day of the bright half of the month of Margshrish. After a fourteen year period of spiritual practices, he attained omniscience. Arhat Sambhavnath gave his first discourse on the ephemeral nature of the mundane existence. For a long period he worked for the spread of religion. He attained Nirvana on the fifth day of the bright half of the month of Chaitra.

Abhinandannath

Abhinandannatha or Abhinandan Swami was the fourth Tirthankara of the present age (Avasarpini). According to Jain beliefs, he became a siddha, a liberated soul which has destroyed all of its Karma. Abhinandannath was born to King Sanvara Raja and Queen Sidharta Rani at Ayodhya in the Ikshvaku clan. His birth date was the second day of the Magh shukla month of the Indian calendar.

Previous Birth

Mahabal was the king of Ratnasanchay/Mangalavati town in Purvavideh. Although a king, he was a simple and humble person. When people praised him, he thought that why people praised him even in absence of any virtues? When someone criticized him he would humbly say, "You are my true well-wisher and a friend who helps my progress by pointing out my faults." when a feeling of detachment grew in him, he found and opportune moment and took Diksha from Vimal Suri. Due to his simplicity and humility he became a very popular and ideal Sharman in his group. It is said that as a result of this rare disposition and deep mediational practices he purified his soul to an extant that he acquired the Tirthankarnam-and-gotra-karma. Completing his age, he reincarnated as a god in the Vijay dimension.

Life as Tirthankara

When the being that was Mahaval left the Vijay dimension, he descended into the womb of queen Siddharth, wife of king Samvar of Ayodhya. As a result of the simplicity of attitude inherited from the earlier birth, the soul in the womb of the queen had a soothing and pacifying influence on the outer world. The people of the kingdom were suddenly filled with the feelings of humility and fraternity. Irrespective of age, caste, creed and status every one started greeting and honoring others. Politeness and polished manners became the thing in vogue. The augurs and other scholars confirmed that as the aura of a pious soul influences all the people around, the effusion of politeness was caused by the soul in the womb. The queen gave birth to the future Tirthankara on the second day of the bright half of the month of Magh. As the influence of this soul was evident in the overt mutual greetings, the king named his son as Abhinandan (greeting).

As time passed Abhinandan lead normal mundane life with least indulgence. He ascended the throne when his father became an ascetic. After a long and peaceful reign, he became an ascetic and indulged in rigorous penance and lofty spiritual practices. He attained omniscience on the fourteenth day of the dark half of the month of Paush. For a long period Bhagavan Abhinandan moved around to show the right path to millions of beings. On the eighth day of the bright half of the month of Vaishakah he attained Nirvana at Sammetshikhar

Sumatinath

Sumatinatha was the fifth Jain Tirthankar of the present age (Avasarpini). According to Jain beliefs, he became a siddha, a liberated soul which has destroyed all of its karma. Sumatinath was born to King Megh Raja and Queen Mangala Rani at Ayodhya in the Ikshvaku clan. His birth date was the eighth day of the Vaishakh shukla month of the Indian calendar.

Previous Birth

Vijayasen was the king of Shankhpur town in the Purva Mahavideh area. He had a son named Purushasimha. While he had gone for a walk in the garden one day, the prince listened to the discourse of Acharya Vinayanandan Dev. He became detached and a turned ascetic. As a result of vigorous penance and higher spiritual practices, he earned the Tirthankarnam-and-gotra-karma. Completing his age, he reincarnated as a god in the Vijayant dimension.

Life as Tirthankara

From Vijayant dimension, the soul that was Purushasimha descended into the womb of queen Mangalavati/Sumangala, wife of king Megh of Ayodhya. The news of the queen being pregnant made the atmosphere of Ayodyha live with happiness and joy.

Story of Disputed Parentage

One day two women and a little boy came to the kings court to seek justice. One of the women put forth her case before the king, "Sire! We both are wives of a rich seafaring merchant. Our husband has left for his heavenly abode leaving behind we two, a son, and heaps of wealth. The child truly belongs to me but this second wife of the merchant claims to be her.

This is nothing but a conspiracy to grab the wealth that would be inherited by the child. Save me, my Lord! I seek my son and justice from you." The story narrated by the other woman was also the same. Shouting charges and counter charges at each other, both the women claimed the possession of the child. The child could not indicate his true mother as he had got equal affection from both. As the boy was born in some remote place, there was no eye witness available.

The king was in a quandary. Even after a lot of probing and weighing the evidence he could not solve the problem. Any ill conceived solution could end up in doing injustice to the innocent. The king and his ministers all could end up in doing injustice to the innocent. The king and his ministers all were in a fix. The night was approaching and the king was getting late for his dinner. He adjourned the case and went into the palace for dinner.

The queen asked, "Today you are late for the dinner, your highness. What is the matter? Was there some complex problem?" The king narrated the case of the two women and their child and said, "No one is able to say firmly, which one of the women is the real mother of the child and which one is the pretender?" The queen said with a smile, "Your Highness, let a woman solve the problems of women. Send the case to me and allow me to resolve the issue." Next morning the queen herself came to the kings court. Both the women and their son were produced before the queen. There was no apparent indication in the behaviour and disposition of the two women that could give any indication of the genuineness of one. All of a sudden, the queen got an inspiration and she said, "This enigma has no simple solution. There is one object and two claimants. The object, being a person, cannot be split into two.

Under the circumstances the only solution I can think of is to keep the matter pending. I carry a pious soul in my womb. Let us wait till it is born and is ready to resolve this issue during the period of waiting, let the son and the property of the deceased be taken into the custody of the state. Till then the claimants may wait." Hearing all of this one of the claimants readily accepted the arrangement but the other started weeping.

In a choked voice she said, "No! Please don't separate me from my son. I will not be able to survive without my son for such a long period, I withdraw my claim. Let the other woman take the child as well as all the property of my husband. My only submission is that I may be allowed at least meet the child. I will be contented with that only." The queen recognized the pain and concern of a mother's heart.

She gave her judgment, "The woman who immediately agreed to my proposal is the impostor. Her attachment is not to the child but to the wealth. She may be imprisoned. The one who wants to surrender her claim is the real mother. The child and the wealth may be given to her with all honor." Everyone present in the assembly was dumbstruck by this witty method of judgment. The impostor pleaded guilty and submitted to be pardoned.

Birth and Omniscience

On the eighth day of the bright half of the month of Vaishakh, the queen gave birth to a son. A wave of peace and goodwill swept the whole world. Appreciating the fact that the marked improvement in wisdom and sense of judgment during the pregnancy was the influence of the presence of the illustrious and pious soul, king Megh named the new born as-Sumati (wisdom or right thinking).

When he became a young man, Sumati Kumar was married, and in due course inherited the kingdom. King Megh became an ascetic. After a long and peaceful reign Sumatinath, too, became an ascetic. He attained omniscience under a Priyangu tree on the eleventh day of the bright half of the month of Chaitra. He established the four pronged religious ford and became a Tirthankar. On the ninth day of the bright half of the month of Chaitra he attained Nirvana at Sammetshikhar

Padmaprabha

Padmaprabha was the sixth Jain Tirthankar of the present age (Avsarpini). According to Jain beliefs, he became a siddha-a liberated soul which has destroyed all of its karma. Padmaprabha (also known as Padhmaprabhu swami) was born to King Shridhar Raja and Queen Susimadevi at Koushambi in the Ikshvaku clan. His birth date was the twelfth day of the Kartik Krishna month of the Indian calendar.

Previous Births

Maharaj Aparajit ruled over Susima town in the Purvavideh area. He was a simple and religious person. He got detached after listening to the discourse of an Arhat and took Diksha from Acharya Pihitashrava. As a result of long spiritual practices he earned Trithankarnama-gotra-karma. Completing his age, he reincarnated as a god in the Graiveyak dimension.

Life as Tirthankara

From the dimension of gods, the being that was Aparajit descended into the womb of queen Susima, wife of the king Kaushambi. One day queen Susima had a desire to sleep on a bed made up of lotus flowers. As this was a desire of a pregnant mother, the gods made arrangements for its fulfillment. On the twelfth day of the dark half of the month of Kartik the queen gave birth to a son. The new born had a soft pink glow like lotus flowers. The king named him as Padmaprabh.

In due course the prince became young and was married. When his father left for spiritual practices, Padmaprabh ascended the throne. After a long and successful reign, when through his threefold knowledge he knew that the right moment has come, he became an ascetic. After six months of spiritual practices, on the full moon day of the month of Chaitra he attained omniscience under a banyan tree. Propagating right religion for a long time, Bhagavan Padmaprabh wandered around and at last arrived at Sammetshikhar. He attained Nirvana on the eleventh day of the dark half of the month of Margshirsh.

There is a huge temple of Padamprabhuji near Jaipur in Rajasthan.

Suparshvanath

Suparshvanath was the seventh Jain Tirthankar of the present age (Avasarpini). According to Jain beliefs, he became a siddha, a liberated soul which has destroyed all of its karma. Suparshvnath was born to King Prathisth Raja and Queen Prithvidevi at Banaras in the Ikshvaku clan. His birth date was the twelfth day of the Jayesth shukla month of the Indian calendar.

Suparshvanath as a Historical Figure

There are some legends about the all the Jain Tirthankaras which may contain some historical matter. In the *Mahavagga* (1. 22. 13), there is a mention of a Jain temple of Lord Suparsva, the seventh Tirthankara situated at Rajagrih of Bihar state of India in the time of Lord Buddha. At Mathura, there is an old stupa of the Jains with the inscription of 157 A. D. This inscription records that an image of the Tirthankar Aranath was set up at the stupa built by the gods.

- Thus, in 157 A. D., this stupa was so old that it was regarded as the work of the gods. It was probably, therefore, erected several centuries before the Christian era. The later authors give us some information about this stupa.

Jinaprabha in the *Tirtha Kalpa*, a work of the 14th century based on ancient materials mentions that the stupa originally of gold was erected in honor of the 7th JainTirthankar Suparsvanatha by the Kubera for two Jain Saints named Acharya Dharmaruchi and Dharmaghosh. In the time of 23rd Jain Tirthankar Parsvanatha, the golden stupa was enclosed in bricks and a stone temple was built outside. Even Somadeva, the author of the Yasastilaka who is nearly four hundred years earlier than Jinaprabha refers to it as built by gods.

- From this type of legendary account, it seems that there was the worship of Suparsvanatha several centuries before the Christian era.

Previous Births

The being that was to be Suparshvanath had done harsh penance and deep spiritual practices in his earlier birth as king Nandisen of Kshetrapuri. He then reincarnated as a god in the sixth Graveyak dimension.

Life as a Tirthankara

From the dimension of gods this soul descended into the womb of queen Prithvi Devi, wife of king Pratishthasen of Varanasi. During her pregnancy the queen did not lose her normal shapely figure, as generally happens. As her flanks still remained attractive, the child, when born, was named Suparshva.

When Suparshva became young he was married and later ascended the throne. He ably conducted the affairs of he state and looked after the well being of his people. One day while he was enjoying the nature sitting at the roof top, he observed the falling of leaves and wilting of flowers. Suddenly he became aware of the transient nature of life. This gave a rising to the feeling of detachment and desire for spiritual upliftment. He gave his kingdom to his son and became an ascetic. After nine months of disciplined practices he became an omniscient on the sixth day of the dark half of the month of Phalgun. For a long period he worked for the spread of right knowledge. He attained Nirvana on the seventh day of the bright half of he month of Palgun at Sammetshikhar.

Chandraprabha

Chandraprabha was the eighth Jain Tirthankar of the present age (Avasarpini). According to Jain beliefs, he became a siddha, a liberated soul which has destroyed all of its karma. Chandraprabha (also known as Chandraprabhu Swami) was born to King Mahasen Raja and Queen Lakshmana Devi at Chandrapuri in the Ikshvaku clan. His birth date was the twelfth day of the Posh Krishna month of the Indian calendar.

Previous Births

In his birth as king Padma of Mangalavati town of Dhatkikhand, the being that was to become Bhagavan Chandraprabh earned Tirthankarnam-and-gotra-karma. Spending a life time as a god in Anuttar Vijay dimension he descended into the womb of queen Lakshmana, wife of king Mahasen of Chandranana town.

Life as Tirthankara

During her pregnancy, one day the queen was looking at the splendors and glowing full-moon. All of a sudden she had a strange desire to drink the glowing streak of moon light. The king cleverly managed to satisfy this strange desire of a pregnant mother. On the thirteenth day of the dark half of the month of Paush the queen gave birth to a healthy son who was fair and glowing like the moon. He was named Chandraprabh (glow of the moon). Chandraprabh was apathetic towards the mundane pleasures and princely grandeur. After he ascended the throne his reign was short lived. He became an ascetic in the prime of his youth and just after three months of acute spiritual practices he became an omniscient. For a considerably long period he continued to enlighten the people and propagate the true religion. When his end approached he went to Sammetshikhar and after a month of long fast and meditation attained Nirvana.

Pushpadanta

Pushpadanta, also known as Suvidhinath, was the ninth Jain Tirthankar of the present age (Avasarpini). According to Jain beliefs, he became a siddha, a liberated soul which has destroyed all of its karma. Pushpadanta was born to King Sugreev Raja and Queen Rama Rani at Kakandi in the Ikshvaku clan. His birth date was the fifth day of the Margshrsha Krishna month of the Indian calendar. In the tradition started by Bhagavan Rishabhdev, the ninth Tirthankar who re-established the four pronged religious ford was Bhagavan Suvidhinath.

Previous Births

During his earlier incarnation as emperor Mahapadma of Pushkalvati Vijay purified his soul to he extant of earning Tirthankaranama-gotra-karma. He took birth in the Vijayant dimension of gods and from there he descended into the womb of queen Rama Devi, wife of king Sugriva of Kakandi town.

Life as a Tirthankara

During the period of pregnancy queen Rama developed a strange capacity to develop processes for doing even the most difficult of tasks. Everyone got astonished at her skill. When the child was born the king accordingly named him as Suvidhi (correct procedure). During the teething period of the child the mother got a craving for playing with flowers. As such, he was also popularly known as Pushpadant (flower-tooth). Suvidhinath had a normal princely life, but with detachment. He became an ascetic at an early age and attained omniscience only after four months rigorous spiritual practices. He attained Nirvana at Sammetshikhar on the ninth day of the dark half of the month of Kartik. The tradition of the four pronged religious ford started by Bhagavan Rishabhdev gradually became extinct after the Nirvana of Bhagavan Suvidhinath. After his death, first the ascetic organization disintegrated and a time came when there was no ascetic left. The religious discourses two were given by common citizens or Shravaks. Slowly the influence of wealth became overpowering and people started forgetting the principals of five vows including Ahimsa and truthfulness. The discipline of spiritual principles gave way to ritualistic exchanges of wealth and total indiscipline.

Sheetalnath

Sheetalnath was the tenth Jain Tirthankar of the present age (Avasarpini). According to Jain beliefs, he became a siddha, a liberated soul which has destroyed all of its karma. Sheetalnath was born to King Dradhrath Raja and Queen Nanda Rani at Bhaddilpur in the Ikshvaku clan. His birth date was the twelfth day of the Magh Krishna month of the Indian calendar.

Previous Births

The being that was to be Bhagavan Sheetalnath, in his previous but one birth was the king of Susima town in the Pushkarvar island. His name was Padmottar. When his son reached adulthood the religious king gave his kingdom to the son and took Diksha from Tristadha Muni. Vigorous spiritual practices and worship of the pious states as mentioned in the scriptures resulted in his acquiring the Tirthankaranama-gotra-karma. Completing his age he reincarnated as the king of the Pranat dimension of gods.

Life as a Tirthankara

In Bhaddilipur town in the subcontinent of Bharat, ruled king Drridhrath. In the womb of his queen, Nanda, descended the being that was Padmottar, when he completed his age in the dimension of gods. One day due to some strange ailment, king Dridhrath had high fever and acute burning sensation in his body. He did not get any relief even after applying a variety of ointments. Out of anxiety and to comfort the king, the queen put her palm on his body. This mere touch of the queen removed the burning sensation and a feeling of soothing relief swept his body. After this incident the king decided to name the new born as Sheetal (cool/ calm). Sheetalnath was born on the twelfth day of the dark half of the month Magh. When he grew older he married at the request of his parents. At proper time, king Dridhrath crowned him and took Diksha. After a long and successful reign Sheetalnath left his home and became an ascetic. He attained omniscience under a Peepal tree on the fourteenth day of the dark half of the month of Paush. After wandering and preaching for a long time, he came to Sammetshikhar and attained attained Nirvana on the second day of the dark half of the month of Vaishakh.

Shreyansanath

Shreyansanath was the eleventh Jain Tirthankar of the present age (Avasarpini). According to Jain beliefs, he became a Siddha- a liberated soul which has destroyed all of its karma. Shreyansanath was born to King Vishnu Raja and Queen Vishnu Devi Rani at Sinhpuri, near Sarnath in the Ikshvaku clan. His birth date was the twelfth day of the Falgun Krishna month of the Indian calendar.

Previous Births

In his earlier incarnation, the being that was to become Bhagavan Shreyansnath purified his soul as king Nalingulm, and went to the Mahashakra dimension of gods.

Life as a Tirthankara

From there he descended and took birth as Shreyans Kumar, the son of king Vishnuraja and queen Vishnu Devi of Simhapur. Shreyans Kumar was born on the twelfth day of the dark half of the month of Bhadrapad. He had a normal princely life and ascended the throne when Vishnuraja retired. After a long reign Shreyans Kumar became a Shraman and within a short span of two months attained omniscience on the fifteenth day of the dark half of the month of Magh under a mango tree. He got Nirvana at Sammetshikhar on the third day of the dark half of the month of Shravan. It was during his period that the being that was to be Bhagavan Mahavir reigned as the first Vasudev Triprishta. After the death of Triprishtha, his brother Baldev Achal became a disciple of Dharmghosh who was a follower of Shreyansnath. Achal got liberated in this birth.

Vasupujya

Vasupujya Swami was the twelve Jain Tirthankar of the present age (Avasarpini). According to Jain beliefs, he became a siddha, a liberated soul which has destroyed all of its karma. Vasupujya was born to King Vasupujya Raja and Queen Jaya Devi Rani at Champapuri in the Ikshvaku clan. His birth date was the fourteenth day of the Falgun Krishna month of the Indian calendar.

Previous Births

King Padmottar ruled over Mangalavati town of Ardhapushkar island. He was a person devoted to spiritual pursuits. In later part of his life he took Diksha from Acharya Vajranabh. Reducing the tarnish of Karma by penance and spiritual practices he earned the Tirthankara-name-gotra-karma and incarnated as a god in the Pranat dimension.

Life as a Tirthankara

Vasupujya was the king of Champa town in the Bharat subcontinent. His queen was Jaya Devi. Besides being a great warrior King Vasupujya was a compassionate and charitable person. The queen too was benevolent and she inspired the king in his charitable activities. The being that was Padmottar was born to queen Jaya Devi. It is said that when the queen was pregnant, the king of gods came to convey his veneration to the future Tirthankar and his mother. As Indra is also known as Vasu, the new born was named Vasupujya (venerated by Vasu).

As Vasupujya grew, so grew his inherent detachment and apathy for mundane affairs. He had no attraction for the regal splendor and grandeur. When he became young his parents wanted him to marry but he declined. He even conveyed that he had no intention of ascending the throne. In spite of all persuasions from his family members, he renounced the worldly life and became a Shraman on the fifteenth day of he dark half of the month of Phalgun along with six hundred other persons.

The intensity of his spiritual practices was so deep that he became an omniscient within one month. At that moment he was practicing under a Patal tree in a garden outside Champa town. He established the four pronged religious ford and preached for a long period. The second Vasudev, Dwiprishtaha, was his devotee. He and his brother Baldev Shrivijay conquered Prativasudev Tark and brought his oppressive rule to an end. Shrivijay later joined the ascetic order of Bhagavan Vasupujya. Bhagavan Vasupujya got Nirvana in Champa town on the fourteenth day of the bright half of the month of Ashad.

Vimalnath

Vimalnath was the thirteenth Jain Tirthankar of the present age (Avasarpini). According to Jain beliefs, he became a Siddha, a liberated soul which has destroyed all of its karma. Vimalnath was born to King Kratvarm Raja and Queen Shyama Devi at Kampilaji in the Ikshvaku clan. His birth date was the third day of the Magh Sukla month of the Indian calendar.

Previous Births

King Kritvarma and queen Shyanan Devi of Kampilpur were both spiritualists and devotees of the Jina. The queen one day saw fourteen auspicious things in her dream and the augurs announced that she will give birth to a Tirthankar. It was the pious soul that in its earlier birth was king Padmasen of Mahapuri town in Datakikhand and had descended into the queens womb from the Mahardhik dimension of gods.

Life as a Tirthankara

During her pregnancy the queen radiated a soothing glow.

Her temperature also became congenial, kind, and generous. When the child was born the whole atmosphere was also filled with a soothing glow. Inspired by this spread of purity, the king named his new born son as Vimal (pure/untarnished). In due course, prince Vimal Kumar became young, was married, and then ascended the throne. After a long and successful reign he became a Shraman along with one thousand other kings and princes on the fourth day of the bright half of the month of Magh. After two years of spiritual practices he attained omniscience and established the religious ford. Merak Prativasudev, Svayambhu Vasudev, and Bhadra Baldev were his contemporaries. Bhagavan Vimalnath got Nirvana at Sammetshikhar on the seventh day of the dark half of the month of Ashadh.

Anantnath

Anantnath was the fourteenth Jain Tirthankar of the present age (Avasarpini). According to Jain beliefs, he became a siddha, a liberated soul which has destroyed all of its karma. Anantnath was born to King Raja Sinhsen and Queen Suyasha Rani at Ayodhya in the Ikshvaku clan. His birth date was the 13th day of the Vaishakh Krishna month of the Indian calendar.

Life as Tirthankara

Queen Suyasha Devi, wife of king Simhasen of Ayodhya, gave birth to an illustrious son on the thirteenth day of the dark half of the month of Vaishakh. During her pregnancy the queen dreamt of a very long strand of beads whose ends were not visible. The power and the glory of the king also increased manifold during this period. Accordingly, the new born was named Anant (endless) Kumar. After leading a normal life, first as a prince and then as the king he became an ascetic along with one thousand other persons.

He became an omniscient on the fourteenth day of the dark half of the month of Vaishakh under an Ashok tree. In his first discourse he elaborated the subject of the fundamentals-matter and life. He had fifty chief disciples including the senior most named Yash. Purushottam Vasudev and Suprabh Baldev reigned during his period of influence. Bhagavan Anantnath got Nirvana at Sammetshikhar on the fifth day of the bright half of the month of Chaitra.

Dharmanath

Dharmanath was the fifteenth Jain Tirthankar of the present age (Avasarpini). According to Jain beliefs, he became a siddha, a liberated soul which has destroyed all of its karma. Dharmanath was born to King Bhanu Raja and Queen Suvrata Rani at Ratnapuri in the Ikshvaku clan. His birth date was the third day of the Magh Sukla month of the Indian calendar.

Previous Life

The being that was to become Bhagavan Dharmnath was king Dridhrath of Bhaddilpur in Mahavideh area, in its earlier incarnation.

Although he had enormous wealth and a large kingdom, he led a detached and pious life like a lotus in a pond. Even great saints praised him as the embodiment of religion. During the later part of his life king Dridhrath became an ascetic and as a result of his unblemished character and sincere spiritual practices he earned the Tirthankarnam-and-gotra-karma. Completing his age he reincarnated as a god in the Vaijayant dimension.

Life as a Tirthankara

This being then descended into the womb of queen Suvrata, wife of king Bhanuraja of Ratnapur. During the pregnancy the queen devoted all her time in religious activities. Even the king and all other members of the family were inclined to devote maximum time to various religious activities like charity, righteousness, penances, studies etc. On the third day of the bright half of the month of Magh a son was born to the queen. Due to the religious influence during the pregnancy period, the king gave him the name Dharmnath.

In due course he became young, was married and then ascended the throne. He ruled successfully for a long period. One day he terminated all worldly attachments and became and ascetic. After two years of spiritual practices he became omniscient. His first religious discourse was attended by the fifth Vasudev Purush Simha and Sudarshan Baldev. In his first discourse he mainly dealt with the subject of form and ill effects of passions. A large audience was benefited by this eloquent discourse. At last he went to Sammetshikhar and got Nirvana.

Shantinath

Shantinath was the sixteenth Jain Tirthankar of the present age (Avasarpini). According to Jain beliefs, he became a siddha, a liberated soul which has destroyed all of its karma. Shantinath was born to King Viswasen Raja and Queen Achira Rani at Hastinapur in the Ikshvaku clan. His birth date is the thirteen day of the Jyest Krishna month of the Indian calendar.

Previous Births

The account of the earlier incarnations of Bhagavan Shantinath indicates that his being had taken the path of discipline that lead toward purity of soul many births before. As a result of this uplifting during his incarnations as Shrisen and Vajrayudh it was born as Meghrath, the son of king Dhanrath of Pundarikini town in Purva Mahavideh area. At the proper time, king Dhanrath gave the kingdom to Meghrat and became an ascetic.

Refugee Protection

Meghrath was a benevolent and religious ruler. He was compassionate and protected all living things. Being a Kshatriya and a warrior he had the chivalry to sacrifice all he had in order to protect those in trouble. One day while observing the partial renunciation vow (Paushadh) he was about to start a discourse on the religion propagated by the Tirthankars.

All of a sudden a pigeon, trembling with fear, fell in his lap and uttered in choking human voice, "Save me, O king! Give me refuge, take me under your protection!" The compassionate king comforted the bird and took it under his protection. The pigeon was followed by a falcon who too uttered in human language, "O king! This pigeon is my food, leave it alone." The king tried to explain, "It has taken refuge with me, as such I am duty bound to protect it.

I will give you any type of food you want; why kill a living thing just to fill your stomach?" The falcon insisted, "If you will not leave it I may die of hunger. I am a carnivore; who will provide me food. If I die, you will be responsible and bear the sin." When the falcon did not yield, Meghrath said at last, "O falcon! As long as I exist, I will not allow you to die.

I will cut out flesh from my body equivalent to the weight of this little pigeon and give it to you. You may satisfy your urge to eat. But under no circumstance I shall allow you to kill the bird that has taken refuge with me." The falcon agreed to this proposal and the king put the pigeon in one pan of balance and in the other started putting pieces of flesh cut out from his own body.

Surprisingly, the weight of the pigeon continued to increase as the king went on putting his flesh in the pan. Witnessing this pathetic scene, the queens and the members of the assembly were moved to tears. They requested the king not to sacrifice his precious life for a mere pigeon. The falcon, was also requested relent but he too declined. The king continued to cut flesh from his body and put it in the pan of the balance.

At last, when the pieces of flesh were not enough, the king got up from his seat and sat down in the pan. Everyone present was dumb struck at this lofty compassion and chivalry displayed by the king. Suddenly there was a flesh of divine light and a divine personage appeared. The pigeon and the falcon disappeared. The god addressed the king, "Maharaj! The king of gods was praising your compassion and courage, in his assembly. I could not contain myself and came around to test you myself.

All this was my creation. You come out with flying colors. You are worthy of the praise bestowed on you by the King of gods. Please forgive me." The god filled Meghrath's wounds instantaneously and left for his abode. Whenever there is a talk about chivalry and compassion king Meghrath's name is taken with respect.

Disturbed by the miseries of the mundane life, one day king Meghrath was doing mediation. He transcended to a very high level of purity. Knowing about this uncommon purity and determination of Meghrath the king of gods bowed to him with reverence, "My salutations to you O citizen Yogi! there are but a few in this world who could reach this level of detachment and purity." Two senior consorts of Indra, Surup and Atirup did not like this gesture of praise of a mere human. They both came to disturb the meditation of Meghrath. They made several beautiful and voluptuous damsels appear before the king.

These beauties tried to disturb Meghrath by a display of dances and inviting gestures. When these night long seductive afflictions failed to disturb king Meghrath, the goddesses, before returning to their abode, appeared themselves and asked the king to forgive them. King Meghrath, then, crowned his son and took Diksha from Arhat Dhanrath. Due to his increasing purity in meditation in the face of many afflictions, he earned the Tirthankarnam-and-gotra-karma. Completing his age he reincarnated in the Sarvarthsiddha dimension of gods.

Birth before Liberation

From the dimension of gods, the being that was Meghrath descended into the womb of queen Achira, wife of king Vishvasen of Ikshvaku clan and ruler of Hastinapur. Once there was a great storm in the Hastinapur area. There were heavy rains and many other calamities. An epidemic followed these calamities and hundreds of people started dying every day. The masses appealed to the king to save them, but the king took a vow that he will not eat or drink as long as peace and normalcy does not return to his kingdom. Moved by this harsh vow of king Vishvasen, the king of gods himself appeared before the king said, "O king! You are disturbed unnecessarily. Is there any death at the place where the wish-fulfilling trio of Chintamani, Kalpavriksha, and Kamdhenu (divine gem, tree and cow) exist? The embodiment of peace is being carried by queen Achira Devi in her womb and you still feel disturbed. It surprises me!" The Indra then sang a panegyric in praise of the Tirthankar and advised the king, "Let the queen got to he roof top and sing this panegyric.

After this, let her throw a glance at the vast expanses of your kingdom all around. This pacifying glance of the queen will remove all miseries from wherever it reaches." On the thirteenth day of the dark half of the month of Jyeshta the queen gave birth to the great and illustrious son.

The whole universe, including even the hell, was pervaded by a soothing glow and a feeling of joy and happiness. Due to the pacifying influence during the period of pregnancy, the new born was named Shanti Kumar (Shanti = Peace). When he came of age he was married to several beautiful princesses. At proper time king Vishvasen gave the kingdom Shantinath and took Diksha.

Chakravarti

After a few years king Shantinath got a son who was named Chakrayudh. Several years later, the divine disc weapon appeared in the armory. When the traditional worship rituals of this weapon were concluded, it started moving toward the east on its own. Shantinath followed the Chakra with his armed forces. Most of the kings on the way surrendered. After defeating the remaining few Shantinath became a Chakravarti.

Life as a Tirthankara

When, after a long and peaceful reign, he realized that the moment for his renunciation was approaching, Shantinath went into the Sahasramra jungle, and, becoming an ascetic commenced his practices. After wandering as an ascetic for one year he returned to the same jungle and there, on the ninth day of the bright half of the month of Paush, he attained omniscience under a Nandi tree. His first discourse was on the subject of disciplining the senses. He came to Sammetshikhar after a long period wandering and propagating true religion. There, along with nine hundred other ascetics, he observed a month long fast that started his final meditation. On the thirteenth day of the dark half of the month of Jyeshta, Bhagavan Shantinath attained Nirvana.

Kunthunath

Kunthunath was the seventeenth Jain Tirthankar of the present age (Avasarpini). According to Jain beliefs, he became a siddha, a liberated soul which has destroyed all of its karma. Kunthunath was born to King Shursen Raja and Queen Srirani Rani at Hastinapur in the Ikshvaku clan. His birth date was the 14th day of the Vaishakh Krishna month of the Indian calendar.

Previous Births

The name of the powerful and illustrious king of Khadgi town in Purva Mahavideh area was Simhavaha. He was a very devoted and religious person when his son became young and capable, he handed over his kingdom to the son and took Diksha from Samvaracharya. As a result of his vigorous penance and devotion for the Arhat, he earned the Tirthankaranama-gotra-karma. Completing his age he reincarnated in the Sarvarthsiddha dimension of gods.

Life as a Tirthankara

From the dimension of gods he descended into the womb of queen Shri Devi, wife of king Shursen of Hastinapur. During her pregnancy the queen saw a heap of gemstones known as Kunthu in her dreams. This inspired the king to name him Kunthu Kumar. The pious deeds of earlier birth resulted in unlimited power and grandeur for Kunthu Kumar. After Shursen became an ascetic, Kunthu Kumar ascended the throne. Soon the disc weapon appeared in his armory and he proceeded to conquer the world with his mighty army. Without any confrontation all the kings accepted his sovereignty and Kunthunath became a Chakravarti.

Many mighty kings and princes used to be present in his court all the time. After a long and peaceful reign of twenty three thousand seven hundred and fifty years he became an ascetic along with one thousand kings immediately after Diksha he acquired Manahparyav Jnan.

He spent sixteen years as an ordinary ascetic. Indulging in penances and other spiritual practices, he attained omniscience on the third day of the bright half of the month of Chaitra under a Tilak tree in Sahasramara jungle outside Hastinapur. His first discourse was on the subject of "inner purity".

As an omniscient ascetic Kunthunath wandered around and preached true religion for a very long period. He then went to Sammetshikhar and observed a month long fast before breathing his last. His followers were deeply devoted to him. As such, a large crowd was present at the moment of his Nirvana and cremation ceremony. They witnessed the ceremony with heavy hearts and tear filled eyes. The mortal remains of Bhagavan Kunthunath were taken away by the gods for worship.

Aranath

Aranath was the eighteenth Jain Tirthankar of the present age (Avasarpini). According to Jain beliefs, he became a siddha-a liberated soul which has destroyed all of its karma. Aranath was born to King Sudarshan Raja and Queen Devi Rani at Hastinapur in the Ikshvaku clan. His birth date was the 10th day of the Migsar Krishna month of the Indian calendar.

Previous Births

King Dhanpati of Susima city in Mahavideh area took Diksha from Samvar Muni and after acquiring Tirthankar-nam-and gotra-karma he reincarnated in the Graiveyak dimension of gods.

Life as a Tirthankara

From here he descended into the womb of queen Maha Devi, wife of king Sudarshan of Hastinapur. Besides the fourteen great dreams that precede the conception of a Tirthankar, queen Maha Devi also saw a gem studded wheel (Ara). accordingly, after the birth the boy was named Ara Kumar.

When Ara Kumar became young he was married to many beautiful princesses. Later king Sudarshan gave the kingdom to Ara Kumar and became an ascetic. For some years Arnath ruled as a regional king. Gradually his power and glory increased and one day the disc weapon appeared in his armory. He conquered the six continents and became a Chakravarti. In his attendance were thirty two thousand kings.

After a long and successful reign, one day emperor Arnath was thinking about the ever changing seasons. This triggered a chain of sublime thoughts that lead to complete detachment. He renounced all the wealth, power and glory and became an ascetic. He did spiritual practices and wandered around. After three years he arrived in the Sahasramra jungle outside Hastinapur and stood in mediation under a mango tree. With the fire of higher meditation he burnt one after another the four vitiating Karmas including illusory, knowledge obstructing, perception obstructing, and power hindering. Consequently he attained omniscience. His first discourse after attaining omniscience was on the subject of "how to win over the enemies like attachment and aversion."

In this first religious assembly thousands of individuals became ascetics including his 32 chief disciples headed by Kumbh. Spending a long period of twenty one thousand years wandering and promoting religion, he finally arrived at Sammethshikhar and attained liberation. The sixth and seventh Vasudevas and Baldevas and the eighth Chakravarti (Subhum) were his followers.

Mallinath

Mallinath was the nineteenth Jain Tirthankar of the present age (Avasarpini). According to Jain beliefs, Mallinath became a siddha-a liberated soul which has destroyed all of its karma. According to members of the Shvetambar sect, she was female, making her the only female to become a Tirthankar during the present age. Digambaras believe that Mallinath was male. Mallinath was born to King Kumbha Raja and Queen Prabhavati Rani at Mithila in the Ikshvaku clan. Their birth date was the 5th day of the Shravan Sukla month of the Indian calendar.

Previous Lives

In the Aparvideh area there was a city named Vitshoka. It was ruled by a powerful king Mahabal. He was very intimate with six other kings who were his childhood friends. Influenced by discourses of ascetics, king Mahabal decided to follow the spiritual path. he sought opinion of his six childhood friends with the remark-I want to became an ascetic, do you also?

All the six friends replied, "We have been together during both good and bad times. When we have been together during both good and bad times. When we have enjoyed the mundane life in company, it would be shameful if we part company on the spiritual path. We shall become ascetics together and we shall do all spiritual practices together."

The seven kings took Diksha from Varadharma Muni and started the spiritual practices earnestly. Mahabal was bitten by the bug of ego. He thought, "I have always been ahead of my friends. Now, if I do the same practices I will remain at the same level. As such I should do a little more and be ahead as before." With this feeling Mahabal started secretly doing more practices than the others. All the seven friends would formally take vow of some specific penance together but when on conclusion, other friends broke their fast, Mahabal would continue his fast on some pretext. The desire to be above the ordinary inspired this competition. As a result of this deception Mahabal feel from the lofty spiritual level he had attained due to his intense practices and acquired the Karma that would result in being born as a woman. However, as he still maintained the purity and intensity in his practices he later also earned the Tirthankarnam-and-gotra-karma. All the seven ascetics breathed their last after sixty days fast and mediation. They reincarnated as gods in the Anuttar dimension.

Shvetambar Accounts

Birth of Malli Kumari

The being that was Mahabal, leaving the abode of gods, descended into the womb of queen Prabhavati, wife of king Kumbh of Mithila town. During the third month of pregnancy the queen had a desire to sleep on a bed made up of fragrant flowers of five colors and to smell a bouquet of flowers (Malladam) all the time. It is said that if a pious soul resides in the womb all the desires are fulfilled. On the eleventh day of the bright half of the month of Margshirsh the Queen gave birth to a pious and beautiful girl. It was unprecedented that a Tirthankar be born as a girl; everyone was surprised. But even the almighty is helpless when the Karmas precipitate into action.

The mother's craving for flower bouquet inspired the king to name the girl as Malli Kumari. She was very fond of having a bouquet of flowers. Florists from far and near used to bring attractive and beautiful bouquets to present her and get desired gifts in return. Strange yarns about her infatuation for flowers and bouquets spread all around.

Divine Earrings

Once a famous and rich merchant, Arhannak, of Champa town, went on a sea voyage with some other people. After earning heaps of wealth when he was returning, a god appeared. In order to test Arhannak's devotion for his religion, the god created a variety of afflictions. Even in the face of death Arhannak did not yield. His devotion for the path shown by Jina was absolutely unwavering. The god was pleased with this unrelenting determination of Arhannak. He gave the merchant a pair of divine earrings as gift.

On the way back the ship stopped at Mithila. All the merchants went to King Kumbh's assembly with gifts. Arhannak gifted the divine earnings for Malli Kumari. The king and his ministers became astonished at the divine beauty of these earrings. Once a joint in these earrings broke. King Kumbh called expert goldsmiths to weld this joint but none of the artisans had skill enough to do its work. In annoyance the king exiled many of these artisans. Wherever these artisans went they talked of the divine beauty of Malli Kumari.

Ignorant Artist

Once Mallidinna, the younger brother of Malli Kumari, constructed an entertainment room in the palace premises. One of the working artists was highly talented. This artist had a glimpse of a toe of Malli Kumari who was standing behind a lattice. This enabled the highly gifted artist to paint a fresco of the princess on a wall of the room. he was under the impression that the prince would be pleased to look at he exact replica of his sister and richly reward him.

When the room was complete, the prince came with his wives to look at and approve the beautiful paintings, some of which were erotic as well. While he was enjoying these works of art, he came across the painting of Malli Kumari. He could not believe what he saw. Ashamed of himself he said, "My elder sister is here and I am shamelessly enjoying these sensual paintings along with my wives." His governess explained, "Prince, You are mistaken. this is not your sister but her life size portrait." The prince carefully examined the painting and was astonished at the realistic work of art and the skill of the artist.

However the feeling of anger overtook the sense of appreciation. He was annoyed at the mindless effrontery of the artist who had painted such a live portrait of his respected elder sister in the entertainment chamber. The angry prince called the painter and asked him when and how he saw the princess. The artist humbly submitted, "Sire! I just saw one toe of the princess from behind a lattice. But I am endowed with this miraculous skill that when I start painting even a part of a thing I automatically complete the thing perfectly." This explanation did not pacify the prince. He exiled the artist after amputating his right thumb. The vexed artist made another painting of the princess and sold it at a very high price to king Adinshatru of Hastinapur. Adinshatru was attracted towards Malli Kumari, as many others who had heard about her divine beauty.

Discussion with Choksha

One day a female mendicant named Choksha came to Mithila. In order to influence the royal family she came to Malli Kumari. Choksha was a scholar of Vedas and other scriptures and her interpretation was that keeping the body clean, indulging in charity and the anointment of Tirth (sacred place)were the only religious activities that lead to liberation. She started preaching her ideas to Malli Kumari, who heard all this with patience. When Choksha had nothing more to say, Malli Kumari said in her magnetic voice, "With due respect to your attire, I am surprised at your ignorance,

Choksha. Know that every charity is not done with religious or pious intent. Even cleaning the body and anointment of a Tirth are not sacred if they are not done with equanimous and pious feelings or if they cause any destruction of any living organism. A blood stained cloth will never be cleaned by washing it with blood. The basis of religion is a discerning attitude. To an irrational person, even penance causes discomfort and irritation." This irrefutable logic of Malli Kumari silenced Choksha, but she became angry and decided to take revenge.

Choksha decided that, in order to shatter the pride of this princess it would be best if she could be manipulated into marrying some king who already had many wives. Cooking up her plan, she approached the king of Kampilyapur in Panchal state. She gave a titillating description of the divine beauty of Malli Kumari and provokingly said to the king, "Your life and palace both are lack luster as long as you do not marry and bring this divine beauty to your palace." King Jitshatru was highly impressed. He decided to seek the hand of Malli Kumari in marriage.

Change of Heart of the Six Kings

The six friends of Malli Kumari's earlier birth were born in six different royal families and inherited the kingdoms.

They were:

1. King Pratibuddha of Saketpur
2. King Chandrachhay of Champa
3. King Rupi of Shravasti
4. King Shankh of Varanasi
5. King Adinshatru of Hastinapur
6. King Jitshatru of Panchal (Kampilyapur).

The fame of the beauty of Malli Kumari inspired all these six kings to send proposing kings and returned the emissaries. These kings felt insulted and marched on Mithila with their armies and lay a seize.

When king Kumbh got the challenge he became worried. Malli Kumari asked about the cause of her father's anxiety. Kumbh replied, "Daughter! All these kings want to marry you. My refusal has irked them and they have surrounded Mithila. I am anxious about what I should do now!"

Malli Kumari was already aware of all these activities due to her Avadhi gnan (the capacity to know all about the physical world). She made a plan to enlighten these friends of her last birth. In the palace garden she got a chamber made and in its center installed a life size statue that was her exact replica. It's inside was hollow and there was an opening hidden under the neck. Six adjacent chambers were also erected around this central circular chamber. These six chambers had windows opening in the main chamber. These windows were so designed that a n onlooker could only see the statue and nothing else. Making all these arrangements, Malli Kumari started putting one handful of the food she ate every day inside the hollow statue.

When the stink of decomposed food, coming out of the statue on opening the lid became intolerable, Malli Kumari went to her father. She said to her father, "Stop worrying, father, and inform the kings individually that I want to meet them to discus about marriage." The king did likewise. Believing that only he had been invited, everyone of the kings accepted the invitation. At the predetermined time they all came one by one and were led to the six chambers allotted for them separately. From the windows in their chambers each one of them gazed at the divinely beautiful statue considering it to be Mali Kumari. Everyone was dreaming of the marriage and the happy moments thereafter. All of a sudden Malli Kumari removed the concealed cover from the hole in the neck of he statue. The obnoxious smell of decomposed food filled the chambers. The hellish smell hit the peeping kings and they were jolted out of their state of day dreaming. Their faces distorted with revulsion.

Panic stricken, the kings shouted, "What is all this? Why have I been locked in this chamber? It is impossible breath here. Please open the doors." It was then that Malli Kumari appeared and said, "O slaves of passions! You are totally infatuated with female beauty. A moment ago you were admiring this earthly beauty and were nurturing a desire to possess and enjoy it. Now a hatred for the same is evident on your distorted faces. What sort of love for beauty is this?"

The kings shouted, "Why are you trying to make fools of us? It is impossible to tolerate this stink?"

Malli Kumari asked the attendants to open the gates of the

chambers. All the six kings rushed out and were surprised to see each other. Finding the right opportunity Malli Kumari said to them, "The stink caused by just a few handfuls of food is intolerable. Mind you, this body is nothing but a statue made of bones and flesh and maintained by the same food. Why such infatuation for such decomposed thing? You are all friends of my last birth. Rise above this infatuation and commence once again the terminated pursuit of purification of the self."

All the six kings acquired Jati-smaran Jnan, They sought pardon from king Kumbh as well as Malli Kumari. Resolving to follow the path of renunciation they left for their respective kingdoms.

Malli Kumari also announced her decision to become an ascetic. After the great charity she became an ascetic along with three hundred males and equal number of females. Immediately after her Diksha, she acquired Vipulmati Manahparyav Jnan (the ultimate Pra normal capacity and started deep meditation. The same afternoon she attained omniscience. In her first discourse she discussed on the subject of philosophy of equanimity. The six kings took Diksha during this first discourse. After enhancing the spread of religion for a long period she attained Nirvana on the fourth day of the bright half of the month of Chaitra at Sammetshikhar.

Munisuvrata

Munisuvrata Swami was the twentieth Jain Tirthankar of the present age (Avasarpini). According to Jain beliefs, he became a siddha, a liberated soul which has destroyed all of its karma. Munisuvrata was born to King Sumitra Raja and Queen Padmavati Rani at Mithila in the HariVansh clan. His birth date was the 15th day of the Shravan Sukla month of the Indian calendar.

The being that was to be Bhagavan Munisuvrat purified its soul during his birth as Surshreshta, the king of Champa city in Mahavideh. He then reincarnated in the Pranat dimension of gods.

Life as a Tirthankara

King Sumitra of the Harivamh clan ruled over Rajgriha town. His wife, queen Padmavati, gave birth to a son, the being that had descended from the Pranat dimension of gods, on the ninth day of the dark half of the month of Jyeshta. After the traditional post birth rituals the name giving ceremony was celebrated. The king announced that since this being had descended into the womb of queen Padmavati, she took a variety of good vows and lead a life as disciplined as an ascetic. As such the new born named Munisuvrat (vow like ascetics).

In due course Munisuvrat was married and ascended the throne. After a successful and long reign he became an ascetic on the eighth day of the dark half of the month of Phalgun. He wandered as an ordinary ascetic for eleven months and attained omniscience under a Champa tree. His first discourse was on the subject of "scriptural and applied philosophy". After a long life devoted to spread of true religion he went to Sammetshikhar and got liberated on the ninth day of the dark half of the month of Jyeshtha.

Bhagavan Munisuvrat's period was an important period of Jain pre-history. His illustrious contemporaries and followers included stalwarts like the ninth Chakravarti-Mahapadma, the eighth Prativasudev, Baldev, and Vasudev, Ravan, Rama and Lakshman respectively. The elder brother of Bahagavan Munisuvrat, ascetic Vishnu Kumar, also became famous for his pioneering effort of saving the Jain organization from the oppressions of mister Namuchi; the Raksha Bandhan festival is celebrated in the memory of that event.

Shani and Lord Munisuvarat (20th Jain Tirthankar)

One who prays to Lord Munisuvarat is protected from Shani as he is great devotee of Lord Munisuvarat Swami (20th jain Tirthankar) as per Jainism and really one can trace from ancient times people worshiping Munisuvarat Swami whose symbol is Tortoise to get protected from ill effects of not properly placed shani in ones horoscope.

Usually Munisuvarat Swamis idol is always found made up of Black colour. Millions of devotees across the world have witnessed miracles of Munisuvarat swami.

At Kankali Tila in Mathura a deity of Muni-Suvrat Swami whose insignia is tortoise, was discovered. One of the nude statues in Mohan-Jodaro (Indus Valley) has the tortoise insignia, which indicates that it must be of Muni-Suvrat Swami. In Vedic history there are descriptions of a Muni in the Puran, connected to the tortoise, which throws light on Muni Suvrat. In the Rigved (23,

27, 32) a sage with tortoise insignia has been mentioned which is none other than Tirthankar Muni-Suvrat Swami. It connection with the tortoise the Puran (40, 27, 41) writes that Vishnu appeared in the form of tortoise in Rishabh race (First Tirthankar).

Nami Natha

Naminatha was the twenty-first Jain Tirthankar of the current era. According to Jain beliefs, he became a siddha, a liberated soul which has destroyed all of its karma. Naminatha was born to King Vijay Raja and Queen Vipra Rani of the Ikshvaku dynasty, who were the rulers of Mithila at that time. His birth date is the 8th day of Shravan Krishna in the Indian calendar.

Previous Births

According to Jain tradition, the soul that would one day be the god Bhagavan Naminath purified itself during its incarnation as King Siddharth of the town of Kshambi in eastern Mhavideh. He reincarnated as a god in the Aparajit dimension, and later reincarnated as the child of Queen Vipra and King Vijay.

Life as a Tirthankara

As the queen had seen fourteen auspicious things in her dream at the moment of conception, the augurs declared that the unborn child was going to be a Chkravarti or a Tirthankar.

During Vipra's pregnancy, Mithila was attacked by a group of powerful kings. Peace-loving King Vijay was at a loss to find a peaceful solution, until an expert augur told the king that the pregnant queen should go to the roof of the palace and look at the attacking armies. The queen followed these instructions and threw a loving glance at the large armies stationed on the fields outside the town. The aura of the pious soul in her womb was so powerful that it cast a pacifying spell on the attackers. The kings, who had been sure of winning the battle, surrendered and bowed before king Vijay.

This incident inspired the king to name his new-born child "Naminath." Born on the eighth day of the dark (second) half of the month of Sravan, Naminath had a happy childhood. When he matured, he was married and later was given the reign of the kingdom. After a long and peaceful reign, he became an ascetic on the ninth day of the dark (second) half of the month of Ashadh.

After nine months he attained omniscience under a Bakul Tree in a garden near Mithila. His first discourse was on the subject of right perception. After a long period of religious and spiritual activities, he went to Sammetsikhar, where he became liberated on the tenth day of the dark half of the month of Vaishakh.

Neminath

Neminatha was twenty-second Jain Tirthankar of the present age (Avsarpini). According to Jain beliefs, he became a Siddha, a liberated soul which has destroyed all of its karma. He is also known as *Aristhnemi* He along with Rishab or Adinath is mentioned in the Rig Veda Samhita. Neminatha was born to King Samudravijay Raja and Queen Shivadevi Rani at Souripur in the HariVansh clan. His birth date is the 5th day of Shravan Sukla in the Indian calendar.

Neminatha as a Historical Figure

There seems to be no doubt about the existence of Jainism in the 7th century BC, but the history of Jainism goes back even earlier than of Parsvanatha. The Jain record mentions the names of twenty two Tirthankaras before him. Neminatha, the 22nd Tirthankara of the Jains, was the son of Samudra Vijaya and grandson of Andhakavrishni. Many Jains and some Hindus is said to be a cousin of Krishna, the lord of the Bhagavad Gita (Hindu scriptures).

According to both religions, Krishna negotiated his marriage with Rajamati, the daughter of Ugrasena, but Neminath, empathizing with the animals which were to be slaughtered for the marriage feast, left the procession suddenly and renounced the world. Some writers of the Jain scriptures say that Tirthankara Neminath was the master of Krishna.

The *Andhakavrishnis* of Dwaraka in Kathiawar Region of present Gujrat state of India, as a republic is referred to in the Mahabharata, Arthasastra and Ashtadhyayi of Panini.

The name of the Vrishni corporation is also found on a coin which on paleographical grounds dates to the first or second century B.C.E. It seems that the republic was named after *Andhakavrishni*, the grandfather of Neminath. If *Andhakavrishni* is a real person, there seems to be little doubt that his grandson Neminatha was real.

It is mentioned in the Chhandogya Upanishads III, that the sage Ghora Angirasa imparted certain instructions of the spiritual sacrifice to Krishna, the son of Devaki. The liberal payment of this sacrifice was austerity, liberality, simplicity, non-violence and truthfulness. These teachings of Ghora Angirasa seem to be the tenets of Jainism. Hence, Ghora Angirasa seems to be a Jain sadhu. The word Ghora Angirasa seems to be an epithet given to him because of the extreme austerities he undertook. It may be possible to suggest that Neminatha was his early name and when he had obtained salvation after hard austerities, he might have been given the name of Ghora Angirasa. In fact, the Jaina traditions about Neminath or Arishtanemi as incorporated in the Harivamsa, Arittha Nemi Chariu and other works may be corroborated to some extent by the Brahaminical traditions. He is mentioned in some of the hymns of the Vedas but their meaning is doubtful.

In the Yajurveda, he seems to be clearly mentioned as one of the important Rishis. He is described as one who is capable of crossing over the ocean of life and death, as the remover of violence, and one who is instrumental is sparing life from injury. The Yajurveda probably belongs to the 12th century B.C.E. This indicates that Neminath was known at this time and flourished even before.

Physical Evidence for Existence

The literary evidence seems to be supported by an epigraphic evidence. In Kathiawar, a copper plate has been discovered on which there is an inscription. King Nebuchadrezzar I of Babylonia, who was also the lord of Reva-nagara (in Kathiawar of Gujarat) had come to the place (Dwarka) of the Yaduraja. He built a temple and paid homage and made the grant perpetual in favour of Lord Neminath, the paramount deity of Mt. Raivata. This inscription is of great historical importance. Nebuchadrezzar was living in the 10th century B.C.E. This indicates that even in the 10th century B.C.E. there was the worship of the temple of Neminath, the 22nd Tirthankara of the Jains.

He is said to be the contemporary of Krishna, the hero of Mahabharata. The Mahbabharta took place in 3138 BC.

Parshva

Parshvanath or Parshvanatha (*pârúvá-nâtha,* occasionally spelled *Parshvanath* or *Parswanath*) was the twenty-third Tirthankara (fordmaker) in Jainism. fl. ca. in the 9th Century BCE, traditionally (877 – 777 BCE). He is the earliest Jain leader generally accepted as a historical figure. He was a nobleman belonging to the Kshatriya caste.

Life as a Tirthankara

He lived a life of a nobleman for 30 years and was married, before he renounced the world to become a monk. He meditated for 84 days before attaining Nirvana. According to the Jain tradition he attained *nirvana* 250 years before the *nirvana* of Mahavira, the 24th Tirthankar. The chronology accepted by most Jains (Svetambaras) places Mahavira's death in 527 BCE. Parshva was the son of king Ashvasena and queen Vama of Varanasi. He renounced the world and became an ascetic when he was 30 years old. He achieved Nirvana atop Sammet Sikhar, now named Parshvanatha after him. He was called *purisdG+ya* ("beloved of men"), a name which shows that he must have been a genial personality. He remains beloved among Jains.

There is a mention of four prominent leaders of the order of Lord Parshvanath:

1. Gandhara Shubhdatta (Shumbh)
2. Arya Haridatta
3. Acharya Samudra Suri
4. Arya Keshi Shraman.

In addition, Parshvanath had ten Ganadhars, or disciples. He also has 108 names. Arya Keshi Shraman is believed to have been born about 166 to 250 years after the death of Bhagawan Parshvanath. He met Ganadhara Gautam Swami, the main disciple of Lord Mahavira. Their discussion about the apparent differences between the teachings of the two Tirthankaras is recorded in Jain texts.

Parsvanatha is the 23rd tirthankara or ford-maker. He lived in Varanasi in India around 800 BCE and is the most popular object of Jain devotion. He is closely associated with compassion, although free from the world of rebirth, like all tirthankaras, and therefore unable to aid his devotees personally.

Iconography

Lord Pârúvanâtha is always represented with the hood of a

nâga shading his head. This nâga usually has three, seven or eleven heads. The Yaksha Dharanendra and the Yakshi Padmavati are often shown flanking him. There is a famous legend about the three of them as follows:

Parshvanath was walking one day when he saw an old man next to a fire. With a special type of knowledge called Avdhignan he could tell that a pair of snakes was in one of the logs in the fire. He quickly warned the man that he was burning the snakes, but instead of acting rapidly to save them, the man became angry at Parshvanath and denied the presence of the snakes. Parshavanath pulled out the right log and put it out, then gently split it, revealing two badly burned snakes. He recited the Navkar Mantra, a prayer, for them before they died. The two nagas reincarnated to become the two Yakshas, Dharanendra and Padmavati.

In Jain canonical literature, Parshvanatha is represented in 'padmasana' (lotus) posture – both palms and feet, with auspicious lotus marks on them, placed upward. He has blue-black complexion – the color of the cosmos. The seven-hooded serpent Shesha – umbrella-like unfurling its hoods over the deity, represented elements of the earth and the ocean and has hence a similar body colour. Parshvanatha has been represented as wearing a gem-studded crown and other ornaments. He has a golden throne as a seat and a rich canopy above.

Famous Temples of Lord Parshvanath

Many temples are dedicated to Lord Parshvanath throughout India. There are at least 108 different images (names/ roop) by which he is honored.

Some of the most famous ones are:

- Shri Jain temples of Khajuraho Parshavanath
- Shri Amijhara Parshavanath
- Shri Andheshwar Parshvanath near Banswara(Raj.)
- Shri Shankheshwar Parshvanath
- Shri Nakoda Parshvanath
- Shri Nageshwar Parshvanath
- Shri Kalikund Parshvanath
- Sammet Sikhar in Jharkand
- Humbaj Padmavati in Karnataka

- Shri Chintamani Parshvanath in Navsari
- Shri Avanti Parshvanath in Ujjain
- Shri Panchasara Parshvanath in Patan, Gujarat
- Shri Adinath Jain Temple, Santhu, Bagra (Marwar), Jalore, Rajasthan.
- Shri Munisuvrata-Nemi-Parsva Jinalaya, Santhu, Bagra (Marwar), Jalore, Rajasthan.
- Shri Uvasagarham Parshavnath Jianalaya, Nagpura, Rajnandgoan, Chhattisgarh.

Mahavira

Mahavira "Great Hero", traditionally 599 – 527 BCE is the name most commonly used to refer to the Indian sage Vardhamana "increasing") who established what are today considered to be the central tenets of Jainism. According to Jain tradition, he was the 24 and the last Tirthankara. He is also known in texts as *Vira* or *Viraprabhu,...Sanmati, Ativira,*and *Gnatputra*. In the Buddhist Pali Canon, he is referred to as Nigantha Nataputta.

Overview of Mahavira's Life

Birth of Prince Vardhaman

In a place called Kshatriyakunda in the ancient kingdom of Lachuar in Jamui District in modern day Bihar, India, Mahavira was born to King Siddartha and Queen Trishala on the 13th day under the rising moon of *Chaitra* (12 April according to the Gregorian calendar). While still in his mother's womb it is believed he brought wealth and prosperity to the entire kingdom, which is why he was also known as Vardhaman. An increase of all good things, like the abundant bloom of beautiful flowers, was noticed in the kingdom after his conception. Queen Trishala had 14 (14 in Swetambar Sect, 16 in Digambar Sect) auspicious dreams before giving birth to Vardhaman, signs foretelling the advent of a great soul.

Jain tradition states that after his birth, Indra bathed him in celestial milk with rituals befitting a future Tirthankar and he was returned to his mother, Trishala.

Vardhaman's birthday is celebrated as Mahavir Jayanti, the most important religious holiday of Jains around the world.

Early Years

As King Siddartha's son, he lived as a prince. However, even at that tender age he exhibited a virtuous nature. He started engaging in meditation and immersed himself in self-contemplation. He was interested in the core beliefs of Jainism and began to distance himself from worldly matters.

Twelve Years of Spiritual Pursuit

At the age of thirty Mahavira renounced his kingdom and family, gave up his worldly possessions, and spent twelve years as an ascetic. During these twelve years he spent most of his time meditating. He gave utmost regard to other living beings, including humans, animals and plants, and avoided harming them. He had given up all worldly possessions including his clothes, and lived an extremely austere life. He exhibited exemplary control over his senses while enduring the penance during these years. His courage and braveness earned him the name *Mahavira*. These were the golden years of his spiritual journey, at the end of which he achieved Kaivlya Gyan. He was now a person of infinite harmony, knowledge and self-control.

Later Years

Mahavira devoted the rest of his life to preaching the eternal truth of spiritual freedom to people around India. He travelled barefoot and without clothes, in the hardest of climates, and people from all walks of life came to listen to his message. At one point Mahavira had over 400,000 followers. Mahavira's preaching and efforts to spread Jain philosophy is considered the real catalyst to the spread of this ancient religion throughout India and into the mainstream.

At the age of 72 years and 4.5 months, he attained Nirvana in the area known as Pawapuri on the last day of the Indian and Jain calendars, Dipavali. Jains celebrate this as the day he attained liberation or Moksha. Jains believe Mahavira lived from 599-527 BCE, though some scholars prefer 549-477 BCE.

Mahavira's Philosophy

Mahavira's philosophy has eight cardinal principals-three metaphysical and five ethical. The objective is to elevate the quality of life. These independent principles reveal exceptional unity of purpose, and aim at achieving spiritual excellence by ethically sound behavior and metaphysical thought. Mahavira's metaphysics consist of three principles-Anekantavada, Syâdvâda, and Karma; and his Panchavrats, five codes of conduct-Ahimsa, Satya, Asteya, Brahmacharya, and Aparigraha. He talks of Tri-ratnas-three gems, which are the means and the goal.

Mahavira preached that from eternity, every living being (soul) is in bondage to karmic atoms accumulated by good or bad deeds. In a state of *karmic* delusion, the individual seeks temporary and illusory pleasure in material possessions, which are the root causes of self-centered violent thoughts and deeds as well as anger, hatred, greed, and other vices. These result in further accumulation of *karma*.

To liberate one's self, Mahavira taught the necessity of right faith (*samyak-darshana*), right knowledge (*samyak-gyana*), and right conduct (*samyak-charitra'*).

At the heart of right conduct for Jains lie the five great vows:

- Nonviolence (*Ahimsa*)-to cause no harm to any living being;
- Truthfulness (*Satya*)-to speak the harmless truth only;
- Non-stealing (*Asteya*)-to take nothing not properly given;
- Chastity (*Brahmacharya*)-to indulge in no sensual pleasure;
- Non-possession/Non-attachment (*Aparigraha*)-to detach completely from people, places, and material things.

These vows cannot be fully implemented without accepting the philosophy of non-absolutism (*Anekantvada*) and the theory of relativity (*Syâdvâda*, also translated "qualified prediction"). Monks and nuns adhere strictly to these vows, while the laypeople observe them as best they can. Mahavira taught that men and women are spiritual equals and that both may renounce the world in search of moksh or ultimate happiness.

Mahavira attracted people from all walks of life, rich and poor, men and women, touchable and untouchable. He organized his followers into a fourfold order; monk (*Sadhu*), nun (*Sadhvi*), layman (*Shravak*), and laywoman (*Shravika*). This order is known as *Chaturvidh Jain Sangh*.

Mahavira's sermons were preserved orally by his immediate disciples in the *Agam Sutras*. Through time many *Agam Sutras* have been lost, destroyed, or modified. About one thousand years after Mahavira's time the *Agam Sutras* were recorded on *Tadpatris* (palm leaf paper used then to form books). Swetambar Jains accept these *sutras* as authentic teachings while Digambar Jains use them as a reference.

Jainism existed before Mahavir, and his teachings were based on those of his predecessors. Thus Mahavira was a reformer and propagator of an existing religion, rather than the founder of a new faith. He followed the well established creed of his predecessor Tirthankar Parshvanath. However, Mahavira did reorganize the philosophical tenets of Jainism to correspond to his times.

A few centuries after Mahavira's Nirvana, the Jain religious order (*Sangh*) grew more and more complex. There were schisms on minor points, although they did not affect Mahavira's original doctrines. Later generations saw the introduction of rituals and complexities that some criticize as placing Mahavira and other *Tirthankars* on the throne similar to those of Hindu deities.

Mahavira in the Visual Arts

Images of Mahavira came to be sculpted more than six hundred years after his 'nirvana'. These images, or rather all Tirthankara images, are employed in Jain devotions. The Jain aesthetic does not focus on physical, but rather upon spiritual versimilitude. Therefore, instead of aiming at discovering a "true" likenesses the primary focus of such images is the depiction of the Tirthankara's spiritual form.

Tirthankara images are considered images of the sacred mind transformed into stone, metal or colors. With locks of hair falling on his shoulders,serpent's hood behind his head and lion's image on his thigh right from birth as a birthmark, the images of Rishabhadeva, Parshvanatha and Mahavirswami respectively have distinct iconographies. Nonetheless, such distinctions, excepting some regional variations and a few minor and remote features, are not seen in other Tirthankara images.

Images of Mahavira are distinguished by his lion emblem and a distinct modeling of the head, otherwise images of Mahavira are mostly identical with images of other Tirthankara. In most images-at least the ancient ones which number in the thousands-the pedestals, which bore emblems of different Tirthankaras, are not intact. Thus, the identity of any particular Tirthankara image is difficult to discern. Mahavira images typically depict him in either 'kayotsarga-mudra' or 'padmasana' postures. Other postures are not as popular-even the 'godohana-mudra', which Mahavira had when he attained 'keval gyan' is rarely displayed.

Images created for devotees of Digambara sect not only lack clothes but also lack all ornamentation. Images rendered for Svetambara devotees are represented with garments, jewels and even a crown. These images are often seated on a throne.

Episodes from Mahavira's life do not figure prominently in Jain visual arts. Both sculptors and painters depict his birth, sometimes with mother Trishala lying on a bed with a number of maids attending upon her, and sometimes as dreaming with sixteen auspicious signs around. A symbolic representation of Mahavira's 'tri-ratnas' is also found in various sculptural panels. Similarly, the diagram of his 'samavasarana' has been the theme of a number of miniatures and wall paintings.

Emphasis on Non-violence in Thought and Practice

Jains believe that every human is responsible for his/her actions and all living beings have an eternal soul, *jîva*. Jains believe all souls are equal because they all possess the potential of being liberated and attaining moksha. Tirthankaras are role models only because they have attained moksha. Jains insist that we live, think and act respectfully and honor the spiritual nature of all life. Jains view divinity as the unchanging traits of the pure soul of each living being, described as Infinite Knowledge, Perception, Consciousness, and Happiness (*Ananta Jnâna, Ananta Darshana, Ananta Caritra* and *Ananta Sukha*). Jains do not believe in an omnipotent supreme being, creator or manager (*kartâ*), but rather in an eternal universe governed by natural laws.

Jains hold that this temporal world inflicts much misery and sorrow. Thus, to attain lasting bliss, one must transcend the cycle of transmigration, lest one remain eternally trapped in its never-ending repetition. The only way to break out of this cycle is to practice detachment through rational perception, rational knowledge and rational conduct. Jain scriptures were written over a long period of time, but the most cited is the *Tattvartha Sutra*, or "Book of Reality", written by the monk-scholar, Umasvati (aka Umâsvâmi) almost 1800 years ago. The protagonists of this Sutra are Tirthankaras. The two main sects of Jainism are called Digambar and Svetambar. Both sects affirm ahimsa (or *ahinsâ*), asceticism, karma, sanskâr, and jiva.

Though practice differs between the two sects, Jain doctrine is uniform, with great emphasis placed on rational perception, rational knowledge and rational conduct.

Compassion for all life, both human and non-human, is central to Jainism. Human life is valued as a unique, rare opportunity to reach enlightenment. To kill any person, no matter their crime, is considered unimaginably abhorrent.

History suggests that various strains of Hinduism became vegetarian due to strong Jain influences.. Jains run animal shelters all over India. For example, Delhi has a bird hospital run by Jains. Every city and town in Bundelkhand has animal shelters run by Jains where all manner of animals are sheltered, even though the shelter is generally known as a Gaushala ("sacred cow").

Jainism's stance on nonviolence goes far beyond vegetarianism. Jains refuse food obtained with unnecessary cruelty. Many practice a lifestyle similar to veganism, due to the violence of modern dairy farms, and others exclude root vegetables from their diets to preserve the lives of these plants. Potatoes, garlic and onions in particular are avoided by Jains.. Traditionally oriented Jains do not eat, drink, or travel after sunset, and prefer to drink water that is boiled and then cooled to room temperature. Many Jains abstain from eating root vegetables as the plant, which is a living organism, is usually uprooted during the harvest. The purpose of these practices is to minimise the harm that may otherwise be caused to living organisms inadvertently.

Anekantavada

Anekntavda is one of the most important and fundamental doctrines of Jainism. It refers to the principles of pluralism and multiplicity of viewpoints, the notion that truth and reality are perceived differently from diverse points of view, and that no single point of view is the complete truth.

This is to contrast attempts to proclaim absolute truth with *adhgajanyâyah,* which can be illustrated through the parable of the "blind men and an elephant". In this story, each blind man felt a different part of an elephant (trunk, leg, ear, etc.). All the men claimed to understand and explain the true appearance of the elephant, but could only partly succeed, due to their limited perspectives. This principle is more formally stated by observing that objects are infinite in their qualities and modes of existence, so they cannot be completely grasped in all aspects and manifestations by finite human perception. According to the Jains, only the *Kevalins*—the omniscient beings—can comprehend objects in all aspects and manifestations; others are only capable of partial knowledge. Consequently, no single, specific, human view can claim to represent absolute truth.

The origins of *anekântavâda* can be traced back to the teachings of Mahavira (599–527 BCE), the 24th Jain *T+rthaGkara*. The dialectical concepts of *syâdvâda* (conditioned viewpoints) and *nayavâda* (partial viewpoints) arose from *anekântavâda*, providing it with more detailed logical structure and expression. The Sanskrit compound *an-eka-anta-vda* literally means "doctrine of non-exclusivity"; it is translated into English as "scepticism" or "non-absolutism". *An-ekânta* "uncertainty, non-exclusivity" is the opposite of *eknta* (*eka+anta*) "exclusiveness, absoluteness, necessity" (or also "monotheistic doctrine"). *Anekântavâda* encourages its adherents to consider the views and beliefs of their rivals and opposing parties. Proponents of *anekântavâda* apply this principle to religion and philosophy, reminding themselves that any religion or philosophy—even Jainism—which clings too dogmatically to its own tenets, is committing an error based on its limited point of view.

Philosophical Overview

The etymological root of *anekântavâda* lies in the compound of two Sanskrit words: *anekânta* ("manifoldness") and *vâda* ("school of thought"). The word *anekânta* is a compound of the Sanskrit negative prefix *an*, *eka* ("singularity"), and *anta* ("attribute"). Hence, *anekânta* means "not of solitary attribute". The Jain doctrine lays a strong emphasis on *samyaktva*, that is, rationality and logic. According to Jains, the ultimate principle should always be logical and no principle can be devoid of logic or reason. Thus, the Jain texts contain deliberative exhortations on every subject, whether they are constructive or obstructive, inferential or analytical, enlightening or destructive.

3

Jain Doctrines of Relativity

Anekântavâda is one of the three Jain doctrines of relativity used for logic and reasoning.

The other two are:

- *syâdvâda*—the theory of conditioned predication and;
- *nayavada*—the theory of partial standpoints.

These Jain philosophical concepts made important contributions to ancient Indian philosophy, especially in the areas of skepticism and relativity.

Syadvada

Syadvada is the theory of conditioned predication which provides an expression to *anekanta* by recommending that the epithet *Syad* be prefixed to every phrase or expression. *Syadvada* is not only an extension of *anekanta* ontology, but a separate system of logic capable of standing on its own. The Sanskrit etymological root of the term *Syad* is "perhaps" or "maybe", but in the context of *Syadvada,* it means "in some ways" or "from a perspective". As reality is complex, no single proposition can express the nature of reality fully. Thus the term *"syat"* should be prefixed before each proposition giving it a conditional point of view and thus removing any dogmatism in the statement. Since it ensures that each statement is expressed from seven different conditional and relative viewpoints or propositions, *Syadvada* is known as *saptibha Eginaya* or the theory of seven conditioned predications.

These seven propositions, also known as *saptibha Egi,* are:

1. *Syad-asti*—in some ways, it is,

2. *Syad-nasti*—in some ways, it is not,
3. *Syad-asti-nasti*—in some ways, it is, and it is not,
4. *syd-asti-avaktavya*—in some ways, it is, and it is indescribable,
5. *syd-nsti-avaktavya*—in some ways, it is not, and it is indescribable,
6. *syd-asti-nsti-avaktavya*—in some ways, it is, it is not, and it is indescribable,
7. *syd-avaktavya*—in some ways, it is indescribable.

Each of these seven propositions examines the complex and multifaceted nature of reality from a relative point of view of time, space, substance and mode. To ignore the complexity of reality is to commit the fallacy of dogmatism.

Nayavada

Nayavada is the theory of partial standpoints or viewpoints. *Nayavada* is a compound of two Sanskrit words—*naya* ("partial viewpoint") and *vada* ("school of thought or debate"). It is used to arrive at a certain inference from a point of view. An object has infinite aspects to it, but when we describe an object in practice, we speak of only relevant aspects and ignore irrelevant ones. This does not deny the other attributes, qualities, modes and other aspects; they are just irrelevant from a particular perspective. Authors like Natubhai Shah explain *nayavada* with the example of a car; for instance, when we talk of a "blue BMW" we are simply considering the colour and make of the car.

However, our statement does not imply that the car is devoid of other attributes like engine type, cylinders, speed, price and the like. This particular viewpoint is called a *naya* or a partial viewpoint. As a type of critical philosophy, *nayavada* holds that all philosophical disputes arise out of confusion of standpoints, and the standpoints we adopt are, although we may not realize it, "the outcome of purposes that we may pursue". While operating within the limits of language and seeing the complex nature of reality, Mahavira used the language of *nayas*. *Naya*, being a partial expression of truth, enables us to comprehend reality part by part.

Syncretisation of Changing and Unchanging Reality

The age of Mahavira and Buddha was an age of intense

intellectual debates, especially on the nature of reality and self. Upanishadic thought postulated the absolute unchanging reality of *Brahman* and *atman* and claimed that change was mere illusion. The theory advanced by Buddhists denied the reality of permanence of conditioned phenomena, asserting only interdependence and impermanence. According to the *Vedânta* (Upanishadic) conceptual scheme, the Buddhists were wrong in denying permanence and absolutism, and within the Buddhist conceptual scheme, the vedântins were wrong in denying the reality of impermanence.

The two positions were contradictory and mutually exclusive from each others' point of view. The Jains managed a synthesis of the two uncompromising positions with *anekantavada*. From the perspective of a higher, inclusive level made possible by the ontology and epistemology of *anekantavada* and *Syadvada*, Jains do not see such claims as contradictory or mutually exclusive; instead, they are seen as *ekantika* or only partially true. The Jain breadth of vision embraces the perspectives of both Vedanta which, according to Jainism, "recognizes substances but not process", and Buddhism, which "recognizes process but not substance". Jainism, on the other hand, pays equal attention to both substance *(dravya)* and process *(Paryaya)*.

Mahavira's responses to various questions asked by his disciples and recorded in the Jain canon *Bhagvatisûtra* demonstrate recognition that there are complex and multiple aspects to truth and reality and a mutually exclusive approach cannot be taken to explain such reality:

Gautama: Lord! Is the soul permanent or impermanent?

Mahavira: The soul is permanent as well as impermanent. From the point of view of the substance it is eternal. From the point of view of its modes it undergoes birth, decay and destruction and hence impermanent.

Jayanti: Lord! Of the states of slumber or awakening, which one is better?

Mahavira: For some souls the state of slumber is better, for some souls the states of awakening. Slumber is better for those who are engaged in sinful activities and awakening for those who are engaged in meritorious deeds. —*Bhagvatisutra*, 12:53–54.

Thousands of questions were asked and Mahavira's responses

suggested a complex and multifaceted reality with each answer qualified from a viewpoint. According to Jainism, even a *T+rthaGkara,* who possesses and perceives infinite knowledge, cannot express reality completely because of the limitations of language, which is of human creation.

This philosophical syncretisation of paradox of change through *anekanta* has been acknowledged by modern scholars such as Arvind Sharma, who wrote:

Our experience of the world presents a profound paradox which we can ignore existentially, but not philosophically. This paradox is the paradox of change. Something – A changes and therefore it cannot be permanent. On the other hand, if A is not permanent, then what changes? In this debate between the 'permanence' and 'change', Hinduism seems more inclined to grasp the first horn of the dilemma and Buddhism the second. It is Jainism that has the philosophical courage to grasp both horns fearlessly and simultaneously, and the philosophical skill not to be gored by either.

However, *anekantavada* is simply not about syncretisation or compromise between competing ideas, as it is about finding the hidden elements of shared truth between such ideas. *Anekantavada* is not about denying the truth; rather truth is acknowledged as an ultimate spiritual goal. For ordinary humans, it is an elusive goal, but they are still obliged to work towards its attainment. *Anekantavada* also does not mean compromising or diluting ones own values and principles.

On the contrary, it allows us to understand and be tolerant of conflicting and opposing views, while respectfully maintaining the validity of ones own view-point. Hence, John Koller calls *anekantavada* as – "epistemological respect for view of others". *Anekantavada,* thus, did not prevent the Jain thinkers from defending the truth and validity of their own doctrine while simultaneously respecting and understanding the rival doctrines. Anne Vallely notes that the epistemological respect for other view-points was put to practice when she was invited by Acarya Tulsi, the head of Jain Terapanthi order, to teach their Jain nuns, the tenets of Christianity. Commenting on their adherence to *ahics* and *anekantavada,* she says:

The Jain *smudges* of Ladnun uncompromisingly maintain *ahics* to be an eternal and unchangeable moral law. Other views and beliefs that contradict this belief would certainly be challenged, and ultimately rejected. But what is significant, is that both the rejection and retention of views is tempered by the belief that our perception conveys only a partial reality, that reality itself is manifold, and that to that, assume one particular viewpoint is final, is to hold a limited picture of reality.

Anekantavada is also different from moral relativism. It does not mean conceding that all arguments and all views are equal, but rather logic and evidence determine which views are true, in what respect and to what extent. While employing *anekantavada,* the 17th century philosopher monk, Ya[ovijaya GaGi also cautions against *anâbhigrahika* (indiscriminate attachment to all views as being true), which is effectively a kind of misconceived relativism. Jains thus consider *anekantavada* as a positive concept corresponding to religious pluralism that transcends monism and dualism, implying a sophisticated conception of a complex reality. It does not merely involve rejection of partisanship, but reflects a positive spirit of reconciliation of opposite views. However, it is argued that pluralism often degenerates to some form of moral relativism or religious exclusivism. According to Anne Vallely, *anekanta* is a way out of this epistemological quagmire, as it makes a genuinely pluralistic view possible without lapsing into extreme moral relativism or exclusivity.

Parable of the Blind Men and Elephant

The ancient Jain texts often explain the concepts of *anekantavada* and *Syadvada* with the parable of the blind men and an elephant (*Andhgajanyayah*), which addresses the manifold nature of truth.

A group of blind men heard that a strange animal, called an elephant, had been brought to the town, but none of them were aware of its shape and form. Out of curiosity, they said: "We must inspect and know it by touch, of which we are capable". So, they sought it out, and when they found it they groped about it. In the case of the first person, whose hand landed on the trunk, said "This being is like a drain pipe". For another one whose hand reached its ear, it seemed like a kind of fan. As for another person, whose hand was upon its leg, said, "I perceive the shape of the elephant to be like a pillar". And in the case of the one who placed his hand upon its back said, "Indeed, this elephant is like a throne".

Now, each of these presented a true aspect when he related what he had gained from experiencing the elephant. None of them had strayed from the true description of the elephant. Yet they fell short of fathoming the true appearance of the elephant.

Two of the many references to this parable are found in *Tattvarthaslokavatika* of Vidyanandi (9th century) and *Syâdvâdamanjari* of Acarya Mallisena (13th century). Mallisena uses the parable to argue that immature people deny various aspects of truth; deluded by the aspects they *do* understand, they deny the aspects they *don't* understand. "Due to extreme delusion produced on account of a partial viewpoint, the immature deny one aspect and try to establish another. This is the maxim of the blind (men) and the elephant." Mallisena also cites the parable when noting the importance of considering all viewpoints in obtaining a full picture of reality. "It is impossible to properly understand an entity consisting of infinite properties without the method of modal description consisting of all viewpoints, since it will otherwise lead to a situation of seizing mere sprouts (i.e., a superficial, inadequate cognition), on the maxim of the blind (men) and the elephant."

History and Development

The principle of *anekantavada* is the foundation of many Jain philosophical concepts. The development of *anekantavada* also encouraged the development of the dialectics of *Syadvada* (conditioned viewpoints), *saptibhaEgî* (the seven conditioned predication), and *nayavada* (partial viewpoints).

Origins

The origins of *anekantavada* lie in the teachings of Mahavira, who used it effectively to show the relativity of truth and reality. Taking a relativistic viewpoint, Mahavira is said to have explained the nature of the soul as both permanent, from the point of view of underlying substance, and temporary, from the point of view of its modes and modification. The importance and antiquity of *anekantavada* are also demonstrated by the fact that it formed the subject matter of *Astinasti Pravada*, the fourth part of the lost *Purva* that contained teachings of the *Tirtha Gkaras* prior to Mahavira. German Indologist Hermann Jacobi believes Mahavira effectively employed the dialectics of *anekantavada* to refute the agnosticism of Sanjaya Belammhaputta. *Sutrakritanga,* the second oldest canon of Jainism, contains the first references to *Syadvada* and *saptibhaegi.* According to *Sûtrakritanga,* Mahavira advised his disciples to use *Syadvada* to preach his teachings:

A monk living single should not ridicule heretical doctrines, and should avoid hard words though they be true; he should not be vain, nor brag, but he should without embarrassment and passion preach the Law. A monk should be modest, though he be of a fearless mind; he should expound the *Syadvada,* he should use the two permitted kinds of speech, living among virtuous men, impartial and wise.

Early History

Sutrakritanga contains references to *Vibhajyavada,* which, according to Jacobi, is the same as *Syadvada* and *saptibhaegi.* The early Jain canons and teachings contained multitudes of references to *anekantavada* and *Syadvada* in rudimentary form without giving it proper structure or establishing it as a separate doctrine. *Bhagvatisutra* mentions only three primary predications of the *saptibha Eginaya.* After Mahavira, Kundakunda (1st century CE) was the first author–saint to expound on the doctrine of *Syadvada* and *saptibhaegi* and give it a proper structure in his famous works *Pravacanasara* and *Pancastikayasara.*

Kundakunda also used *nayas* to discuss the essence of the self in *Samayasara.* Proper classification of the *nayas* was provided by the philosopher monk, Umasvati (2nd century CE) in *Tattvarthasutra.* Samantabhadra (2nd century CE) and Siddhasena Divâkara (3rd century CE) further fine-tuned Jain epistemology and logic by expounding on the concepts of *anekantavada* in proper form and structure.

Acarya Siddhasena Divakara expounded on the nature of truth in the court of King Vikramaditya:

Vikramaditya: What is 'truth'? That which is said repeatedly, that which is said loudly, that which is said with authority or that which is agreed by the majority?

Divakara: None of the above. Every one has his own definition of 'truth' and that it is conditional.

Vikramaditya: How about traditions? They have been established by our ancestors and have passed the test of time?

Divakara: Would the system established by ancestors hold true on examination? In case it does not, I am not here to justify it for the sake of saving the traditional grace of the dead, irrespective of the wrath I may have to face. —Acarya Siddhasena Divakara, *Vardhamana Dvtrimcik.*

In Sanmatitarka, Divakara further adds: "All doctrines are right in their own respective spheres—but if they encroach upon the province of other doctrines and try to refute their view, they are wrong. A man who holds the view of the cumulative character of truth never says that a particular view is right or that a particular view is wrong."

Age of Logic

The period beginning with the start of common era, up to the modern period is often referred to as the age of logic in the history of Jain philosophy. By the time of Akalanka (5th century CE), whose works are a landmark in Jain logic, *anekantavada* was firmly entrenched in Jain texts, as is evident from the various teachings of the Jain scriptures.

Acarya Haribhadra (8th century CE) was one of the leading proponents of *anekantavada*. He was the first classical author to write a doxography, a compendium of a variety of intellectual views. This attempted to contextualise Jain thoughts within the broad framework, rather than espouse narrow partisan views. It interacted with the many possible intellectual orientations available to Indian thinkers around the 8th century. Acarya Amrtacandra starts his famous 10th century CE work *Purusathasiddhiupaya* with strong praise for *anekantavada*: "I bow down to the principle of *anekanta,* the source and foundation of the highest scriptures, the dispeller of wrong one-sided notions, that which takes into account all aspects of truth, reconciling diverse and even contradictory traits of all objects or entity."

Acarya Vidyanandi (11th century CE) provides the analogy of the ocean to explain the nature of truth in *Tattvarthaslokavartikka,* 116: "Water from the ocean contained in a pot can neither be called an ocean nor a non-ocean, but simply a part of ocean. Similarly, a doctrine, though arising from absolute truth can neither be called a whole truth nor a non-truth."

Yaovijaya Gagi, a 17th century Jain monk, went beyond

anekantavada by advocating *madhayastha,* meaning "standing in the middle" or "equidistance". This position allowed him to praise qualities in others even though the people were non-Jain and belonged to other faiths. There was a period of stagnation after Yasovijayaji, as there were no new contributions to the development of Jain philosophy.

Role in Ensuring the Survival of Jainism

Anekantavada played a pivotal role in the growth as well as the survival of Jainism in ancient India, especially against onslaughts from Eaivas, Vaic Gavas, Buddhists, Muslims, and Christians at various times. According to Hermann Jacobi, Mahavira used such concepts as *Syadvada* and *saptbhangi* to silence some of his opponents. The discussions of the agnostics led by Sanjaya Belammhaputta had probably influenced many of their contemporaries and consequently *Syadvada* may have seemed to them a way out of *ajnanavada.* Jacobi further speculates that many of their followers would have gone over to Mahavira's creed, convinced of the truth of the *saptbhanginaya.* According to Professor Christopher Key Chapple, *anekantavada* allowed Jains to survive during the most hostile and unfavourable moments in history. According to John Koller, professor of Asian studies, *anekantavada* allowed Jain thinkers to maintain the validity of their doctrine, while at the same time respectfully criticizing the views of their opponents.

Anekantavada was often used by Jain monks to obtain royal patronage from Hindu Kings. Acarya Hemacandra used *anekantavada* to gain the confidence and respect of the Calukya Emperor Jayasimha Siddharaja. According to the Jain text *Prabandhacantamani,* Emperor Siddharaja desired enlightenment and liberation and he questioned teachers from various traditions. He remained in a quandary when he discovered that they all promoted their own teachings while disparaging other teachings. Among the teachers he questioned was Hemacandra, who, rather than promote Jainism, told him a story with a different message. According to his story, a sick man was cured of his disease after eating all the herbs available, as he was not aware which herb was medicinal. The moral of the tale, according to Hemacandra, was that just as the man was restored by the herb, even though no one knew which particular herb did the trick, so in the *kaliyuga* ("age of vice") the wise should obtain salvation by supporting all religious traditions, even though no-one can say with absolute certainty which tradition it is that provides that salvation.

Influence

Jain religious tolerance fits well with the ecumenical disposition typical of Indian religions. It can be traced to the analogous Jain principles of *anekantavada* and *ahics*. The epistemology of *anekantavada* and *Syadvada* also had a profound impact on the development of ancient Indian logic and philosophy. In recent times, Jainism influenced Gandhi, who advocated *ahics* and *satyagraha*.

Intellectual Ahimsa and Religious Tolerance

The concepts of *anekantavada* and *Syadvada* allow Jains to accept the truth in other philosophies from their own perspective and thus inculcate tolerance for other viewpoints. *Anekantavada* is non-absolutist and stands firmly against all dogmatisms, including any assertion that Jainism is the only correct religious path. It is thus an intellectual *ahics*, or *ahics* of the mind. Burch writes, "Jain logic is intellectual *ahics*. Just as a right-acting person respects the life of all beings, so a right-thinking person acknowledges the validity of all judgments. This means recognizing all aspects of reality, not merely one or some aspects, as is done in non-Jain philosophies."

Mahavira encouraged his followers to study and understand rival traditions in his *Acaranga Sutra*: "Comprehend one philosophical view through the comprehensive study of another one."

In *anekantavada*, there is no "battle of ideas", because this is considered to be a form of intellectual *himsa* or violence, leading quite logically to physical violence and war. In today's world, the limitations of the adversarial, "either with us or against us" form of argument are increasingly apparent by the fact that the argument leads to political, religious and social conflicts. *Sutrakrtanga*, the second oldest canon of Jainism, provides a solution by stating: "Those who praise their own doctrines and ideology and disparage the doctrine of others distort the truth and will be confined to the cycle of birth and death."

This ecumenical and irenical attitude, engendered by *anekantavada*, allowed modern Jain monks such as Vijayadharmasuri to declare: "I am neither a Jain nor a Buddhist, a Vaisnava nor a Saivite, a Hindu nor a Muslim, but a traveler on the path of peace shown by the supreme soul, the God who is free from passion."

Criticism

The doctrines of *anekantavada* and *Syadvada* are often criticised on the grounds that they engender a degree of hesitancy and uncertainty, and may compound problems rather than solve them. It is also pointed out that Jain epistemology asserts its own doctrines, but at the cost of being unable to deny contradictory doctrines. Furthermore, it is also argued that this doctrine could be self-defeating. It is argued that if reality is so complex that no single doctrine can describe it adequately, then *anekantavada* itself, being a single doctrine, must be inadequate. This criticism seems to have been anticipated by Acarya Samantabhadra who said: "From the point of view of *pramana* (means of knowledge) it is *anekanta* (multi-sided), but from a point of view of *naya* (partial view) it is *ekanta* (one-sided)."

In defense of the doctrine, Jains point out that *anekantavada* seeks to reconcile apparently opposing viewpoints rather than refuting them.

Anekantavada received much criticism from the Vedantists, notably Adi Sankarâcârya (9th century C.E.). Sankara argued against some tenets of Jainism in his *bhasya* on *Brahmasutra* (2:2:33–36). His main arguments centre on *anekantavada*:

It is impossible that contradictory attributes such as being and non-being should at the same time belong to one and the same thing; just as observation teaches us that a thing cannot be hot and cold at the same moment.

The third alternative expressed in the words — they either are such or not such — results in cognition of indefinite nature, which is no more a source of true knowledge than doubt is. Thus the means of knowledge, the object of knowledge, the knowing subject, and the act of knowledge become all alike indefinite. How can his followers act on a doctrine, the matter of which is altogether indeterminate? The result of your efforts is perfect knowledge and is not perfect knowledge. Observation shows that, only when a course of action is known to have a definite result, people set about it without hesitation. Hence a man who proclaims a doctrine of altogether indefinite contents does not deserve to be listened anymore than a drunken or a mad man. —Adi Sankaracarya, *Brahmasutra,* 2.2:33–36

However, many believe that Sankara fails to address genuine *anekantavada*. By identifying *Syadvada* with *sansayavada,* he instead addresses "agnosticism", which was argued by Sanjaya Belammhaputta. Many authors like Pandya believe that Sankara overlooked that, the affirmation of the existence of an object is in respect to the object itself, and its negation is in respect to what the object is not. Genuine *anekantavada* thus considers positive and negative attributes of an object, at the same time, and without any contradictions.

Another Buddhist logician Dharmakirti ridiculed *anekantavada* in *Pramânavarttikakârika*: "With the differentiation removed, all things have dual nature. Then, if somebody is implored to eat curd, then why he does not eat camel?" The insinuation is obvious; if curd exists from the nature of curd and does not exist from the nature of a camel, then one is justified in eating camel, as by eating camel, he is merely eating the negation of curd. Acarya Akalanka, while agreeing that Dharmakirti may be right from one viewpoint, took it upon himself to issue a rejoinder:

The person who criticises without understanding the prima facie view is acting like a jester and not a critic. The Buddha was born a deer and the deer was born as Buddha; but Buddha is adorable and deer is only a food. Similarly, due to the strength of an entity, with its differences and similarities specified, nobody would eat camel if implored to eat curd.

Creation and Cosmology

Jain cosmology considers the loka or universe as an uncreated entity, existing since infinity having no beginning or an end. Jain texts describe the shape of the universe as similar to a man standing with legs apart and arm resting on his waist. This Universe, according to Jainism, is narrow at the top, broad at the middle and once again becomes broad at the bottom. MahpurGa of Acarya Jinasena is famous for this quote:

"Some foolish men declare that a creator made the world. The doctrine that the world was created is ill advised and should be rejected. If God created the world, where was he before the creation? If you say

he was transcendent then and needed no support, where is he now? How could God have made this world without any raw material? If you say that he made this first, and then the world, you are faced with an endless regression."

The Concept of Reality – The Constituents of the Universe

This Universe is made up of what Jains call six dravya or reals or substances classified as follows –

- Jiva i.e. Living Substances : Jiva i.e. Souls-Soul (Jiva) exists as a reality, having a separate existence from the body that houses it. It is characterised by chetana i.e. consciousness and upayoga i.e. knowledge and perception. Though the soul experiences both birth and death, it is neither really destroyed nor created. Decay and origin refer respectively to the disappearing of one state of soul and appearing of another state, these being merely the modes of the soul.
- Ajiva i.e. or Non-Living Substances :
    - o Pudgala i.e. Matter-Matter is classified as solid, liquid, gaseous, energy, fine Karmic materials and extra-fine matter i.e. ultimate particles. ParamGu or ultimate particle (atoms) is the basic building block of all matter. One of the qualities of the ParamGu and Pudgala is that of permanence and indestructibility. It combines and changes its modes but its basic qualities remain the same. According to Jainism, it cannot be created nor destroyed.
    - o Dharma-tattva i.e Principle of Motion and
    - o Adharma-tattva i.e. Principle of Rest-Dharmastikâya and Adharmastikaya are distinctly peculiar to Jaina system of thought depicting the principle of Motion and Rest. They are said to pervade the entire universe. Dharma and Adharma are by itself not motion or rest but mediate motion and rest in other bodies. Without Dharmastikaya motion is not possible and without Adharmastikaya rest is not possible in universe.
    - o Akaua i.e Space-Space is a substance that accommodates the living souls, the matter, the principle of motion, the principle of rest and time. It is all-pervading, infinite and made of infinite space-points.

- o Kala i.e. Time-Kala is a real entity according to Jainism and all activities, changes or modifications can be achieved only through the progress of time.

Time Cycle

According to Jainism, the time is beginningless and eternal. The Klacakra, the cosmic wheel of time rotates ceaseless. The wheel of time, is divided into two half-rotations-UtsarpiGi or ascending time cycle and AvasarpiGi, the descending time cycle, occurring continuously after each other. UtsarpiGi is a period of progressive prosperity and happiness where the time spans and ages are at an increasing scale, while AvsarpiGi is a period of increasing sorrow and immorality with decline in timespans of the epochs. Each of this half time cycle consisting of innumerable period of time is further sub-divided into six Aras or epochs of unequal periods.

The currently, the time cycle is in AvasarpiGi or descending phase with the following epochs :

- Sucama-sucam-During the first ara of Sucama-sucam of the Avsarpini, the age of the people was three palyopama years. They took their food on every fourth day; they were very tall and devoid of anger, pride, deceit, greed and other sinful acts. Various kinds of the kalpa trees fulfilled their wishes and needs like food, clothing, homes, entertainment, jewels etc.
- Sucam-During the second ara, Sucam, the people lived for two palyopama years. They took their food at an interval of three days, but the kalpa trees supplied their wants, less than before. The land and water became less sweet and fruitful than they were during the first ara.
- Sucama-ducam-During the third ara of Sucama-dictum, the age limit of the people became one palyopama year. They took their food on every second day. The earth and water as well as height and strength of the body went on decreasing and they became less than they were during the second ara. The first three ara the children were born as twins, one male and one female, who married each other and once again gave birth to twins. On account of happiness and pleasures, the religion, renunciation and

austerities was not possible. At the end of the third ara, the wish-fulfilling trees stopped giving the desired fruits and the people started living in the societies. The first Tirthankara, Zcabhdeva was born at the fag end of this ara. He taught the people the skills of farming, commerce, defence, politics and arts and organised the people in societies. That is why he is known as the father of human civilisation.

- Ducama-sucam-The fourth ara was the age of religion, where the renunciation, austerities and liberation was possible. The Zalkpuruca's or the illustrious persons who promote the Jain religion regularly appear in this ara. The balance 23 Tirtha Ekars, including lord Mhavira appeared in this area. This area came to an 3 years and 8 months after the nirvGa of Mhavira.
- Dictum-As per Jain cosmology, currently we are in the 5th area, wherein exactly 2,536 years have elapsed and 18,464 years are still left. It is an age of sorrow and misery. No liberation is possible, although people practice religion in lax and diluted form. However, at the end of this area, even the Jain religion will disappear, only to appear back with the advent of 1st Tirthankara in the next cycle.
- Dictum-dictum-The sixth Area, Dictum-dictum will be the age if intense misery and sorrow, making it impossible to practice religion in any form. The age, height and strength of the human beings will decrease to a great extent. This trend will start reversing at the onset of utsarpi Gikl.

In utsarpiGi, the order of the aras is reversed; starting from Dictum-dictum, it ends with Sucama-sucam and thus this never ending cycle continues. Each of these aras progress into the next phase seamlessly without any apocalyptic consequences. The increase or decrease in the happiness, life spans and length of people and general moral conduct of the society changes in a phased and graded manner as the time passes. No divine or supernatural beings are credited or responsible with these spontaneous temporal changes, either in a creative or overseeing role, rather the human beings and creatures are born under the impulse of their own karmas.

Jain Geography

The early Jains contemplated over the nature of the earth and universe and developed a detailed hypothesis on the various aspects of the astronomy and cosmology.

According to the Jain texts, the universe is divided into 3 parts–

- Urdhva Loka – the realms of the gods or heavens
- Madhya Loka – the realms of the humans, animals and plants
- Adho Loka – the realms of the hellish beings or the infernal regions.

The Jain Texts on Geography

The Jain texts provide a detailed description on The following Upanga Agamas describe the Jain cosmology and geography in a great detail :-

1. Suyaprajnapti – Treatise on Sun
2. Jambudvipaprajnapti-Treatise on the island of Roseapple tree; it contains a description of Jambudvi and life biographies of Zcabha and King Bharata
3. Candraprajnapti-Treatise on moon.

Additionally, the following texts describe the Jain cosmology and related topics in details:-

1. Trilokasara – Essence of the three worlds (heavens, middle level, hells)
2. Trilokaprajnapti – Treatise on the three worlds
3. Trilokadipika – Illumination of the three worlds
4. Tattvarthasutra – Description on nature of realities
5. Kcetrasamasa – Summary of Jain geography
6. Bruhatsamgrahni – Treatise on Jain cosmology and geography.

Urdhva Loka, the Upper World

Udharva loka consists of 12 Dev Lok, 9 Greveyak and 5 Anutar Viman, which are the realms of the Vaimaniks or the astral gods who are non-liberated gods. Above the Anutar vimans, at the apex of the universe, is the Siddhasila, the realms of the infinite liberated gods also known as the Siddhas, the perfected omniscient and blissful beings, who are venerated by the Jains. Below the siddhasila are the five Anutar Vimans named :

1. Vijay
2. Vijayant
3. Jayant
4. Aparajit
5. Savarthsiddha.

Below the Anutar Vimas are the 9 Greveyaks whose names are:

1. Bhadre
2. Subhadre
3. Sujae
4. Sumanase
5. Priydansne
6. Sudansne
7. Aamohe
8. Supadibaddhe
9. Jasodhare.

Below the Greveyaks, are the 12 Devalokas whose names are :

1. Sudharma
2. Ishan
3. Sanatkumar
4. Mahendra
5. Brahmloka
6. Lantak
7. Mahashukra
8. Sahastrar
9. Aanat
10. Pranat
11. Aaran
12. Achyuta.

Vaimanik devas are divided into, two groups i.e. –

- The higher groups, dwelling in 9 Greveyak and 5 Anutar

Viman. They are independent and dewelling in their own vehicles. The anuttara devas attain liberation within one or two lifetimes.

- The lower groups, organized like earthly kingdoms-rulers (Indra), organized like earthly kingdoms-rulers (Indras), counselors, guards, queens, followers, armies etc.

Madhya Loka, the Middle World

Madhya Loka, at the centre of the universe consists of 900 yojans above and 900 yojans below earth surface. It is inhabited by :

1. Jyotishka devas (luminous gods)-790 to 900 yojans above earth
2. Human, Tiryanch (Animals, birds, plants) on the surface
3. Vyantar devas (Intermediary gods)-100 yojan below the ground level.

Madhyaloka consists of many continent-islands surrounded by oceans, first eight whose names are :-

Continent/Island	*Ocean*
Jambudvipa	Lavanoda (Salt-ocean)
Ghatki Khand	Kaloda (Black sea)
Puskarvardvipa	Puskaroda (Lotus Ocean)
Varunvardvipa	Varunoda (Varun Ocean)
Kshirvardvipa	Kshiroda (Ocean of milk)
Ghrutvardvipa	Ghrutoda (Butter milk ocean)
Ikshuvardvipa	Iksuvaroda (Sugar Ocean)
Nandishwardvipa	Nandishwaroda

Mount Meru is at the centre of the world surrounded by Jambudvipa, in form of a circle forming a diameter of 100,000 yojans. continent has 6 mighty mountains, dividing the continent into 7 zones (Ksetra).

The names of these zones are:

1. Bharat Kshetra
2. Mahavideh Kshetra
3. Airavat Kshetra

4. Ramyak
5. Hairanyvat Kshetra
6. Haimava Kshetra
7. Hari Kshetra.

The three zones i.e. Bharat Kshetra, Mahavideh Kshetra and Airavat Kshetra are also known as Karma bhoomi because practice of austerities and liberation is possible and the Tirthankaras preach the Jain doctrine. The other four zones, Ramyak, Hairanyvat Kshetra, Haimava Kshetra and Hari Kshetra are known as akarmabhoomi or bhogbhumi as humans live a sinless life of pleasure and no religion or liberation is possible.

Adho Loka, the lower world

The lower world consists of seven hells which is inhabited by Bhavanpati demigods and the hellish beings. Hellish beings reside in the following hells-

1. Ratna prabha-dharma.
2. Sharkara prabha-vansha.
3. Valuka prabha-megha.
4. Pank prabha-anjana.
5. Dhum prabha-arista.
6. Tamah prabha-maghavi.
7. Mahatamah prabha-maadhavi.

Zalkpurucas-The Deeds of the 63 Illustrious Men

During the each motion of the half-cycle of the wheel of time, 63 Zalkpuruca or 63 illustrious men, consisting of the 24 T+rthaEkaras and their contemporaries regularly appear.. The Jain universal or legendary history is basically a compilation of the deeds of these illustrious men.

They are categorised as follows :-

- 24 Tirtha Ekaras – The 24 Tirtha Ekaras or the ford makers appear in succession to activate the true religion and establish the community of ascetics and laymen.
- 12 Chakravartis – The Chakravartis are the universal monarchs who rule over the six continents.
- 9 Baladevas and 9 Vasudevas or Naraya Gas (heros) –

Baladeva and Vasudeva are half brothers who jointly rule over three continents.

- 9 Prativasudevas (anti-heros) – They are anti-heros who are ultimately killed by the Vasudevas.

Jain Monks and Nuns (Sadhu or Muni Maharaj)

Jain Muni or simply Muni is the term often used for Jain monks.

A Jain monk does not have a permanent home and does not have any possessions. He wanders barefoot from place to place except for the four months of the rainy season. A Jain monk is not a priest; rather he is himself a worshipped one.

A full Jain monk in either Svetambar or Digambar tradition can belong to one of these ranks:

- Acharya: leader of the order
- Upadhyaya: a learned monk, who both teaches and studies himself
- Muni: an ordinary monk.

Thse three are mentioned is the three lines of the Namokar Mantra.

In the Digambar tradition, a junior monk can be a:

- Ailak: they use one piece of cloth
- Kshullak: they may use two pieces of cloth.

The Svetambar Terapanthi sect has a new rank of junior monks who are called samana.

The nuns are called Aryikas in Digambar tradition and Sadhvi in the Svetambar tradition.

Famous Historical Jain Monks

Some of the famous Jain Acharyas in approximate chronological order, are:

- Gautam Ganadhara
- Ganahar Sudharma Swami

Sudharmaswami (607 BC to 507 BC) was the fifth Ganadhar of Lord Mahavir. All the current Jain acharya's and monks follow his rule. Ganadhar means a group leader. Lord Mahavir had many pupils. They were divided into 11 groups and each of them was placed under one Ganadhar. As such, there were 11 Ganadhars in all.

The first and foremost was Gautam Swami, whose idol you might have seen in the temple. Actually, Gautam is his last name, because he belonged to the Gautam clan. His first name was Indrabhuti, but he is popularly known as Gautam swami. Even Lord Mahavira used to call him Goyam, which is the Ardhamagadhi version of Gautam.

Biography as Jain Literature

Sudharma swami was the son of a learned Brahmin named Dhammil, who lived in a village called *Kollag* situated in the present state of Bihar,India. The place is now known as Kollua and according to the archaeologists, it is the place where great Pundits like Vyakta and Sudharma had their schools in ancient times. Dhammil was childless. His wife Bhaddila was therefore craving for a child and worshipped the goddess Saraswati for that purpose. It is said that the Hindu goddess was pleased by her devotion and blessed her to get a highly accomplished son. Soon after that, Bhaddila became pregnant, and in due course, she gave birth to a son, who was named Sudharma.

That happened in 607 BC, which means Sudharma swami was 8 years older than Lord Mahavira. The boy grew up under the loving care of his parents. At the proper age he was sent to a well known Ashram school, where he studied Vedas, Upanishads and all other Brahmanical literature. By the time he came back from the school, he was known as a learned Pundit and his fame had spread round about. He then started his own school, which became a great center of learning. Pupils used to come there from all over the country. There were more than 500 students studying under him.

At that time in Pavapuri, a city of Bihar in India, there was a prosperous Brahmin named Somil. Once, he decided to organize a great sacrifice. He wanted all the well-known learned men to come on that occasion. Indrabhuti Gautam, who was the most learned Brahmin of that time, was going to be the presiding priest. His equally learned brothers, Agnibhuti and Vayubhuti, were going to sit by his side. Vyakta and other well known Pundits were also scheduled to remain present on that occasion. Somil had come to know about Sudharma and had sent the invitation to him.

Sudharma did not wish to miss the opportunity to attend that great sacrifice. Moreover, he was eager to see the Gautam brothers. He therefore, willingly accepted Somil's invitation.

At the appointed time, the sacrifice started in right earnest. Oblations began to be offered together with the recitation of the appropriate verses. As the sacrificial smoke rose towards the sky, they noticed the celestial vehicles coming down. Indrabhuti and other priests were satisfied that they could induce the celestial beings to come down to accept the oblations. They were, however, disappointed to see that the vehicles had diverted their direction and were descending at the other end of the city. They could not make out why, forsaking their great performance, the vehicles were bound towards a different destination.

What had happened was that after attaining omniscience, Lord Mahavira had arrived at Pavapuri that very time. The heavenly beings were therefore coming down to pay their homage to the Lord and to listen to his sermon. *Indrabhuti* was surprised to know that. He had never come across anyone more knowledgeable than himself. He therefore guessed that Mahavira might be an impostor who could have somehow impressed the heavenly beings. It was therefore necessary to counter his tactics immediately.

With that intention, *Indrabhuti* went towards the camping ground of the Lord. As he approached, the Lord welcomed him by calling his name. *Indrabhuti* was astonished that the impostor even knew his name. But as he looked at the Lord, he was impressed by his personality. His pride began to melt.

The Lord Mahavira soon asked him, 'Gautam, a doubt still lurks in your mind about the independent existence of the soul. Isn't that?' *Indrabhuti* was dumbfounded to hear those words, because he did have such a doubt. The Lord then quoted the relevant Sutra from Veda itself and explained that there was no reason to hold such a doubt. With that clarification, the doubt of Indrabhuti was eradicated. Thereupon, he decided to accept the Lord Mahavira as his Guru. So falling at the feet of the Lord Mahavira, he requested to be accepted as a pupil. The Mahavira was pleased to accede to the request and initiated him as the first pupil.

As *Indrabhuti* did not come back, his brothers Agnibhuti, Vayubhuti and other Pundits like Vyakta went to the Lord Mahavira one after another.Mahavira welcomed them, and, pointing out their doubts pertaining to the soul, he gave them the convincing replies. All of them were satisfied with the Mahavira's elucidation and became his pupils along with their own followers.

Now, it came the turn of Sudharma. He had the concept that every living being could reincarnate in its own species. In other words, human beings could be reborn as human only. His belief was based on the analogy of plant life. An apple tree, for instance, would produce the seeds from which only apple trees can come out. The Lord welcomed him, too, and, pointing out his doubt, he explained that as different types of plants could be produced by cross breeding, so human beings could be reincarnated as human or heavenly beings or even as animals depending upon their tendencies and longings. Sudharma was convinced with that explanation and became the Mahavira's pupil along with his 500 followers. As a Ganadhar of the Lord he came to be known as Sudharmaswami. This happened during the 42nd year of the Lord Mahavira.

The eleven Pundits who had come from Somil's sacrifice became his first pupils and later came to be known as Ganadhars. Thereafter the Lord Mahavira lived for 30 years. During that period, he continued to move in different parts of the country in order to lay down the path of liberation. During his discourses, Sudharma swami always sat in front of him and carefully listened to what the Mahavira had to say. That enabled him to compose the Lord's teaching in the form of Agams. By the time of the Lord'Mahaviras Nirvan in 527 BC nine of the eleven Ganadhars had passed away and only Gautam swami and Sudharma swami had survived. Since Gautam swami had attained omniscience on the very night of Lord's Nirvan, the administration of the order was left to Sudharma swami. During the next 12 years that he remained at the helm, he efficiently managed the order set up by the Lord Mahavira and spread his message far and wide.

Work

He gained omniscience in 515 BC and attained Nirvana in 507 BC at the ripe age of 100. After gaining omniscience, the religious order was entrusted to his principal pupil Jambuswami. During the period of his stewardship, Sudharmaswami composed the Lord's teachings in 12 parts, which are known as 12 Anga Agamas.

They are known as our original Agamas and are collectively known as Dwädashängi. Dwadash means 12, and Anga means limb. As there are various limbs of the body, so there are these 12 limbs of the spiritual science. Many of the Agamas are composed in the form of questions asked by the disciple Jambuswami and the replies given by Ganadhar Sudharmaswami.

- Jambu Swami
- Bhadrabahu (undivided sangha, Chandragupta Maurya was his disciple) (325 BCE).

Acharya Bhadrabahu (433 B.C.-357 B.C. ?) was a Jain monk. He is more famously known as a spiritual teacher of Chandragupta Maurya and author of several texts related to Jainism, including some of the most important works, Upsargahara Stotra and Kalpasutra.

Early Life

Bhadrabahu was born in Pundravardhan, (now in Bangladesh). During this time, the secondary capital of the Mauryas was Ujjain. While there Bhadrabahu was able to foresee through his *nimitta jnan* (subtle cognition of causes and effects) that there would be a 12-year famine across North India. He decided the famine would make it harder for monks to survive and migrated with a group of monks to South India, bringing with him Chandragupta, the founder of the Mauryan Empire turned Jain monk.

Career

While Bhadrabahu was away the monks staying in the North realized that the sacred scriptures were being forgotten. A monk named Sthulabhadra convened a council to recompile the Purva scriptures. However, because Sthulabhadra's own knowledge of these texts was imperfect, he went to Bhadrabahu to study the sections missing from his memory. Bhadrabahu taught Sthulabhadra, but forbade him to teach the Purva to others upon witnessing a demonstration by Sthulabhadra of certain extra corporal powers, which suggested that with time these sacred scriptures would become corrupted. Thus, the Purvas in their original form perished with these two men.

Bhadrabahu remains an exemplar of dedication to first principles at any cost. After him, the Sangha split into two separate teacher-student lineages of monks. Digambar monks belong to the lineage of Acharya Vishakha and Shvetambar monks follow the tradition of Sthulabhadra. Bhadrabahu composed some new texts as well. In the Shvetambar tradition, Brihatkalpa, Vyavahara, and Nisitha are considered his works.

Bhadrabahu is considered to be the last expert of 14 Purvas, of 12th Anga called Dristivaad, one of the scriptures of Jainism. Of these, 10 Purvas were passed on to Sthulibhadra, his chief disciple. Bhadrabahu went to Nepal for twelve years to perform the "Mahaprana Sadhana" a tantric exercise. According to the Digambaras, he died after committing Sallekhana.

Acharya Bhadrabahu had a brother named Varahmihir. Both were in the same kingdom. When a son was born to the king, Varahmihira declared that he would live for a hundred years but Bhadrabahu declared that he would live for only seven days, and that he would be killed by a cat.

According to the story Varahmihira became evil and tortured and terrorized the Jains, especially disciples and followers of Bhadrabahu. Acharya Bhadrabahu then formed a mantric prayer to 23rd Jain Tirthankara Parshvanath called the *Upsarga stotra* (now known as *Uvassagaharam Stotra*) and called upon Dharnendra, the divine follower (a "devta") of Parshvanath. As an effect of it, Varahmihira was defeated and Jain society was relieved. That mantric prayer is still famous among the Jains and they chant it with due respect and faith. And that prayer had made Bhadrabahu's name immortal among Jain ascetics.

- Sthulabhadra (Svetambar tradition) : Sthulabhadra (297-198 BCE) was a disciple of Acharya Bhadrabahu. The Swetambar tradition of Jainism trace their lineage through Sthulabhadra.

He was a son of the Nanda's minister Sakadala. He became a disciple of Sambhutavijaya. Later he became a disciple of Bhadrabahu to learn the Purvas. Bhadrabahu refused to teach him the last 4 Purvas because Sthulabhadra used his knowledge in vain. Sthulabhadra became a leader of the sangha when Bhadrabahu migrated to South India during a famine. He was succeeded by his disciples Mahagiri and Suhasti.

Sthulabhadra permitted the use of white cloth by his order during the famine. He is thus sometimes thought to be the originator of the Swetambara order.

- Kundakunda, (Digambar tradition) (2nd century CE) : Kundakunda (also Kundkund) is a celebrated Jain Acharya, Jain scholar monk, 2nd century CE, composer of spiritual classics such as: *Samayasara, Niyamasara, Pancastikayasara, Pravacanasara, Atthapahuda* and *Barasanuvekkha.* He occupies the highest place in the tradition of the Jain acharyas.

He belonged to the Mula Sangh order. His proper name was Padmanandi, he is popularly referred to as Kundakunda because he was born in a place named Kaundakunda in south India. He is closely associated with the Digambara sect, also in recent decades, his books have become popular among Svetambaras also. He was known also as:

1. Padmanandi
2. Elacarya
3. Vakragriva
4. Grddhapiccha.

For Digambaras, his name has auspicious significance and occupies third place after Bhagavan Mahavira and Gautama Ganadhara in the sacred litany. Kundakunda's singular contribution consists in his compiling a number of liturgical tracts and creating several masterly doctrinal works of his own, which provided a parallel canon for the Digambara tradition. This earned him the everlasting gratitude of the Digambaras, who have for centuries invoked his name together with that of Mahavira and his chief ganadhara Indrabhuti Gautama, placing him ahead even of Bhadrabahu, Visakha, and some forty other elders (sthaviras) in the lineage, thus making him virtually the founder of the Digambara sect, as illustrated by the following verse:

mangalam bhagavan Virah, mangalam Gautamo ganih,

mangalam Kundakundadyah, Jainadharmo 'stu mangalam.

Works

The works attributed to Kundakunda, all of them in Prakrit, can be divided in three groups. The first group is a collection of ten bhaktis (devotional prayers), short compositions in praise of the acaryas (Acaryabhakti), the scriptures (Srutabhakti), the mendicant conduct (Caritrabhakti), and so forth. They form the standard liturgical texts used by the Digambaras in their daily rituals and bear close resemblance to similar texts employed by the Svetambaras, suggesting the possibility of their origin in the canonical period prior to the division of the community.

The second group comprises four original works described as "The Essence" (sara)— namely, the Niyamasara (The Essence of the Restraint, or the mendicant discipline, in 187 verses), the Pancastikayasara (The Essence of the Five Existents, in 153 verses), the Samayasara (The Essence of Self-Realization, in 439 verses), and the Pravacanasara (The Essence of the Teaching, in 275 verses), all of which, because of their nonconventional or absolute (niscayanaya) approach, have exerted a tremendous influence not only on the Digambara psyche but, as will be seen in Chapter VI, even on some of the leading members of the Svetambara community, both old and new.

The last group consists of eight short texts called Prabhrta (Pkt. pahuda, i.e., a gift or a treatise), probably compilations from some older sources, on such topics as the right view (Darsanaprabhrta, in 36 verses), right conduct (Caritraprabhrta, in 44 verses), the scripture (Sutraprabhrta, in 27 verses), and so forth. Dr. A. N. Upadhye in his critical edition of the Pravacanasara has examined at great length the problems concerning the date and author-ship of these and other works attributed to Kundakunda and has placed him in the middle of the second century A.D.

Kundakunda wrote in Shauraseni Prakrit. Amongst the modern followers of Kundakunda, two names are remarkable, Banarasidasa, a 16th century lay poet from Agra who began his spiritual quest after reading kundakunda's "Samayasara"; and Rajachandra, the Gujarati merchant who trod famously on the spiritual path highlighted by Acarya Kundakunda.

- Spolniodnos, (Digambar tradition) (3–4th century CE)
- Siddhasen Diwakar, (claimed by both) (5th century CE).

Siddhasen Diwakar (Fifth century A. D.) was a highly intelligent Jain acharya of his time. Siddhasen could study the scriptures and realize their truth in a short time. In due course he became the most well known Jain scholar of the time. He was like the illuminating lamp of the Jain order and therefore came to be known as Siddhasen Diwakar. He is credited with the authorship of many books but most of them unfortunately are not available.

Sanmatitarka is his best book on logic and is widely read even at present. The well known *Kalyanmandir Stotra* was also composed by him.

Life

Approximate 2000 years ago there lived a preceptor (sicsic) named Devarshi in the court of King Vikramaditya. Devarshi's son, Kumud (this was the birth name of Siddhasen Diwakar) was very handsome, smart and highly intelligent and so Devarshi sent him to the best monastery school of the time. There Kumud quickly mastered all the arts and sciences. Devarshi was very proud of his son. It was customary in those days to hold contests to determine who was more knowledgeable. Devarshi believed that Kumud would defeat anyone in such contests and Kumud did not belie his expectations. In a short amount of time, Kumud defeated everyone in the court of King Vikramaditya. From there he went to other prominent courts of India and was victorious every time. However these successive triumphs generated a sense of vanity in his mind and he started believing that there was no one was more learned than himself.

He announced for an open contest with any one who claimed superior knowledge and also vowed that if any one could beat him, he would instantly become the winner s disciple. No one however came forward to accept his challenge. This made him even more egotistical. His vanity now knew no bounds. He sewed the emblems of a lamp, a net, a fork, a ladder and a spade onto his clothes and when any one inquired about the purpose of such amazing emblems, he would say that they were meant for his rivals.

If any of his opponents, out of fear of defeat, escaped in the dark, he would locate him with his lamp, if one escaped in water, he would trap him with the net, if one escaped in fire, he would get him out with the fork, if one escaped in the sky, he would bring him back with his ladder and if one escaped in the nether world, he would dig him out with the spade. At that time, Jain Acharya Vriddhivadi was the head of the Jain religious order. He was very learned but because he was a Jain saint he would not come out to challenge Kumud. Someone told Kumud that his universal conquest would remain incomplete until he vanquished the Jain Acharya.

Acharya Vriddhivadi was then camping at Mandu (Madhya Pradesh, India), a little away from Ujjayini (Ujjain). Kumud rode out to meet him, however, Jain monks do not stay at any one place very long. Accordingly the Acharya happened to move towards the next camp that very morning. As Kumud arrived in Mandu, he came to know that the Acharya had left. He felt that the Acharya was scared of him and had escaped knowing about his arrival. He sped towards the place where the Acharya was headed and intercepted him near the river Kshipra.

He informed the Acharya that he was Kumudchandra, the most learned man of India and since the latter claimed to be very learned, he had come to have a contest. The Jain Acharya was rather indifferent but Kumud insisted upon the contest. Acharya then suggested to have the contest in the nearby court but Kumud was rather impatient and insisted upon the contest right there with the ranchers of the Kshipra as their judges. Acharya had heard about Kumud and was aware of his reputation as a well known scholar. He saw that the knowledge of Kumud was obscured by the vanity, however he also visualized the immense contribution that Kumud could make to the religious order, if he accepted the Jain faith. Acharya thereupon agreed and asked Kumud to first make his presentation.

Kumud seized that opportunity and started exposing the weakness of different schools of thought including Jainism. The ranchers had no idea what he was talking about. Then came the turn of the Jain Acharya. He knew the real caliber of the ranchers and asked them to form a circle and recite a song. Then with his melodious voice he started singing a song with the following lines:

"Nonviolence is the path of peace; That ultimately leads to bliss."

The ranchers liked the song and merrily recited the same in chorus. Simultaneously they played flute in tune. At the end of the song, Acharya said that he did not want to say anything else. Kumud was sure that he had made his exposition very well and asked the ranchers about the outcome. Ranchers unanimously declared Acharya to be the winner. Kumud immediately realized his folly. His vanity disappeared and he fell at the feet of the Jain Acharya begging him to accept him as the pupil.

Acharya however did not intend to take advantage of that unfair contest. He therefore declined the offer and asked Kumud to a rematch at a nearby court. Kumud replied that the "Acharya was his true preceptor because he made him realize that the real essence of knowledge lay in equanimity of mind and not in vanity with which his own knowledge had been clouded." At the insistence of the Acharya he however agreed to have one more contest in the nearby court where Acharya decisively defeated him. So Kumud became his pupil and was renamed Siddhasen that is known as Siddhasen Diwakar.

Work

He inspired the Jain monks to study profoundly the Jain scriptures. He himself devoted to the deep study of Jain works. He was bitterly opposed to the storage of Jain works in isolated places; he eagerly desired to bring them to light for the propagation of Jainism. He himself wrote collected and edited certain important Jain works. He complied the famous *Kalyanmandir Stotra*. It is a monumental work in Sanskrit poetry. Sanmatitarka is his best book on logic and is widely read even at present. He wrote well known *Sakal tirth stotra* with the details of all Jain Tirtha of that time. This work itself places Siddhasen Diwakar on a high pedestal of Jain scholars and pioneers of religious Acharya's of the fifth century.

- Manatunga composer of Bhaktamar Stotra, (claimed by both)
- Haribhadra, (Svetambar tradition), (700–750 CE).

Haribhadra Suri (c.700-c.770, or 459-529, traditional) was a Svetambara mendicant Jain leader and author.

History

There are multiple contradictory dates assigned to his birth. These include 459, 478, and 529. However, given his familiarity with Dharmakirti, a more likely choice would be sometime after 650. In his writings, Haribhadra identifies himself as a student of Jinabhadra and Jinadatta of the Vidyadhara Kula. There are several, somewhat contradictory, accounts of his life.

The earlier of these, which dates to the 12th century, says that Haribhadra was an educated Brahmin who made the boast that he would become a pupil of anyone who stated a sentence which he could not understand. After hearing a Jain nun named Yâkinî Mahattara recite a verse that he could not understand, he was sent to her teacher Jinabhama, who promised Haribhadra that he would instruct him if Haribhadra accepted initiation into Jainism. Haribhadra agreed, and took the name Yakiniputra, or "Spiritual Son of Yakking".

The second account, which bears similarities to the story of Akalanka Digambara, also shows the state of relations between Buddhist and Jain mendicants at the time. In this story, Haribhadra was teaching two of his nephews. These nephews went to secretly study logic at a Buddhist temple, and fled after being discovered there. One of them was killed by the Buddhists, and the other died of grief later. Haribhadra engaged the monks of this monastery in a philosophical debate, and emerged victorious. He then ordered the losing monks to jump into a vat of hot oil. When Haribhadra's own teacher heard of this, he ordered Haribhadra to undertake severe penances for his unseemly display of anger and attachment. Haribhadra did so, and took the title "Virahânka", which means "having separation (or viraha, from his nephews) as a distinguishing characteristic".

Tradition ascribes some 1400 different works to him. A more creditable number is in the vicinity of 100, some of which are among the most highly regarded works in Jainism. Some have even suggested that, based on the language and subject material of the books ascribed to Haribhadra, there were two Haribhadras, the first of which, Haribhadra Virahanka, may have lived around the sixth century, and the second, Haribhadra Yakiniputra, was a monk who lived in a temple around the eighth century. Scholars of the Svetambara community itself tend to hold with the belief that there was only one Haribhadra.

Among his important teachings were tolerance for other traditions, and that ultimate reality can be grasped from multiple different perspectives.

Philosophy and Influence

With his writings, he established that Sanskrit, rather than Prakrit, would be the language of Jain study. He used his only familiarity with the techniques of brahminical study and wrote in the same style. He is also noted for the great respect he displays toward other religious traditions. He even did what few other Jain scholars have done, and wrote a commentary on the *Nyayapraveua,* a text on Indian logic by the Buddhist scholar Dignaga. He does however ultimately support Jain thought, arguing that the other beliefs tend to display only a one-sided view of the greater reality.

Works

Among his other works are:

- *Anekantajayapataka* (*The Victory Banner of Relativism*)-which puts forward arguments about anekantavada
- *Ashtakaprakarana* (*The Eightfold Explanation*)
- *Dharmabindu*-which outlines the duties of the laity, outlines rules for mendicants, and describes the bliss of moksha
- *Dhurtakhyana* (*The Rogue's Stories*)-a satire of Hinduism
- *Pancaikha*-a Prakrit work on rituals and spiritual matters
- *badarœanasamuccaya (*Compendium of Six Philosophies*)-which compares Jainism with other schools of Indian philosophy*
- *Samaraiccakaha* (*The Story of Samaraicca)*-a narrative which outlines the effects of karma in a story about the enmity of its characters which endures over several reincarnations
- *Sastravartasamuccaya* (*The Array of Explanatory Teachings*)
- *Yogabindu* (*The Seeds of Yoga*)-a work on yoga
- *Yogadrishtisamuccaya* (*An Array of Views on Yoga*)-another work on yoga
- *Yogaœataka*-a third work on yoga. In these three volumes, he compares the yoga of Jainism with the other varieties of yoga prevalent in India at the time.
- Sanmatti Prakaran
- Akalanka, (Digambar tradition), (620–680 CE)
- Virasena, (Digambar tradition), (790–825 CE).

Virasena was an 8th century mathematician in India who gave the derivation of the volume of a frustum by a sort of infinite procedure. He also dealt with logarithms to base 2 (*ardhaccheda*) and knew its laws, and was also the first to deal with logarithms to base 3 (*trakacheda*) and base 4 (*caturthacheda*).

- Jinasena, (Digambar tradition), preceptor of Rashtrakuta rulers, (800–880 CE).

Jinasena is the name of several famous Jain Acharyas of the Digambar tradition.

- The author of *Harivamsha Purana* in the 8th century. He belonged to the Punnata branch of Jain monks.
- The author of Mahapurana in the 9th century, he was the disciple of Virasena and he completed his teacher's famous commentary "Dhavala" on Kashayaprabhrita. Mahapurana includes Adipurana and Uttarapurana, the project was completed by his pupil Gunabhadra.
- The legendary founder of the Khandelwal Jain community.
- Jinasena is also the traditional name of the Bhattarakas of the Sena Gana seat.

Mahapurana is the source of the famous quote:

Some foolish men declare that Creator made the world. The doctrine that the world was created is ill-advised, and should be rejected. If god created the world, where was he before creation? If you say he was transcendent then, and needed no support, where is he now? No single being had the skill to make the world-for how can an immaterial god create that which is material? How could god have made the world without any raw material? If you say he made this first, and then the world, you are face with an endless regression. If you declare that the raw material arose naturally you fall into another fallacy, for the whole universe might thus have been its own creator, and have risen equally naturally.

If god created the world by an act of will, without any raw material, then it is just his will made nothing else and who will believe this silly stuff? If he is ever perfect, and complete, how could the will to create have arisen in him? If, on the other hand, he is not perfect, he could no more create the universe than a potter could. If he is formless, actionless, and all-embracing, how could he have created the world? Such a soul, devoid of all modality, would have no desire to create anything. If you say that he created to no purpose, because it was his nature to do so then god is pointless. If he created in some kind of sport, it was the sport of a foolish child, leading to trouble. If he created out of love for living things and need of them he made the world; why did he not make creation wholly blissful, free from misfortune? Thus the doctrine that the world was created by god makes no sense at all.

Mahapurana was the model for Saiva Siddhanta Periyapuranam which gives biographies of 63 individuals. Jinasena belonged to the Panchastupanvaya lineage of Jain monks. The spiritual lineage of Jinasena continues today and is called Senagana.

- Nemichandra, (Digambar tradition) : Nemichandra Siddhanta Chakravarty (ca. 9th century), was the celebrated author of Gomattasara (Jivkand and Karmakand), Triloksara, Labdhisara and Kshapanasara. He was among the most distinguished of the Jain Acharyas.

At the request of Chamundaraya, he wrote Gomattasar taking the essence of all available works of the great Acharyas. He also supervised the consecration of the Gomateshwara statue.

The *Dravyasamgraha* of Nemichandra (ca. 9th century) is a sacred text of Jainism.

- Hemachandra, (Svetambar tradition), preceptor of Kumarapala, (1089–1172 CE).

Nemichandra Siddhanta Chakravarty (ca. 9th century), was the celebrated author of Gomattasara (Jivkand and Karmakand), Triloksara, Labdhisara and Kshapanasara. He was among the most distinguished of the Jain Acharyas.

At the request of Chamundaraya, he wrote Gomattasar taking the essence of all available works of the great Acharyas. He also supervised the consecration of the Gomateshwara statue.

The *Dravyasamgraha* of Nemichandra (ca. 9th century) is a sacred text of Jainism.

- Jagadguru Hira Vijaya Suri, (Svetambar tradition), who was invited by Akbar, the Mughal emperor

Hiravijaya (1526–1595 C.E) (also known as Muni Hiravijayji and Hiravijay Suri) was the supreme pontiff of Tapa Gachcha order of Jain Svetambara tradition. He is famous for propounding the Jain philosophy to Emperor Akbar and turning him towards vegetarianism.

Early Life and Monkhood

Hiravijaya was born in a Jain Oswal family in Palanpur in Gujarat in 1527. His parents had died when he was still an infant, and he was brought up by his two elder sisters. He became the disciple of a Jain monk, Vijayadana Suri in 1540 at the age of 13, and a new name Hira Harsh was given to him. He was taken to Devagiri – a center of Sanskrit learning in those days, for further education. He successively won the title of *Pandit* in 1550, *Upadhyaya* in 1552 and *Suri* in 1553. This last title he won at Sirohi. Henceforth he was known as Hiravijaya Suri. In 1556 when his guru died, the Svetambara community of Gujarat selected him as their Acarya. At that time there was a large community of around 2,000 students studying under him.

Influence on Akbar

In 1582, Emperor Akbar invited Hiravijaya Suri to explain him the principles of Jainism. He first discussed the various aspects of religion and philosophy with Abul Fazal and the later with Akbar. The emperor was so impressed with the Suri that he bestowed on him the title of *Jagatguru* which means World Teacher or the Preceptor of the World. Akbar was so much influenced by the religion of non-violence preached by the Jain monk that he became vegetarian most of the days, prohibited slaughter of animals and birds, released prisoners and gave up fishing and hunting which were his favourite pastime.

Hiravijaya is reported to have told Akbar: "*How could a man's stomach be a tomb of animals?*" creating an aversion for meat eating in mind of Akbar. Out of respect for Jainism, Akbar declared firmans (royal decree) for *Amari Ghosana* banning the killing of animals during the Jain festivals of Paryusana and Mahavir Jayanti. He rolled back the Jazia tax from Jain pilgrim places like Palitana. Furthermore, he issued firmans for ban on slaughter of animals for six months in Gujarat, abolishing the confiscation of property of deceased persons and removal of the Sujija Tax (Jazia) and a Sulka (possibly a tax on pilgrims).

Indologist and biographer of Akbar, Vincent Smith notes: "Akbars action in abstaining almost wholly from meat and in issuing stringent prohibitions, resembling those of Asoka, restricting to the narrowest limit the destruction of animal life, certainly was taken in obedience to the doctrine of his Jaina teachers." Akbar developed such fondness for the Jain ideology that he repeatedly requested Suri to send his itinerary one after another. At the request of the Emperor he left behind his brilliant disciple Santichandra with the Emperor, who in turn left his disciples Bhanucandra and Siddhicandra in the Royal court. Akbar again invited Hiravijaya Suri's successor Vijayasena Suri in his court who visited him between 1593 to 1595.

In Literature

In Ain-i-Akbari, Abul Fazal gives a list of 140 influential learned persons during Akbars time. Out of this, he places 21 persons in the highest class as "persons who understands the mysteries of the both worlds" He thus places Hiravijaya Suri in this list of twenty-one most learned persons in the Mughal Empire. His ardent disciples Devavimal Gani composed *Hira Saubhagya Kavya* and another disciple Padmasagara composed *Jagatguru Kavya* in his honour. Both works of poetry written in Sanskrit were composed in 1590 C.E. and give an authenticate account of relationship of Suri with Akbar.

Famous Historical Jain Nuns

- Aryika Chandanbala
- Sadhvi Yakking Mahattara

Chaturmas (VarshaYog) for Jain Monks

Chaturmas means the four months of the monsoon, a practice observed by both Digamber and Shwetamber Jain monks and nuns. Chaturmas is related to the staying of the Jain monks and nuns in one place during this period. Because during this time the Jain monks and nuns have settled in the city/town for a longer duration, it is a suitable time for the householders to have an annual renewal of the faith by listening to the statement of the Dharma and by meditation and vartas (self-control). And for the Jain monks, almost as importantly, staying in one place during the monsoon reduces the risk of causing accidental death to numerous insects and smaller forms of life that thrive during the rains. There are two categories of ascetics, *Sadhu* (monk) and *Sadhvi* (nun). They practice the five *Mahavratas*, three *Guptis* and five *Samitis*:

Five Mahavratas:

- Ahimsa: Non-violence in thought, word and deed
- Satya: Truth which is (hita) beneficial, (mita) succinct and (priya) pleasing
- Acaurya: Not accepting anything that has not been given to them by the owner

- Brahmacarya: Absolute purity of mind and body
- Aparigraha: Non-attachment to non-self objects.

Three Guptis:

- Managupti: Control of the mind
- Vacanagupti: Control of speech
- Kayagupti: Control of body.

Five Samitis:

- Irya Samiti: Carefulness while walking
- Bhasha Samiti: Carefulness while communicating
- Eshana Samiti: Carefulness while eating
- Adana Nikshepana Samiti: Carefulness while handling their fly-whisks, water gourds, etc.
- Pratishthapana Samiti: Carefulness while disposing of bodily waste matter.

Male Digambara monks do not wear any clothes and are nude. They practice non-attachment to the body and hence, wear no clothes. Shvetambara monks and nuns wear white clothes. Shvetambaras believe that monks and nuns may wear simple un-stitched white clothes as long as they are not attached to them. Jain monks and nuns travel on foot. They do not use mechanical transport.

Digambar followers take up to eleven *Pratimaye* (oath). Monks take all eleven oaths. They eat only once a day. The Male Digambar monk (*Maharajji*) eat standing at one place in their palms without using any utensil.

Jain Festivities (Parva)

- Paryushan Parva, 10/8 (Digambar/Svetamber) day fasts, and for observe, 10/8 important principles.
- Mahavir Janma Kalyanak, Lord Mahavir's birth, it is popularly known as *Mahavir Jayanti* but the term 'jayanti' is inappropriate for a Tirthankar, as this term is used for mortals.
- Kshamavaani, The day for asking everyone's forgiveness.
- diwali, the nirvana day of Lord Mahavira
- astami/ Chaturdashi, The day to learn the eight karmas.

To release from the four gathis or bhava, Manushya, triyancha, Nariki, deva

- Veerashasana jayanthi, The day divya dvani of lord mahaveera was heard from the samvathsarana.
- Shrutha panchami, The completion day of the first grantha of shatkandagama. On this day the we do the jinavani pooja or stuti and read the granthas or Aagamas. i.e. Davala, Jayadavala, Mahadavala (39 volumes).

4

Karma Theory

In Jainism, karma is the basic principle within an overarching psycho-cosmology, in which human moral actions form the basis of the transmigration of the soul (*Java*)—constrained *within* the temporal world—until one achieves liberation (*mokca*) from this cycle, by following a path of purification.

In Jain philosophy, karma not only encompasses the causality of transmigration, but is also conceived of as an extremely subtle matter, which infiltrates the soul—obscuring its natural, transparent and pure qualities. Karma is thought of as a kind of pollution, that taints the soul with various colours. Based on its karma, a soul undergoes transmigration and reincarnates in various states of existence—like heavens or hells, or as humans or animals.

Jains cite inequalities, sufferings, and pain as evidence for the existence of karma. Jain texts have classified the various types of karma according to their effects on the potency of the soul. The Jain theory seeks to explain the karmic process by specifying the various causes of karmic influx and bondage (*bandha*), placing equal emphasis on deeds themselves, and the intentions behind those deeds. The Jain karmic theory attaches great responsibility to individual actions, and eliminates any reliance on some supposed existence of divine grace or retribution. The Jain doctrine also states that it is possible for us to both modify our karma, and to obtain release from it, through the austerities of purity of conduct.

Most scholars are of the view that the doctrine of karma predates the migration of Indo-Aryan peoples, later being developed by the ZramaGas, and finally being assimilated into brahmanical Hinduism, by the time of the Upanicads. The Jain concept of karma has been subject to criticism from rival Indian philosophies—like Vedic Hinduism, Buddhism, and Sekhya.

Philosophical Overview

According to Jains, all souls are intrinsically pure in their inherent and ideal state, possessing the qualities of infinite knowledge, infinite perception, infinite bliss and infinite energy. However, in contemporary experience, these qualities are found to be defiled and obstructed, on account of the association of these souls with karma. The soul has been associated with karma in this way throughout an eternity of beginningless time. This bondage of the soul is explained in the Jain texts by analogy with gold ore, which—in its natural state—is always found unrefined of admixture with impurities. Similarly, the ideally pure state of the soul has always been overlaid with the impurities of karma. This analogy with gold ore is also taken one step further: the purification of the soul can be achieved if the proper methods of refining are applied. Over the centuries, Jain monks have developed a large and sophisticated corpus of literature describing the nature of the soul, various aspects of the working of karma, and the ways and means of attaining *mokca*.

Material Theory

Jainism speaks of karmic "dirt", as karma is thought to be manifest as very subtle and microscopically imperceptible particles pervading the entire universe. They are so small that one space-point—the smallest possible extent of space—contains an infinite number of karmic particles. It is these karmic particles that adhere to the soul and affect its natural potency. This material karma is called *dravya karma;* and the resultant emotions—pleasure, pain, love, hatred, and so on—experienced by the soul are called *bhava karma,* psychic karma. The relationship between the material and psychic karma is that of cause and effect.

The material karma gives rise to the feelings and emotions in worldly souls, which—in turn—give rise to psychic karma, causing emotional modifications within the soul. These emotions, yet again, result in influx and bondage of fresh material karma. Jains hold that the karmic matter is actually an agent that enables the consciousness to act within the material context of this universe. They are the material carrier of a soul's desire to physically experience this world. When attracted to the consciousness, they are stored in an interactive karmic field called *krmana rarira,* which emanates from the soul. Thus, karma is a subtle matter surrounding the consciousness of a soul. When these two components—consciousness and ripened karma—interact, the soul experiences life as known in the present material universe.

Self Regulating Mechanism

According to Indologist Robert J. Zydenbos, karma is a system of natural laws, where actions that carry moral significance are considered to cause certain consequences in the same way as physical actions. When one holds an apple and then lets it go, the apple will fall. There is no judge, and no moral judgment involved, since this is a mechanical consequence of the physical action. In the same manner, consequences occur naturally when one utters a lie, steals something, commits senseless violence or leads a life of debauchery. Rather than assume that these consequences—the moral rewards and retributions—are a work of some divine judge, Jains believe that there is an innate moral order in the cosmos, self-regulating through the workings of the law of karma.

Morality and ethics are important in Jainism not because of a God, but because a life led in agreement with moral and ethical principles (*mahavrata*) is considered beneficial: it leads to a decrease—and finally to the total loss of—karma, which in turns leads to everlasting happiness. The Jain conception of karma takes away the responsibility for salvation from God and bestows it on man himself. In the words of the Jain scholar, J. L. Jaini:

> Jainism, more than any other creed, gives absolute religious independence and freedom to man. Nothing can intervene between the actions which we do and the fruits thereof. Once done, they become our masters and must fructify. As my independence is great, so my responsibility is co-extensive with it. I can live as I like; but my voice is irrevocable, and I cannot escape the consequences of it. No God, his Prophet or his deputy or beloved can interfere with human life. The soul, and it alone is responsible for all it does.

Predominance of Karma

According to Jainism, karmic consequences are unerringly certain and inescapable. No divine grace can save a person from experiencing them. Only the practice of austerities and self-control can modify or alleviate the consequences of karma. Even then, in some cases, there is no option but to accept karma with equanimity. The second-century Jain text, Bhagavati Aradhana (verse no. 1616) sums up the predominance of karma in Jain doctrine: "There is nothing mightier in the world than karma; karma tramples down all powers, as an elephant a clump of lotuses." This predominance of karma is a theme often explored by Jain ascetics in the literature they have produced, throughout all centuries. Paul Dundas notes that the ascetics often used cautionary tales to underline the full karmic implications of morally incorrect modes of life, or excessively intense emotional relationships. However, he notes that such narratives were often softened by concluding statements about the transforming effects of the protagonists' pious actions, and their eventual attainment of liberation.

The biographies of the exploits of legendary persons like Rama (Rma) and Krishna, in the Jain versions of the Ramayana and Mahabharata, also have karma as one of the major themes. The major events, characters and circumstances are explained by reference to their past lives, with examples of specific actions of particular intensity in one life determining events in the next. Jain texts narrate how even Mahavira, the 24th *tirthaGkara* (ford-maker), had to bear the brunt of his previous karma before attaining *kevala Junin* (enlightenment). He attained it only after bearing twelve years of severe austerity with detachment. The cranga Sktra speaks of how Mahavira bore his karma with complete equanimity, as follows.

He was struck with a stick, the fist, a lance, hit with a fruit, a clod, a potsherd. Beating him again and again many cried. When he once sat without moving his body many cut his flesh, tore his hair under pain, or covered him with dust. Throwing him up they let him fall, or disturbed him in his religious postures; abandoning the care of his body, the Venerable One humbled himself and bore pain, free from desires.

Reincarnation and Transmigration

Karma forms a central and fundamental part of Jain faith, being intricately connected to other of its philosophical concepts like transmigration, reincarnation, liberation, non-violence (*ahics*) and non-attachment, among others. Actions are seen to have consequences: some immediate, some delayed, even into future incarnations. So the doctrine of karma is not considered simply in relation to one life-time, but also in relation to both future incarnations and past lives. *Uttaradhyayana-Sutra* 3.3–4 states: "The *Jiva* or the soul is sometimes born in the world of gods, sometimes in hell. Sometimes it acquires the body of a demon; all this happens on account of its karma. This *Jiva* sometimes takes birth as a worm, as an insect or as an ant." The text further states (32.7): "Karma is the root of birth and death. The souls bound by karma go round and round in the cycle of existence."

Actions and emotions in the current lifetime affect future incarnations depending on the nature of the particular karma. For example, a good and virtuous life indicates a latent desire to experience good and virtuous themes of life. Therefore, such a person attracts karma that ensures that his future births will allow him to experience and manifest his virtues and good feelings unhindered. In this case, he may take birth in heaven or in a prosperous and virtuous human family. On the other hand, a person who has indulged in immoral deeds, or with a cruel disposition, indicates a latent desire to experience cruel themes of life. As a natural consequence, he will attract karma which will ensure that he is reincarnated in hell, or in lower life forms, to enable his soul to experience the cruel themes of life.

There is no retribution, judgment or reward involved but a natural consequences of the choices in life made either knowingly or unknowingly. Hence, whatever suffering or pleasure that a soul may be experiencing in its present life is on account of choices that it has made in the past. As a result of this doctrine, Jainism attributes supreme importance to pure thinking and moral behaviour. Apart from Buddhism, Jainism may be the only religion that does not invoke the fear of God as a reason for moral behaviour.

Four States of Existence

The Jain texts postulate four *gatis,* that is states-of-existence or birth-categories, within which the soul transmigrates. The four *gatis* are: *deva* (demi-gods), *manucya* (humans), *nâraki* (hell beings) and *tiryanca* (animals, plants and micro-organisms). The four *gatis* have four corresponding realms or habitation levels in the vertically tiered Jain universe: demi-gods occupy the higher levels where the heavens are situated; humans, plants and animals occupy the middle levels; and hellish beings occupy the lower levels where seven hells are situated. Single-sensed souls, however, called *nigoda,* and element-bodied souls pervade all tiers of this universe. *Nigodas* are souls at the bottom end of the existential hierarchy. They are so tiny and undifferentiated, that they lack even individual bodies, living in colonies. According to Jain texts, this infinity of *nigodas* can also be found in plant tissues, root vegetables and animal bodies. Depending on its karma, a soul transmigrates and reincarnates within the scope of this cosmology of destinies. The four main destinies are further divided into sub-categories and still smaller sub–sub categories. In all, Jain texts speak of a cycle of 8.4 million birth destinies in which souls find themselves again and again as they cycle within *samsara.*

In Jainism, God has no role to play in an individual's destiny; one's personal destiny is not seen as a consequence of any system of reward or punishment, but rather as a result of its own personal karma. A text from a volume of the ancient Jain canon, *Bhagvati Sutra* 8.9.9, links specific states of existence to specific karmas. Violent deeds, killing of creatures having five sense organs, eating fish, and so on, lead to rebirth in hell. Deception, fraud and falsehood leads to rebirth in the animal and vegetable world. Kindness, compassion and humble character result in human birth; while austerities and the making and keeping of vows leads to rebirth in heaven.

Each soul is thus responsible for its own predicament, as well as its own salvation. Accumulated karma represent a sum total of all unfulfilled desires, attachments and aspirations of a soul. It enables the soul to experience the various themes of the lives that it desires to experience. Hence a soul may transmigrate from one life form to another for countless of years, taking with it the karma that it has earned, until it finds conditions that bring about the required fruits. In certain philosophies, heavens and hells are often viewed as places for eternal salvation or eternal damnation for good and bad deeds. But according to Jainism, such places, including the earth are simply the places which allow the soul to experience its unfulfilled karma.

Lesya – Colouring of the Soul

According to the Jain theory of karma, the karmic matter imparts a colour to the soul, depending on the mental activities behind an action. The colouring of the soul is explained through the analogy of crystal, that acquires the colour of the matter associated with it. In the same way, the soul also reflects the qualities of taste, smell and touch of associated karmic matter, although it is usually the colour that is referred to when discussing the *leuyas*. *Uttaradhyayana-Sutra* 34.3 speaks of six main categories of *leuya* represented by six colours: black, blue, grey, yellow, red and white. The black, blue and grey are inauspicious *leuya*, leading to the soul being born into misfortunes. The yellow, red and white are auspicious *leuyas*, that lead to the soul being born into good fortune. *Uttaradhyayana-Sutra* describes the mental disposition of persons having black and white *leuyas*:

A man who acts on the impulse of the five sins, does not possess the three *guptis*, has not ceased to injure the six (kinds of living beings), commits cruel acts, is wicked and violent, is afraid of no consequences, is mischievous and does not subdue his senses– a man of such habits develops the black *leuya*. — *Uttaradhyayana-Sutra*, 34.21:22

A man who abstains from constant thinking about his misery and about sinful deeds, but engages in meditation on the law and truth only, whose mind is at ease, who controls himself, who practises the *samitis* and *guptis*, whether he be still subject to passion or free from passion, is calm, and subdues his senses— a man of such habits develops the white *leuya*. — *Uttaradhyayana-Sutra*, 34.31:32

The Jain texts further illustrate the effects of *leuyas* on the mental dispositions of a soul, using an example of the reactions of six travellers on seeing a fruit-bearing tree. They see a tree laden with fruit and begin to think of getting those fruits: one of them suggests uprooting the entire tree and eating the fruit; the second one suggests cutting the trunk of the tree; the third one suggests simply cutting the branches; the fourth one suggests cutting the twigs and sparing the branches and the tree; the fifth one suggests plucking only the fruits; the sixth one suggests picking up only the fruits that have fallen down. The thoughts, words and bodily activities of each of these six travellers are different based on their mental dispositions and are respectively illustrative of the six *leuyas*. At one extreme, the person with the black *leuya*, having evil disposition, thinks of uprooting the whole tree even though he wants to eat only one fruit. At the other extreme, the person with the white *leuya,* having a pure disposition, thinks of picking up the fallen fruit, in order to spare the tree.

Role of Deeds and Intent

The role of intent is one of the most important and definitive elements of the karma theory, in all its traditions. In Jainism, intent is important but not an essential precondition of sin or wrong conduct. Evil intent forms only one of the modes of committing sin. Any action committed, knowingly or *unknowingly,* has karmic repercussions. In certain philosophies, like Buddhism, a person is guilty of violence only if he had an intention to commit violence. On the other hand, according to Jains, if an act produces violence, then the person is guilty of it, whether or not he had an intention to commit it.

John Koller explains the role of intent in Jainism with the example of a monk, who unknowingly offered poisoned food to his brethren. According to the Jain view, the monk is guilty of a violent act if the other monks die because they eat the poisoned food; but according to the Buddhist view he would not be guilty.

The crucial difference between the two views is that the Buddhist view excuses the act, categorising it as non-intentional, since he was not aware that the food was poisoned; whereas the Jain view holds the monk to have been responsible, due to his ignorance and carelessness. Jains argue that the monk's very ignorance and carelessness constitute an intent to do violence and hence entail his guilt. So the absence of intent does not absolve a person from the karmic *consequences* of guilt either, according to the Jain analysis.

Intent is a function of kacaya, which refers to negative emotions and negative qualities of mental (or deliberative) action. The presence of intent acts as an aggravating factor, increasing the vibrations of the soul, which results in the soul absorbing more karma. This is explained by *Tattvarthasutra* 6.7: "[The] intentional act produces a strong karmic bondage and [the] unintentional produces weak, short-lived karmic bondage." Similarly, the physical act is also not a necessary condition for karma to bind to the soul: the existence of intent alone is sufficient. This is explained by Kundakunda (1st Century CE) in *Samayasara* 262–263: "The intent to kill, to steal, to be unchaste and to acquire property, whether these offences are actually carried or not, leads to bondage of evil karmas." Jainism thus places an equal emphasis on the physical act as well as intent for binding of karmas.

Origins and Influence

The doctrine of karma is central to all Indian religions, however, it is difficult to say just when and where in India the concept of karma originated. According to Glasenapp, the doctrine of karma must have existed at least a thousand years before the beginning of the Christian era. There is no clear consensus amongst scholars as to its origins, although it is believed by some that the concept of karma has a philosophical background that is non-Vedic and non-brahmanical origin. According to the scholars, the Jain conception of karma—as something material that encumbers the soul—is probably the oldest distinct element, common to all the karmic theories. It is probable that the concept of karma and reincarnation entered the mainstream brahaminical thought via the Sramana—literally "renouncer (of tradition)"—movement, to which Jainism and Buddhism belong. Historian G. C. Pande opines that early Upananicadic thinkers like Yajnavalkya were acquainted with the Sramanic philosophy and tried to incorporate ideas of karma, *Soccer* and *mokca* into the Vedic thought.

Jain and Buddhist scholar, Dr. Padmanabh Jaini observes: "Perhaps the entire concept that a person's situation and experiences are in fact the results of deeds committed in various lives may not be Aryan origin at all, but rather may have developed as a part of the indigenous Gangetic traditions from which the various Sramana movements arose. In any case we shall see, Jaina views on the process and possibilities of rebirth are distinctly non-Hindu; the social ramifications of these views, moreover, have been profound." The earliest works of the Jain canon, Acaranga Sutra and Sutrakritanga, contain a general outline of the doctrines of karma and reincarnation, with only minimal technical details and classification. Detailed codification of types of karma and their effects is not attested until the time of Umasvati in 2nd century CE. With regards to the influence of the theory of karma on development of various religious and social practices in ancient India, Dr. Padmanabh Jaini states:

The emphasis on reaping the fruits only of one's own karma was not restricted to the Jainas; both Hindus and Buddhist writers have produced doctrinal materials stressing the same point. Each of the latter traditions, however, developed practices in basic contradiction to such belief. In addition to *uraddha* (the ritual Hindu offerings to the dead ancestors), we find among Hindus widespread adherence to the notion of divine intervention in one's fate, while (Mahayana) Buddhists eventually came to propound such theories like boon-granting Bodhisattvas, transfer of merit and like. Only Jainas have been absolutely unwilling to allow such ideas to penetrate their community, despite the fact that there must have been tremendous amount of social pressure on them to do so.

The Jain socio-religious practices like regular fasting, practicing severe austerities and penances, the ritual death of *sallekhana* and rejection of god as the creator and operator of the universe can all be linked to the Jain theory of karma. Jaini notes that the disagreement over the karmic theory of transmigration resulted in the social distinction between the Jains and their Hindu neighbours. Thus one of the most important Hindu ritual of *uraddha* offerings was not only rejected but strongly criticised by the Jains as superstition. Certain authors have also noted the strong influence of the concept of karma on the Jain ethics, especially the ethics of non-violence. It is suggested that, belief in the doctrine of rebirth may have led to the idea of the unity of all life and, consequently, to the ethical concept of non-violence in ancient India. Once the doctrine of transmigration of souls came to include rebirth on earth in animal as well as human form, depending upon one's karmas, it is quite probable that, it created a humanitarian sentiment of kinship amongst all life forms and thus contributed to the notion of *ahics*.

The Process of Bondage and Release

The karmic process in Jainism is based on seven truths or fundamental principles of Jainism which explain the human predicament. Out that the seven, the four—influx , bondage, stoppage and release—pertain to the karmic process.

Attraction and Binding

The karmic bondage occurs as a result of the following two processes: *asrava* and *bandha*. *Asrava* is the inflow of karma. The karmic influx occurs when the particles are attracted to the soul on account of *yoga*. *Yoga* is the vibrations of the soul due to activities of mind, speech and body. However, the *yoga* alone do not produce bondage. The karmas have effect only when they are bound to the consciousness. This binding of the karma to the consciousness is called *bandha*. Out of the many causes of bondage, emotions or passions are considered as the main cause of bondage.

The karmas are literally bound on account of the stickiness of the soul due to existence of various passions or mental dispositions. The passions like anger, pride, deceit and greed are called sticky (*kacayas*) because they act like glue in making karmic particles stick to the soul resulting in *bandha*. The karmic inflow on account of *yoga* driven by passions and emotions cause a long term inflow of karma prolonging the cycle of reincarnations. On the other hand, the karmic inflows on account of actions that are not driven by passions and emotions have only a transient, short-lived karmic effect. Hence the ancient Jain texts talk of subduing these negative emotions: When he wishes that which is good for him, he should get rid of the four faults—anger, pride, deceit and greed—which increase the evil. Anger and pride when not suppressed, and deceit and greed when arising: all these four black passions water the roots of re-birth. —*Dauavaikalika Sutra, 8:36–39*

Causes of Attraction and Bondage

The Jain theory of karma proposes that karma particles are attracted and then bound to the consciousness of souls by a combination of four factors pertaining to actions: instrumentality, process, modality and motivation.

- The instrumentality of an action refers to whether the instrument of the action was: the body, as in physical actions; one's speech, as in speech acts; or the mind, as in thoughtful deliberation.
- The process of an action refers to the temporal sequence in which it occurs: the decision to act, plans to facilitate the act, making preparations necessary for the act, and ultimately the carrying through of the act itself.
- The modality of an action refers to different modes in which one can participate in an action, for example: being the one who carries out the act itself; being one who instigates another to perform the act; or being one who gives permission, approval or endorsement of an act.

- The motivation for an action refers to the internal passions or negative emotions that prompt the act, including: anger, greed, pride, deceit and so on.

All actions have the above four factor present in them. When different permutations of the sub-elements of the four factors are calculated, the Jain teachers speak of 108 ways in which the karmic matter can be attracted to the soul. Even giving silent assent or endorsement to acts of violence from far away has karmic consequences for the soul. Hence, the scriptures advise carefulness in actions, awareness of the world, and purity in thoughts as means to avoid the burden of karma. According to *Tattvarthasutra*, the causes of *bandha* or the karmic bondage—in the order they are required to be eliminate by a soul for spiritual progress—are:

- *Mithyatva* (Irrationality and a deluded world view) – The deluded world view is the misunderstanding as to how this world really functions on account of one-sided perspectives, perverse viewpoints, irrational scepticism, pointless generalisations and ignorance.
- *Avirati* (non-restraint or a vowless life) – The second cause of bondage, *avirati* is the inability to refrain voluntarily from the evil actions, that harms oneself and others. The state of *avirati* can only be overcome by observing the minor vows of a layman.
- *Pyramid* (carelessness and laxity of conduct) – This third cause of bondage consists of absentmindedness, lack of enthusiasm towards acquiring merit and spiritual growth, and improper actions of mind, body and speech without any regard to oneself or others.
- *Kacya* (passions or negative emotions) – The four passions—anger, pride, deceit and greed—are the primary reason for the attachment of the karmas to the soul. They keep the soul immersed in the darkness of delusion leading to deluded conduct and unending cycles of reincarnations.
- *Yoga* (activities of mind, speech and body) – The threefold activities of mind, body and speech attract and bind the karmas when such actions are influenced by passions.

Each cause presupposes the existence of the next cause, but the next cause does not necessarily pre-suppose the existence of the previous cause. A soul is able to advance on the spiritual ladder called *gugasthna,* only when it is able to eliminate the above causes of bondage one by one.

Experiencing the Effects

The nature of experience of the effects of the karma depends on the following four factors:

- *Prikriti* (nature or type of karma) – According to Jain texts, there are eight main types of karma which categorized into the 'harming' and the 'non-harming'; each divided into four types. The harming karmas (*ghatiya karmas*) directly affect the soul powers by impeding its perception, knowledge and energy, and also brings about delusion. These harming karmas are: *daruanavaraga* (perception-obscuring karma), *ajnanavada* (knowledge-obscuring karma), *antaraya* (obstacle-creating karma) and *mohaniya* (deluding karma). The non-harming category (*aghatiya karmas*) is responsible for the reborn soul's physical and mental circumstances, longevity, spiritual potential and experience of pleasant and unpleasant sensations. These non-harming karmas are: *name* (body-determining karma), *ayu* (life-span-determining karma), *gotra* (status-determining karma) and *vedaniya* (feeling-producing karma), respectively. Different types of karmas thus affect the soul in different ways as per their nature.
- *Stithi* (the duration of the karmic bond) – The karmic bond remains latent and bound to the consciousness up to the time it is activated. Although latent karma does not affect the soul directly, its existence limits the spiritual growth of the soul. Jain texts provide minimum and the maximum duration for which such karma is bound before it matures.
- *Anubhava* (intensity of karmas) – The degree of the experience of the karmas, that is, mild or intense, depends on the *anubhava* quality or the intensity of the bondage. It determines the power of karmas and its effect on the soul. *Anubhava* depends on the intensity of the passions at the time of binding the karmas. More intense the emotions—like anger, greed etc.— at the time of binding the karma, the more intence will be its experience at the time of maturity.

- *Pradesha* (The quantity of the karmas) – It the quantity of karmic matter that is received and gets activated at the time of experience.

Both emotions and activity play a part in binding of karmas. Duration and intensity of the karmic bond are determined by emotions or *"kacya"* and type and quantity of the karmas bound is depended on *yoga* or activity.

Maturity

The consequences of karma are inevitable. The consequences may take some time to take effect but the karma is never fruitless. To explain this, a Jain monk, Ratnaprabhacharya says: "The prosperity of a vicious man and misery of a virtuous man are respectively but the effects of good deeds and bad deeds done previously. The vice and virtue may have their effects in their next lives. In this way the law of causality is not infringed here."

The latent karma becomes active and bears fruit when the supportive conditions arise. A great part of attracted karma bears its consequences with minor fleeting effects, as generally most of our activities are influenced by mild negative emotions. However, those actions that are influenced by intense negative emotions cause an equally strong karmic attachment which usually does not bear fruit immediately. It takes on an inactive state and waits for the supportive conditions—like proper time, place, and environment—to arise for it to manifest and produce effects.

If the supportive conditions do not arise, the respective karmas will manifest at the end of maximum period for which it can remain bound to the soul. These supportive conditions for activation of latent karmas are determined by the nature of karmas, intensity of emotional engagement at the time of binding karmas and our actual relation to time, place, surroundings. There are certain laws of precedence among the karmas, according to which the fruition of some of the karmas may be deferred but not absolutely barred.

Modifications

Although the Jains believe the karmic consequences as inevitable, Jain texts also hold that a soul has energy to transform and modify the effects of the karmas.. Karma undergoes following modifications:

1. *Udaya* (maturity) – It is the fruition of karmas as per its nature in the due course.
2. *UdiraGa* (premature operation) – By this process, it is possible to make certain karmas operative before their predetermined time.
3. *Udvartana* (augmentation) – By this process, there is a subsequent increase in duration and intensity of the karmas due to additional negative emotions and feelings.
4. *Apavartana* (diminution) – In this case, there is subsequent decrease in duration and intensity of the karmas due to positive emotions and feelings.
5. *SaCkramaGa* (transformation) – It is the mutation or conversion of one sub-type of karmas into another sub-type. However, this does not occur between different types. For example, *papa* (bad karma) can be converted into *punya* (good karma) as both sub-types belong to the same type of karma.
6. *Upauamana* (state of subsidence) – During this state the operation of karma does not occur. The karma becomes operative only when the duration of subsidence ceases.
7. *Nidhatti* (prevention) – In this state, premature operation and transformation is not possible but augmentation and diminution of karmas is possible.
8. *Nikâcanâ* (invariance) – For some sub-types, no variations or modifications are possible—the consequences are the same as were established at the time of bonding.

The Jain karmic theory, thus speaks of great powers of soul to manipulate the karmas by its actions.

Release

Jains assert that emancipation is not possible as long as the soul is released from bondage of the karmas. This is possible by *samvara*, that is, stoppage of inflow of new karmas, and *nirjara*, that is, shedding of existing karmas through conscious efforts. *Samvara* or stoppage of karmic influx is achieved through practice of:

1. Three *guptis* or three controls of mind, speech and body,
2. Five *samitis* or observing carefulness in movement, speaking, eating, placing objects and disposing refuse.

3. Ten *dharmas* or observation of good acts like – forgiveness, humility, straightforwardness, contentment, truthfulness, self control, penance, renunciation, non-attachment and continence.
4. *Anuprekshas* or meditation on the truths of this universe.
5. *Paricahajaya,* that is, a man on moral path must develop a perfectly patient and unperturbed attitude in the midst of trying and difficult circumstances.
6. *Caritra,* that is, endeavour to remain in steady spiritual practices.

Nirjara or annihilation of the existing karmas is possible through *tapas*, that is, austerities and penances. *Tapas* can be either external or internal. Six forms of external *tapas* are—fasting, control of appetite, accepting food under certain conditions, renunciation of delicious food, sitting and sleeping in lonely place and renunciation of comforts. Six forms of internal *tapas* are—atonement, reverence, rendering of service to worthy ones, spiritual study, avoiding selfish feelings and meditation.

Rationale

Justice Tukol notes that the supreme importance of the doctrine of karma lies in providing a rational and satisfying explanation to the apparent unexplainable phenomenon of birth and death, of happiness and misery, of inequalities and of existence of different species of living beings.

Here in the east, west, north, and south many men have been born according to their merit, as inhabitants of this our world—some as Aryas, some as non-Aryas, some in noble families, some in low families, some as big men, some as small men, some of good complexion, some of bad complexion, some as handsome men, some as ugly men. And of these men one man is king.

Jains thus cite inequalities, sufferings, and pain as evidence for the existence of karma. The theory of karma is able to explain day-to-day observable phenomena such as inequality between the rich and the poor, luck, differences in life-span, and the ability to enjoy life despite being immoral. According to Jains, such inequalities and oddities that exist even from the time of birth can be attributed to the deeds of the past lives and thus provide evidence to existence of karmas:

One is stout while another is lean; one is a master while another is a slave and similarly we find the high and the low, the mutilated and the lame, the blind and the deaf and many such oddities. The thrones of mighty monarchs are gone. The proud and the haughty have been humiliated in a moment and reduced to ashes. Even amongst the twins born of the same mother, we find one a dullard and another intelligent, one rich and another poor, one black and another white. What is all this due to? They could not have done any deeds while they were in their mother's womb.

Then, why then should such oddities exist? We have then to infer that these disparities must be the result of their deeds in their past births though they are born together at one time. There are many oddities in this world and it will have to be admitted that behind all this some powerful force is at work whereby the world appears to be full of oddities. This force is called 'karma'. We are unable to perceive karma by our naked eyes, yet we are able to know it from its actions.

Scientific Interpretation

Jain philosopher-monks postulated the existence of karma as subtle and microscopic particles that cannot be perceived by senses, some two millennia before modern science proved the existence of atoms and subatomic particles. However, these and other elementary particles that have been either discovered or postulated cannot be equated with karmic particles. Some authors have sought to explain the concept of karmic particles in the context of modern science and physics. Hermann Kuhn points out that, although the idea of "karmic particles" is not yet proven, one only needs to recall that science found proof of the existence of molecules and atoms only the 19th and 20th century.

Anyone who would have suggested that these "indivisible" particles were made up of even subtler units like quarks and leptons only a hundred years ago may have been dismissed, though such theories were in existence. With regards to interaction of consciousness and karmic matter, he further states that, it can be easily understood considering that ideas like the mind fundamentally affecting matter are now accepted in scientific circles. While admitting that though science has not discovered karmic matter yet, he is of opinion that it does not state anything against its existence. K. V. Mardia, in his book *The Scientific*

Foundations of Jainism, has interpreted karma in terms of modern physics, suggesting that the particles are made of *karmons*, dynamic high energy particles which permeate the universe. However, most scientists do not consider karma and reincarnation to be within the bounds of science, as it is neither a testable nor a falsifiable theory.

Criticisms

The Jain theory of karma has been challenged since ancient times by Vedic Hindu, Buddhist and Sekhya philosophies. In particular, Vedic Hindus considered the Jain position on the supremacy and potency of karma, specifically its insistence on non-intervention by any Supreme Being in regard to the fate of souls, as worthy of the label *nastika* or atheistic.

Strong emphasis on the doctrine of karma and intense asceticism was also criticised by the Buddhists, even though they also believe in karma. The ancient Buddhist scripture *SaCyutta Nikaya* narrates the story of Asibandhakaputta, a headman who was originally a disciple of Mahavira. He debates with the Buddha, telling him that, according to Mahavira (NigaGmha Nataputta), a man's fate or karma is decided by what he does habitually. The Buddha responds, considering this view to be inadequate, stating that even a habitual sinner spends more time "not doing the sin" and only some time actually "doing the sin."

In another Buddhist text *Majjhima Nikaya*, the Buddha criticizes Jain emphasis on the destruction of unobservable and unverifiable types of karma as a means to end suffering, rather than on eliminating evil mental states such as greed, hatred and delusion, which are observable and verifiable. In the Upalisutta dialogue of this *Majjhima Nikaya* text, Buddha contends with a Jain monk who asserts that bodily actions are the most criminal, in comparison to the actions of speech and mind. Buddha criticises this view, saying that the actions of *mind* are most criminal, and not the actions of speech or body. Buddha also criticises the Jain ascetic practice of various austerities, claiming that he, Buddha, is happier when *not* practising the austerities.

While admitting the complexity and sophistication of the Jain doctrine, Padmanabh Jaini compares it with that of Hindu doctrine of rebirth and points out that the Jain seers are silent on the exact moment and mode of rebirth, that is, the re-entry of soul in womb after the death. The concept of *nitya-nigoda*, which states that there are certain categories of souls who have always been *nigodas*, is also criticized. According to Jainism, *nigodas* are lowest form of extremely microscopic beings having momentary life spans, living in colonies and pervading the entire universe. According to Dr. Jaini, the entire concept of *nitya-nigoda* undermines the concept of karma, as these beings clearly would not have had prior opportunity to perform any karmically meaningful actions.

Karma is also criticised on the grounds that it leads to the dampening of spirits with men suffering the ills of life because the course of one's life is determined by karma. It is often maintained that the impression of karma as the accumulation of a mountain of bad deeds looming over our heads without any recourse leads to fatalism. However, as Paul Dundas puts it, the Jain theory of karma does not imply lack of free will or operation of total deterministic control over destinies. Furthermore, the doctrine of karma does not promote fatalism amongst its believers on account of belief in personal responsibility of actions and that austerities could expatiate the evil karmas and it was possible to attain salvation by emulating the life of the Jinas.

Customs and Practices

The hand with a wheel on the palm symbolizes the Jain Vow of Ahimsa, meaning non-violence. The word in the middle is "Ahimsa." The wheel represents the dharmacakra, to halt the cycle of reincarnation through relentless pursuit of truth.

Jain monks and nuns practice strict asceticism and strive to make their current birth their last, thus ending their cycle of transmigration. The laity, who pursue less rigorous practices, strive to attain rational perception and to do as much good as possible and get closer to the goal of attaining freedom from the cycle of transmigration. Following strict ethics, the laity usually choose professions that revere and protect life and totally avoid violent livelihoods.

Jains practice *Samayika*, which is a Sanskrit word meaning *equanimity* and derived from *samaya* (the soul). The goal of *samayika* is to attain equanimity. *Samayika* is begun by achieving a balance in time. If this current moment is defined as a moving line between the past and the future, *samayika* happens by being fully aware, alert and conscious in that moving time line when one experiences *atma,* one's true nature, common to all life forms. *Samayika* is especially significant during *Paryushana,* a special period during the monsoon, and is practiced during the *Samvatsari Pratikramana* ritual.

Jains believe that *Devas* (gods or celestial beings) cannot help *jiva* to obtain liberation, which must be achieved by individuals through their own efforts. In fact, devas themselves cannot achieve liberation until they reincarnate as humans and undertake the difficult act of removing karma. Their efforts to attain the exalted state of *siddha,* the permanent liberation of *jiva* from all involvement in worldly existence, must be their own.

The strict Jain ethical code for monks/nuns is:

1. *Ahimsa* (Non-violence)
2. *Satya* (truth)
3. *Achaurya* or *Asteya* (non-stealing)
4. *Brahmacharya* (Celibacy)
5. *Aparigraha* (Non-attachment to materialistic things).

Common men and women also have the five vows of non-violence, truth, non-stealing, celibacy and non-possession. It is not possible to observe these vows completely in day-to-day life and therefore followed to a limited extent. As these vows are limited in their scope, they are called 'Anuvratas'. Apart from these, additionally there are seven vows designed to assist the householders in their spiritual journey.

Nonviolence includes vegetarianism. Jains are expected to be non-violent in thought, word, and deed, both toward humans and toward all other living beings, including their own selves. Jain monks and nuns walk barefoot and sweep the ground in front of them to avoid killing insects or other tiny beings. Even though all life is considered sacred by the Jains, human life is deemed the highest form of life. For this reason, it is considered vital never to harm or upset any person.

For laypersons, *brahmacharya* means either confining sex to marriage or complete celibacy. For monks and nuns, it means complete celibacy.

While performing holy deeds, Svetambara Jains wear cloths, *muhapatti,* over their mouths and noses to avoid saliva falling on texts or revered images. It is not the case, as is sometimes believed, that this is to avoid accidentally inhaling insects. Many healthy concepts are entwined. For example, Jains drink only boiled water. In ancient times, a person might get ill by drinking unboiled water, which could prevent equanimity, and illness may engender intolerance.

True spirituality, according to enlightened Jains, starts when one attains *Samyak darshana,* or true perception. Such souls are on the path to moksha, striving to remain in the nature of the soul. This is characterized by knowing and observing only all worldly affairs, without *raag* (attachment) and *dwesh* (repulsion), a state of pure knowledge and bliss. Attachment to worldly life collects new karmas, and traps one in birth, death, and suffering. Worldly life has a dual nature (for example, love and hate, suffering and pleasure, etc.), for the perception of one state cannot exist without the contrasting perception of the other. Jain Dharma shares some beliefs with Hinduism. Both believe in karma and reincarnation. However, the Jain version of the Ramayana and Mahabharata is different from Hindu beliefs, for example. Generally, Hindus believe that Rama was a reincarnation of God, whereas Jains believe he attained moksha (liberation)

Along with the Five Vows, Jains avoid harboring ill will and practice forgiveness. They believe that *atma* (soul) can lead one to becoming *parmatma* (liberated soul) and this must come from one's inner self. Jains refrain from all violence (Ahimsa) and recommend that sinful activities be avoided.

Jainism has a distinct idea underlying Tirthankar worship. The physical form is not worshiped, but their Gunas (virtues, qualities) are praised. Tirthankaras remain role-models, and sects such as the Sthanakavasi stringently reject statue worship.

Jain Fasting

. Fasting is very common among Jains and as a part of Jain festivals. Most Jains fast at special times, during festivals, and on holy days. Paryushan is the most prominent festival, lasting eight days in Svetambara Jain tradition and ten days in Digambar Jain tradition during the monsoon. The monsoon is a time of fasting. However, a Jain may fast at any time, especially if he or she feels some error has been committed. Variations in fasts encourage Jains to do whatever they can to maintain whatever self control is possible for the individual.

Purpose of Fasting

Monks, nuns and laity fast as penance and to control desires. Jains believe fasting purifies the body and the mind, reminding one of Mahavir's emphasis on renunciation and asceticism.

Mahavir spent months fasting and in contemplation. It is not sufficient simply to stop eating when fasting; the person must also stop wanting to eat. Control over one's mind is a major goal. If one continues to desire food, the fast is fruitless.

Types of Fasting

There are several types of fasts:

- Santhara or "complete fasting": To give up food and water entirely. This leads to death and is undertaken by someone who has finished all his/her duties and wishes to leave this world peacefully. It gives control over when one dies so everything may be completed and a person may leave of his or her own free will.
- Partial fasting: Eating less than you desire and to simply avoid hunger.
- Vruti Sankshep: Limiting the number of items eaten.
- Rasa Parityag: Giving up favourite foods.
- Great fasts: Some monks fast for months at a time, following Mahavir, who fasted for over 6 months.
- Varsitap: To eat on alternate days, and Upvas on the rest, for a whole year. Thus this fast is very rigorous since it entails a whole year of "tap" with eating no food on alternate days and eating food on rest of the days, while following the prescribed rules like not eating in the evening after sunset, not eating root vegetables (like potatoes, onions, ginger), and various other rules. In Swetamber Varsitap they do Ekasanu as mentioned below alternet days and Upavas on the rest days.
- Chauvihar Upvas: To give up food and water for the whole day.
- Upvas: To give up only food for the whole day.
- Digambar Upvas: One may drink water only once a day, before sunset.

- Shvetamber Upvas: One may drink boiled and cooled water after Porsi, provided this is done before sunset.
- Tivihar Upvas: One may drink boiled water between sunrise and sunset.
- Ekasanu: To eat one meal a day at one sitting and drink boiled water as desired between sunrise and sunset.
- Beasanu: To eat two meals a day in two sittings and drink boiled water anytime between sunrise and sunset.
- Ayambil: Eating food once in one sitting. The food contains only cereals and pulses not sprouted and it is spice free and boiled or cooked, without milk, curds, ghee, oil, oil seeds, or green/raw vegetables, fruits and sugar and its products.
- Bela/ Chhath: To give up both food and water or only food continuously for two days.
- Tela / Aththam : To give up food and water or only food continuously for three days.
- Aththai: To give up food and water or only food continuously for eight days. "Lagtu nathi aththai kari ne farak pade" is a common saying
- Masaksaman: To give up food and water or only food continuously for a whole month.
- Navkarsi: Food and water is consumed a minimum forty-eight (48) minutes after sunrise. Devout Jains brush their teeth and rinse their mouths only after sunrise.
- Porsi: Taking food and water three hours after sunrise.
- Sadh-porsi: Taking food and water four hours and thirty minutes after sunrise.
- Purimuddh: Taking food and water six hours after sunrise.
- Avadhdh: Taking food and water eight hours after sunrise.
- Tivihar: After sunset no food or juice shall be taken, but one may drink water. Many Jains practise this daily.
- Navapad Oli: During every year for 9 days starting from the 6/7th day in the bright fortnight until the full moon day in Ashwin and Chaitra months, one does Ayambil. This is repeated for the next four and half years. Ayambils may be restricted to one kind of grain per day.

Jain Worship and Rituals

Every day most Jains bow and say their universal prayer, the "Namokara Mantra", a.k.a. the Navkar Mantra, Parmesthi Mantra, Panch Namaskar Mantra. Jains have built temples, or *Basadi* or *Derasar*, where idols of tirthankaras are revered. Rituals may be elaborate because symbolic objects are offered and Tirthankaras praised in song. But some sects refuse to enter temples or revere images. All Jains accept that images of Tirthankaras are merely symbolic reminders of their paths to attain moksha. Jains are clear that the Jinas reside in moksha and are completely detached from the world.

Jain rituals include:

- *Pancakalyanaka Pratishtha* : Panch-kalyanak Pratishtha (installation with five auspicious events) is a traditional Jain ceremony that consecrates one or more Jain Tirthankara pratimas.

The five kalyanakas are the five major events associated with a tirthankara:

1. Garbh (conception)
2. Janma (birth)
3. Tapa (austerities)
4. Gyan (omniscience)
5. Moksha (liberation).

After the pratishtha the statue represents the Tirthankara, and becomes a worshippable object.

A pratishtha must be authorised by an acknowledged leader of the sangha, an Acharya or a Bhattaraka, or a representative (pratishthacharya), who can recite the sacred suri-mantra to mark the final step in the installation ceremony. The Shvetambara sect requires a ceremony called anjana-shalaka. Once an idol is fully installed, it must be worshipped daily.

Pratikramana

Pratikraman (literally Sanskrit "introspection"), is a process of repentance of sins (prayaschit) during which Jains repent for their wrongdoings during their daily life, and remind themselves to refrain from doing so again. Devout Jains often do Pratikraman at least twice a day.

There are five types of Pratikraman:

1. Devasi
2. Rayi
3. Pakhi
4. Chaumasi
5. Samvatsari.

Devasi Pratikraman is performed daily in the evening, Raysi Pratikraman is performed in the early morning, Pakhi Pratikraman is done once every fifteen days. Chaumasi Pratikraman is done once in four months on purnima (full moon day) of Kartik, Falgun and Ashah months of lunar calendar year for the sins committed during that period. Samvatsari Pratikraman is done once per year on the last day of paryushana mahaparv for the sins committed during the whole year.

Samvatsari Pratikraman includes all six things a Jain must do:

1. Samayik-maintain equanimity
2. Chauvisanttho-honour the Tirthankars
3. Vandana-honor all sadhus and sadhvis
4. Pratikraman-repent wrongdoings
5. Kayotsarg-meditation and prayer
6. Pratyakhan-take vows to keep self-control.

The soul, in its pure form, has infinite perception, infinite knowledge, infinite vigor, and is non-attached. These attributes are not seen in a worldly soul because it is soiled with karmas. By following religious principles principals and activities, we overcome our karmas and uplift our souls to liberation. There are various kinds of religious activities, sometimes called rituals, and among them Pratikraman is the most important ritual. During pratikraman we repent for our non-meritorious activities on a daily basis. We realize our mistakes and ask for forgiveness which helps us to minimize the intensity of the karmaic bondage. Pratikraman is a combination of six avshyakas (essential rituals).

Samayika

Jain meditation is called Samayika. The word Samayika means being in the moment of continuous real-time. This act of being conscious of the continual renewal of the universe in general and one's own renewal of the individual living being (*Jiva*) in particular is the critical first step in the journey towards identification with one's true nature, called the Atman. It is also a method by which one can develop an attitude of harmony and respect towards other humans and Mother Nature.

One begins by achieving a balance in time. By being fully aware, alert and conscious of the constantly moving present, one will experience their true nature, Atman.

The 24 Jain Tirthankaras are always seen in meditative posture.

Samayika gains a special significance during Paryushana.

Postures

The Samayika is done to practice meditation generally by sitting in the Kayotsarga (khadgasana), Padmasana or Paryankasana postures. Although other postures have been used by yogis and others, the 24 Jain Tirthankaras are always seen in one of these two postures. The image to the right shows Jain monks in Samayika. Jains visit their temples and are seen sitting in this posture in one-on-one Samayika sessions in front of Tirthankar statues, for example, a Jain temple in Blairstown, NJ USA. Also included is an image of the Jain temple in Mt. Abu Rajastan, India.

Etymology

Samayika word comes from Prakrit language. The aim of Samayika is to transcend our daily experiences as the "constantly changing" human beings, called Jiva, and allow identification with the "changeless" reality in us, called the Atman. Is it possible to identify with the "changelessness" in us when constant change and renewal in and around us dominate our attention and energies? Samayika addresses this question. One begins in Samayika by achieving a balance in time. If the present fine moment of time could be defined as the moving line between the past and the future, Samayika happens by being fully aware, alert and conscious in that moving timeline when one experiences one's true nature, Atman, which is considered common to all living beings. The Samayika is derived from the word samay-meaning time-in the Prakrit language. The Samayika takes on special significance during special 8-day period practiced by the Jains called Paryushana. Also see Jainism for more.

Preksha Meditation

Acharya Mahaprajna, The Tenth Head of Jain Svetambara Terapanth sect formulated Preksha Meditation in 1970s. He practiced various meditation techniques for nearly 30 years and developed this well organized meditation system and presented it in scientific light. Preksha Meditation is the combination of knowledge from ancient religious books, modern science and experience. Acharya Mahaprajna made a deep research on Agam-Jain holy scriptures, ancient scriptures, medical science, Yoga science, Naturopathy, Ayurveda, modern Physics, etc while developing this meditation system.

Preksha meditation is the practice of purifying the emotions and conscious (*chitta*) and realizing the own self. It helps in leading a peaceful life and is a system of mediation for attitudinal change, behavioural modification and integrated development of personality.

The word preksha means 'to perceive carefully and profoundly'. In *preksha*, perception always means experience bereft of the duality of like and dislike, pleasure and pain. Impartiality and equanimity are synonymous with *Preksha*. *Preksha* is impartial perception, where there is neither the emotion of attachment nor aversion, neither pleasure or displeasure.

Both these states of emotion are closely and carefully perceived but not experienced. And because both are perceived from close quarters, it is not difficult to reject both of them and assume a neutral position. Thus equanimity is essentially associated with preksha.

It aims at reaching and purify the deeper levels of existence. Regular practice strengthens the immune system, builds up stamina to resist against ageing, pollution, chemical toxins, viruses, diseases.

Important elements in the system are *Kayotsarg*-Full awareness with complete relaxation, Perception of the breath, body, the psychic centres, psychic colours (*lesya* meditation), contemplation processes, Yoga and Pranayaam, Mantra.

Important disciplines in the system are-Synchrony of mental and physical actions or simply present mindedness or complete awareness of one's actions, disciplining the reacting attitude, friendliness, diet, silence, spiritual vigilance.

One commences the practice of this technique with the perception of the body. Body contains the soul. Therefore, one must pierce the wall of the container to reach the content (the soul). Again, breathing is a part of the body and essence of life. To breath is to live; and so breath is naturally qualified to be the first object of perception, while the body itself would become the next one. The vibrations, sensations and other physiological events are worthy of attention. Conscious mind becomes sharpened to perceive these internal realities in due course, and then it will be able to focus itself on the minutest and the most subtle occurrences within the body. The direct perception of emotions, urges and other psychological events will then be possible. And ultimately the envelope of *karmic* matter, contaminating the consciousness could be clearly recognized.

The meditation training camps are organized on a regular basis. Major training centres in India are in Ladnun, Rajasthan, Delhi, Ahemedabad. Centres are also present in many countries like the US, UK, Russia, Germany, Ukraine, Australia, Singapore, Netherland, etc.

Existing and Historical Meditation Techniques in Jainism

According to the some commonly practiced *yoga* systems, high concentration is reached by meditating in an easy (preferably lotus) posture in seclusion and staring without blinking at the rising sun, a point on the wall, or the tip of the nose, and as long as one can keep the mind away from the outer world, this strengthens concentration. *Garuda* is the name Jainism gives to the yoga of self-control and control of mind, body and speech, so that even earth, water, fire and air can come under one's control. *Eiva* is in Jainism control over the passions and the acquisition of such self-control that under all circumstances equanimity is maintained.

Pranayama – breathing exercises – are performed to strengthen the flows of life energy. Through this, the elements of the constitution – earth, water, fire and air – are also strengthened. At the same time the five *chakras* are controlled. *Prânayâma* also helps to stabilize one's thinking and leads to unhampered direct experience of the events around us.

Next one practices pratyahara. Pratyahara means that one directs the senses away from the enjoyment of sensual and mental objects. The senses are part of the nervous system, and their task is to send data to the brain through which the mind as well as the soul is provided with information. The mind tends to enjoy this at the cost of the soul as well as the body. *Pratyahara* is obtained by focusing the mind on one point for the purpose of receiving impulses: on the eyes, ears, tip of the nose, the brow, the navel, the head, the heart or the palate.

Contemplation is an important wing in Jain meditation. The practitioner meditates or reflects deeply on subtle facts or philosophical aspects. The first type is *Agnya vichaya*, in which one meditates deeply on the seven elementary facts-life and non-life, the inflow, bondage, stoppage and removal of *karmas*, and the final accomplishment of liberation. The second is *Apaya vichaya*, in which incorrect insights and behaviour in which "sleeping souls" indulge, are reflected upon. The third is *Vipaka vichaya dharma dhyana*, in which one reflects on the eight causes or basic types of *karma*. The fourth is *Sansathan vichaya dharma dhyana*, when one thinks about the vastness of the universe and the loneliness of the soul, which has had to face the results of its own causes all alone.

Practitioner can apply a number of meditation techniques known as *pindastha-dhyana, padastha-dhyana, rupastha-dhyana, rupatita-dhyana, savîrya-dhyana*, etc.

In *pindastha-dhyana* one imagines oneself sitting all alone in the middle of a vast ocean of milk on a lotus flower, meditating on the soul. There are no living beings around whatsoever. The lotus is identical to *Jambudvipa*, with Mount *Meru* as its stalk. Next the meditator imagines a 16-petalled lotus at the level of his navel, and on each petal are printed the (Sanskrit) letters "arham" and also an inverted lotus of 8 petals at the location of his heart. Suddenly the lotus on which one is seated flares up at the navel and flames gradually rise up to the inverted lotus, burning its petals with a rising golden flame which not only burns his or her body, but also the inverted lotus at the heart.

The flames rise further up to the throat whirling in the shape of a swastika and then reach the head, burning it entirely, while taking the form of a three-sided pyramid of golden flames above the head, piercing the skull sharp en straight up. The whole physical body is charred, and everything turns into glowing ashes. Thus the *pinda* or body is burnt off and the pure soul survives. Then suddenly a strong wind blows off all the ashes; and one imagines that a heavy rain shower washes all the ashes away, and the pure soul remains seated on the lotus. That pure Soul has infinite virtues, it is Myself. Why should I get polluted at all? One tries to remain in his purest nature. This is called *pindastha dhyana,* in which one ponders the reality of feeling and experiencing.

In *padastha dhyana* one focuses on some mantras, words or themes. Couple of important mantra are, OM-it signifies remembrance of the five classes of spiritual beings (the embodied and non-embodied Jinas, the ascetics, the monks and the nuns), pronouncing the word "Arham" makes one feel "I myself am the omniscient soul" and one tries to improve one's character accordingly.

One may also pronounce the holy name of an *arhat* and concentrate on the universal richness of the soul.

In *rupastha dhyana* one reflects on the embodiments of arhats, the svayambhuva (the self-begotten), the omniscients and other miraculous people and their attributes, such as three umbrellas and whiskers – as seen in many icons – unconcerned about one's own body, but almighty and benevolent to all living beings, destroyer of attachment, enmity, etc. Thus the meditator as a human being concentrates his or her attention on the virtues of the omniscients to acquire the same virtues for himself.

Rupatita dhyana is a meditation in which one focuses on bodiless objects such as the liberated souls or *siddhas,* which stand individually and collectively for the infinite qualities that such souls have earned. That omniscient, potent, omnipresent, liberated and untainted soul is called a *niranjana,* and this stage can be achieved by right vision, right knowledge and right conduct only. Right vision, right knowledge and right conduct begin the fourth stage of the 14-fold path.

The ultimate aim of such yoga and meditation is to pave the way for the spiritual elevation and salvation of the soul. Some yogis develop their own methods for meditation.

The *kayotsarg* method is found to be very useful by many Jains. It means full awareness with complete relaxation. The practitioner takes a comfortable posture either lying down or sitting or standing and breathes calmly. Then auto suggests each and every part and entity of the body to be relaxed and feel the same. Once the body is completely relaxed, the practitioner forgets about the body and tries to identify the Self. Then one practices of complete awareness of the self without any hindrance.

Lord Mahavira and Meditation

Meditation was an integral part of Lord Mahavira's life. Lord Mahavira had meditated in different ways :

- Meditation by fixing the gaze for hours on an oblique wall and also for acquiring high levels of magnetism in the eyes.
- Adoption of various steady postures in meditation. He meditated on various spaces in the universe, the higher *loka*-upper, in the downward direction-lower *loka* and in the transverse direction-the transverse *loka,* making them objects for meditation.
- Meditating mostly in standing posture.
- Practiced *Kayotsarga* for full awareness and deep relaxation.
- Meditating in the open without clothes and shelter.
- Being ceaselessly conscious at every moment of the day and night. Total vigilance in the sixth step, and Samadhi, the seventh step of the meditative path.
- Practicing meditation, both with the support of an object and without any support of any object.
- Usage of different objects for his meditation sessions. He would change the targets of his attention.

Objects on which he had meditated:

- The *Karmas* moving upward, downward and in a transverse direction.
- Bondage, the cause of bondage and its consequences.
- Salvation, its cause and its bliss.
- The head, the navel and the big toe.
- Matter, its characteristic and modes (its changing conditions).
- The origin, permanence and transitory nature of Matter.
- The gross world and the cosmos.
- Subtle objects like the molecular structure.
- The soul, by intuition.

- Practice of contemplations (*Bhawanas*) during practice of meditation. The main subjects were: Loneliness, transitoriness and absence of protection, etc.
- Concentration on the body for a long stretch of time; he could change it on the mental and vocal level. He could change his meditations from matter to mode and from word to silence.
- Guru Vandana, *Chaitya Vandana,* and other sutras to honor ascetics.

Guru Vandana means "Reverence for the Teacher" – it is the thanksgiving from a student to a teacher, expressing his or her gratitude. The Guru Vandana program provides a platform for students to honor their teachers for imparting knowledge and wisdom to them.

Guru

The concept of Guru is as old as humanity itself. Primarily, the word Guru means a 'teacher' and as such it is a universal concept based on the idea of transmitting knowledge from a person, who knows something, to an ignorant student or disciple. In an extended view, a Guru can also be a priest, a rabbi, a master, a school teacher, even a father or a mother. Guru does not mean a teacher imparting formal training but a person who contributes to the overall development and learning of an individual.

Guru transforms his disciple through his presence and spiritual knowledge. According to RamaKrishna Prarahamsa Spiritual knowledge can not be attained completely by reading books. But for obtaining complete spiritual enlightenment Guru's presence is a must. Only when there is a strong bond between Guru and Shishya spiritual enlightenment might takes place.

5

Origins of Guru-Shishya Parampara

Thus our great sanathana darma tradition has been enriched by the Guru-Sishya relationship. Lord Rama's greatness lay in His relationship with His most loyal disciple Hanuman who taught the essence of Ramanamamritim. Lord Krishna gave us the Bhagavad Gita, thanks to his devoted and most trusted disciple Arjuna. Saint Ramakrishna Paramahamsa gave to the world Swami Vivekananda who in turn gave to the world the Ramakrishna Mission, embodying the soul of India.

Saint Thyagaraja, an avatar of Sage Valmiki, composed hundreds of soulful Krithis in praise of God. Two Krithis, in particular, refer to the GURU'S role in guiding the seeker on the right path. Guru leka in 'Gowrimanohari' raga is a Krithi in which the Saint of Thiruvaiyar sings how one who is trapped in the jungle of desire, can come out of it with help of the right Guru. Saint Thyagaraja says however learned and good a person might be, life would be meaningless without the guidance of a Satguru. In another Krithi, Sri Naradamuni Gururaya ganti in Bhairavi raga, Thyagaraja explains how Satguru Smaranam helps one in getting rid of ignorance.

History

Parshvanatha, the twenty-third Tirthankar, is the earliest Jain leader who can be reliably dated. As noted, however, Jain mythology asserts that the line of Tirthankars began with Rushabhdeva; moreover, Jains themselves tend to believe that Jainism has no single founder, and believe that Jainism is the one of the world's oldest religions, predating Hinduism. According to scholars, Parshvanatha probably lived in the 9th Century BCE. In the sixth century BCE, Vardhamana Mahavira became one of the most influential Jainism teachers. He built up a large group of disciples that learned from his teachings and followed him as he taught an ascetic doctrine in order to achieve enlightenment. The disciples referred to him as Jina, which means "the conqueror" and later his followers would use this title to refer to themselves.

It is generally accepted that Jainism started spreading in south India from the third century BCE. i.e. since the time when Badrabahu, a preacher of this religion and the head of the monks' community, came to Karnataka from Bihar.

Kalinga (modern Orissa and Osiaji) was home to many Jains in the past. Rushabh, the first Tirthankar, was revered and worshipped in the ancient city Pithunda. This was destroyed by Mahapadma Nanda when he conquered Kalinga and brought the statue of Rushabhanatha to his capital in Magadh. Rushabhanatha is revered as the *Kalinga Jina*. Ashoka's invasion and his Buddhist policy also subjugated Jains greatly in Kalinga. However, in the 1st century BCE Emperor Kharvela conquered Magadha and brought Rushabhnath's statue back and installed it in Udaygiri, near his capital, Shishupalgadh. The Khandagiri and Udaygiri caves near Bhubaneswar are the only surviving stone Jain monuments in Orissa. Earlier buildings were made of wood and were destroyed.

Deciphering of the Brahmi script by James Prinsep in 1788 enabled the reading of ancient inscriptions in India and established the antiquity of Jainism. The discovery of Jain manuscripts has added significantly to retracing Jain history. Archaeologists have encountered Jain remains and artifacts at Maurya, Sunga, Kishan, Gupta, Kalachuries, Rashtrakut, Chalukya, Chandel and Rajput as well as later sites. Several western and Indian scholars have contributed to the reconstruction of Jain history. Western historians like Bühler, Jacobi, and Indian scholars like Iravatham Mahadevan, worked on Tamil Brahmi inscriptions.

Geographical Spread and Influence

Jainism has been a major cultural, philosophical, social and political force since the dawn of civilization in Asia, and its ancient influence has been noted in other religions, including Buddhism and Hinduism. This pervasive influence of Jain culture and philosophy in ancient Bihar may have given rise to Buddhism. The Buddhists have always maintained that during the time of Buddha and Mahavira (who, according to the Pali canon, were contemporaries), Jainism was already an ancient, deeply entrenched faith and culture there. Over several thousand years, Jain influence on Hindu philosophy and religion has been considerable, while Hindu influence on Jain rituals may be observed in certain Jain sects. Certain Vedic Hindu holy books contain beautiful narrations about various Jain Tirthankaras (e.g., Lord Rushabdev). There have been no wars fought in the name of Jainism.

For instance, the concept of *puja* is Jain. The Vedic Religion prescribed *yajnas* and *havanas* for pleasing the gods. *Puja* is a specifically Jain concept, arising from the Kannada words, "pu" (flower) and "ja" (offering).

There are many Jain communities in different parts of India and around the world. They may speak local languages or follow different rituals but essentially follow the same principles.

Outside India, the United States, United Kingdom, Canada and East Africa (Kenya, Tanzania and Uganda) have large Jain communities. The first Jain temple to be built outside India was constructed and consecrated in the 1960s in Mombasa, Kenya, although Jainism in the West mostly came about came about after the Oshwal and Jain diaspora spread to the West in the late 1970s and 1980s. Jainism is presently a strong faith in the United States and several dozen Jain temples have been built there. American Jainism accommodates all the sects. Smaller Jain communities exist in Nepal, South Africa, Japan, Singapore, Malaysia, Australia, Fiji, and Suriname. In Belgium the very successful Indian diamond community, almost all of whom are Jain, are also establishing a temple to strengthen Jain values in and across Western Europe.

Denominations

It is generally believed that the Jain *sangha* divided into two major sects, Digambar and Svetambar, about 200 years after Mahavira's nirvana. Some historians believe there was no clear division until the 5th century. In the book *Outlines of Jainism*, it states, "It seems certain that even at the time of Mahavira the two sects were in existence, though he was able to maintain at least a semblance of unity between them. The final 'parting of ways' came much later". The best available information indicates that the chief Jain monk, Acharya Bhadrabahu, according to the Svetambara version of the split between the two sects, foresaw a 12-year famine and led about 12,000 Digambar followers to southern India. Twelve years later they returned to find the Svetambara sect, and in 453 the Valabhi council edited and compiled the traditional Svetambara scriptures.

The differences between the two sects are primarily minor and relatively obscure. Digambar Jain monks do not wear clothes because they believe clothes, like other possessions, increase dependency and desire for material things, and desire for anything ultimately leads to sorrow. Svetambar Jain monks, on the other hand, wear white, seamless clothes for practical reasons, and believe there is nothing in Jain scripture that condemns wearing clothes. Sadhvis (nuns) of both sects wear white. In Sanskrit, *ambar* refers to a covering generally, or a garment in particular. *Dig*, an older form of *disha*, refers to the cardinal directions. *Digambar* therefore means "covered by the four directions", or "sky-clad". *Svet* means white and Svetambars wear white garments.

There is one major difference between the sects. Digambars believe that women cannot attain moksha in the same birth, while Svetambars believe that women may attain liberation and that Mallinath, a Tirthankar, was a woman. The difference is because Digambar asceticism requires nudity. As nudity is impractical for women, it follows that without it they cannot attain moksha. This is based on the belief that women cannot reach perfect purity (yathakhyata), "Their lack of clothes can, therefore, be a hindrance to their leading a holy life". The earliest record of this belief is contained in the Prakrit Suttapahuda of the Digambara mendicant Kundakunda (c. second century A.D.). This of course has extreme consequences for women and effectively polarises the two sects in this regard.

Digambars believe that Mahavir was not married, whereas Svetambars believe Mahavir was married and had a daughter. The two sects also differ on the origin of Mata Trishala, Mahavira's mother.

Digambars believe that only the first five lines are formally part of the Namokara Mantra (the main Jain prayer), whereas Svetambaras believe all nine form the mantra. Other differences are minor and not based on major points of doctrine. Excavations at Mathura revealed many Jain statues from the Kushana period. Tirthankaras, represented without clothes, and monks with cloth wrapped around the left arm are identified as Ardhaphalaka and mentioned in some texts. The Yapaniya sect, believed to have originated from the Ardhaphalaka, follows Digambara nudity, along with several Svetambara beliefs.

Svetambaras are further divided into sub-sects, such as Sthanakavasi, Terapanthi and Deravasi. Some are *murtipujak* (revering statues) while non-Murtipujak Jains refuse statues or images. Svetambar follow the 12 *agam* literature (voice of omniscient).

Most simply call themselves Jains and follow general traditions rather than specific sectarian practices. In 1974 a committee with representatives from every sect compiled a new text called the Samana Suttam.

Digambar

Digambar (alternate orthographies: *Digambara*), has many different meaning and associations throughout Dharmic traditions. Many representations of deities within these traditions are depicted as sky-clad, eg. Samantabhadra/Samantabhadri in yab-yum. Certain traditions and lineages also practice Digambar as a lifelong vow as evidenced by numerous sadhus throughout India.

Distinctives of Digambar

Digambara is one of the two main sects of Jainism, the other being Svetambar.

Until the leadership of Acharya Bhadrabahu, there was no significant division. After that some divisions gradually arose. Generally Digambar monks wear no clothes (*dig ambar* = sky clad) whereas Svetambar (*svet ambar* = white clad) monks usually wear white clothes.

Although Senior Digambar monks wear no clothes, following the practice of Lord Mahavira, they do not consider themselves to be nude. Rather, they are wearing the environment, that is the quintessential, akasha or space. Digambaras believe that this practice represents a refusal to give in to the demands of the body for comfort and private property. Only Digambara ascetics are required to forsake clothing and not the laity. Digambara ascetics have only two possessions: a peacock feather broom and a water gourd. Conversely, Svetambara monks usually wear white maintaining that nudism is no longer practicable. While there are some differences in some practices, the main principles of each sect such as Mahavratas, Anuvratas and so forth are the same.

Digambara Monasticism

The prominent Acharyas of the Digambar tradition were:

- Acharya Kundakunda: author of Samayasar, etc.
- Acharya Virasena: author of Dhavala
- Acharya Aryanandi (monk).

In around 10th century Digambar tradition was divided into two main orders:

- Mula Sangh: includes Sena gana, Deshiya gana, Balatkara gana etc.
- Kashtha Sangh: includes Mathura gana, Lat-vagad gana, etc.

The Bhattarakas of Shravanabelagola and Mudbidri belong to Deshiya gana and Bhattara of Humbaj belongs to Balatkara gana.

Sub-Sects of Digambara

Those following the Terapanth reforms are called Terapanth and others following more traditional practices are called Bisapanthai. In practice, the Bisapantha / Terapanth division is not important, and separate institutions do not exist.

Among the Digambaras, the Taran Panthi follow Taran Swami and Kanji Panthi follow Kanji Swami.

Taran Panth

The Taran Panth or Taran (a) panthi sect of Digambar Jainism was founded by Taran Svami in Bundelkhand in 1506. Taran Svami is also referred to as Taran Taran, the one who can help the swimmers to the other side, i.e. towards nirvana.

During this time several reform movements arose in Jainism. Lonka Shah of Gujarat founded his Dhundhia order in Sam 1508 (1451 CE). The Terapantha (Adhyatma movement) among the Digambaras arose in Sam. 1683 in Agra. The main founders of this movement were Banarasidas of Agra and Amarachanda of Sanganer near Jaipur.

The Digambara Terapantha movement was against the domination of the Bhattarakas. They opposed worship of various demi-gods and demi-goddesses, which was indulged in by the Bhattarakas. Some Terapanthi practices, like not using flowers in worship, gradually spread throughout North India among the Digambaras. In fact, today, Digambara Jainism in North India is Terapanthi whereas Digambara Jainism in Western (Gujarat) and Southern India (Maharashtra, Karnataka and Tamil Nadu) is Bisapanthi.

The Taranpanthis on the other hand traditionally do not have idols in their shrines at all.

The birth name of Taran Svami is not known. He was born in Pushpavati (now Bilahari near Katni) in the Paravar Jain community. His father was a government official there. His uncle lived in Sironj, where a Bhattaraka institution of Balatkara Gana was present. When he was 8 years old, while accompanying his father to Sironj, he came across Bhattaraka Shrutakirti. The Bhattaraka persuaded the boy to start attending the lectures where "Samayasara" was discussed. Later Taran Svami organized his group and meditated and preached at Semalkheri, Sukha and Rakh. His chief disciples were Ruiaraman and Kamanavati. His samadhi is at Nisaiji in Dist Guna. A mystical account of his life, perhaps an autobiography, is given in Chadmastha Vani.

The language in his 14 books is a unique blend of Prakrit, Sanskrit and Apabhramsha. Note that at this time Jains had not been using Prakrit for several centuries. His language was perhaps influenced by his reading of the books of Acarya Kundakunda.

Commentaries on six of the main texts composed by Taran Svami were written by Brahmacari Shitala Prasad in the 1930s. Commentaries on other texts have also been done recently. Osho (Rajnish), who was born into a Taranpanthi family, has included Shunya Svabhava and Siddhi Svabhava as among the books that influenced him most.

The number of Taranpanthis is very small. Their shrines are called Caityalaya (or sometimes Nisai/Nasia). At the altar (vimana) they have a book instead of an idol. The Taranpanthis were originally from 6 communities.

Kashtha Sangh

Kashtha Sangha was a Digambar Jain monastic order once dominant in several regions of North and Western India. It is considered to be a branch of Mula Sangh itself. It is said to have originated from a town named Kashtha. The origin of Kashtha Sangha is often attributed to Lohacharya in several texts and inscriptions from Delhi region. The Kashtasangh Gurvavali identifies Lohacharya as the last person who knew Acharanga in the Digambara tradition, who lived until the 683th year of the nirvana of Lord Mahavira. the The Darshanasara of Devasena (VS 990) attributes the origin to Kumarasena in Vikram Samvat 753. Several of the Jain communities were affiliated with the Kashtha Sangha. The Agrawals were the major supporters of Kashtha Sangha. They are said to have been initiated by Lohacharya in antiquity

Kashta Sangha included several orders :

- Nanditat gachchha: associated with Nanded. It is also called Ramasenanvaya, after Acharya Ramasena, the founder of the Narsingpura community.
- Mathura Sangha: The Agrawals were associated with this order. It was founded by Ramasena according to Darshanasar. The oldest known inscription is of 1170 AD.
- Bagada gachha: associated with Vagad region of Rajasthan
- Lata-bagada gachha: associated with Vagad and Lata region of Gujarat.

The 1145 AD inscription of Dubkunda mentions this order. The acharyas of this order formerly used to reside in the Punnata region of Karnataka. Jinasena, the author Harivansh Purana in shaka 705 belonged to this order. Kashta Sangha eventually merged into Mula Sangh. The celebrated poet and pratishthacharya Raighu was a disciple of the Kashtha Sangh Bhattarakas of Gwalior.

The rock carved Jain statues in the Gwalior Fort were mostly consecrated by the Kashtha Sangh Bhattarakas, as stated in the inscriptions dated between 1441 and 1474.

Svetambara

The Svetambara is one of the two main sects of Jainism, the other being Digambar. Svetambar literally means "white-clad", describing its ascetics' practice of wearing white clothes, which sets it apart from Digambar ("sky clad"), whose ascetic practitioners wear no clothes.

Svetambaras, unlike Digambaras, do not believe that ascetics must practice nudity, or that women are unable to obtain moksha. Svetambaras maintain that the 19 Tirthankara, Mallinath, was a woman.

At present in Svetambara sects, there are 2,510 Monks and 10,228 nuns, while in Digambaras there are 548 monks and 527 nuns (According to 'Smagra Jain chaturmas suchi-2006').

The Svetambara tradition follows the lineage of Acharya Sthulibhadra suri. Kalpasutra mentions some of the lineages in ancient times. from the Kottiya Gana, which was once prominent. The Svetambara monastic orders are branches of Vrahada-gachchha founded in 937 AD. The most prominent among the classical orders today are Kharatara-gachchha (1024 AD), Tapa Gachchha (1228 AD) and Tristutik Gachchha.

A major dispute was initiated by Lonka Shaha, who started a movement opposed to idol worship in 1476. The Sthanakvasi and Terapanthi (Svetambara) (1780) orders are branches of this movement.

The major reforms by Vijayananda Suri (1827 – 1906) in 1880, as the leader of the Tapa Gachchha, led a movement to restore orders of wandering monks, which brought about the near extinction of the Yati institutions. Acharya Rajendrasuri restored shraman sanstha in the "Tristutik" gachchha.

Some Svetambara monks and nuns cover their mouth with a white cloth (muhpatti) to practise ahimsa even when they talk. By doing so they minimize the possibility of inhaling small organisms.

Svetambara Sub-Sects

Svetambara is divided into two sub-sects, those practitioners who worship images in temples, known as the Murtipujak ("image-worshiping") or Mandirmargi ("temple-going"), and those who do not, the reformist sub-sects of the Sthanakvasis and the Terapanthis:

- Murtipujak, headed by various Acharyas as their sect and sub-sects.

In the Murtipujak sect there are 4 main sub-sects as follows:

- o Tapa gachchha In Tapa Gachchha there are 21 sub-sects headed by different Acharya
- o Achal gachchhaKhartar gachchha
- o Parshwachandra gachchha.

- non-Murtipujak (Sadhumargi).
  - o Sthanakvasi
  - o Terapanthi.

Tapa Gachchha

Tapa Gachchha is the largest monstic order of Svetambara Jainism. It was founded by Acharya Jagat Chandra Suri in Vikram Samvat 1285 (1229 A.D.). He was given the title of "Tapa" (i.e. the meditative one) by the ruler of Mewar. It was a branch of the Brihad gachchha founded by Udyotan Suri. Shri Vijayananda suri was responsible for reviving the wandering orders among the Svetambara monks. As a result of this reform, most Svetambara Jain monks today belong to the Tapa gachchha.

Differences among Subsects

All the Tapa Gachchha sects and subsects are followers and disciples of Acharya Vijay Dev suri M.S. (1600-1657 A.D.) It is remarkable here that Acharya Vijay Dev suri was worshiped end number of time with Navangi puja which is still exists with Acharya Prem suri, and Acharya Shantichandra suri sects (Samudaya). In all sub sects of Tapa gachchha there are a few differences as below:

- 'Navangi Puja of monk' (worship).
- Tithi (calendar).
- Palitana Chaturmas yatra.
- 'Santikaram' Chanting in Chaturdasi.

Acharya Vijay Dev suri (1600-1657) was above all this controversy and never chanting Santikaram after Chaumasi pratikraman, always worshiped by Navangi Puja by followers and plenty of examples in his disciples who has established pratishtha on palitana hills in so called chaturmas times.

In the Tapa Gachchha now there are total 8000 monks and nuns with nearly 24 different sects belongs to Tapa Gachchha. Tapa Gachchha is having different 24 branches in different groups or subsects. The biggest group is Achary Prem suri, where nearly 2200 monks and nuns are with highest number. One is followed by Acharya Ramchandra Suri who was established by Acharya shri Prem Suriji himself (1350 monks and nuns), another is Acharya shri Bhuvan Bhanu Suri ji (850 monks and nuns) who disassociated himself from Prem Suri group's original way of rites and rituals. Other big group is "Sager Samuday" and "Acharya Nemi Suri Samudaya" which are counted as big group in Tapa Gachchha. Mainly Prem Suri sect has more than 50% of Jain monks.

Acharya Ramchandra Suri group (first disciple of Acharya Premsuri ji) is biggest having more than 1324 monks and nuns, Acharya Shri Hembhushan Suri was Head (Gachchha Nayak) of this Jain monk's group who passed away last year and Shri Lalit Shekhar Suriji will be new gachchhadhipati. Acharya shri Bhuvan Bhanu suri group (another prominent disciple of Acharya Premsuri ji) is also another group in Tapaa Gachchha having 826 monk and nuns. Currently Acharya Shri Jayghosh Suri ji is Head (Gachchha Nayak) in this group. It is important that Shri Jaygosh suri ji has highest number of monks in any singal samudaya that is 435 monks.

Murtipujaka

Murtipujaka is also known as Deravasi and is the term for a sect of Jainism which includes most members of the Shvetambar sect. Murtipujaka Deravasis differ from the Sthanakvasi division of the sect in that they go to a Jain Temple (Derasar) and pray towards an idol of a Jain Tirthankar instead of a sthanak (empty room), which the Sthanakvasi sect prefers. Deravasi Jains believe that siddhas, or liberated souls, have a form, whereas Sthanakvasi Jains believe they do not. Murtipujaka monks and worshipers do not use the muhapatti, a piece of cloth over the mouth, during prayers, whereas it is permanently worn by Sthanakvasi and Terapanthi Jains. The Sthankvasis and Terapanthis do so to protect the living beings in the air around them from any injury or death due to their speech. There are more Murtipujaka Deravasi Jains in comparison to Sthanakvasi Jains in India.

Tristutik

Tristutik was an origin of Tapa Gachchha of shvetambar sect of Jainism. It was established in 1194 A.D. (Vikram Samvat 1250.) It was known as Agama Gachchha in ancient times.

The 'Tristutik' Gachchha was reformed by Acharya Rajendrasuri. As in the Tristutik' way of worship, there is only devotion to Jain Tirthankar, they do not believe in worshiping other gods known as "devi-devata" like Padmavati, Bharava, Gantakarna, Manibhadra etc during the rituals like Pratikraman, Samayik, Bhaavanusthans. They respect them as extraordinary living beings & sadharmik and do remember and honour in special rituals of Derasar Pratistha, Big Pujas etc. This sect of Jainism is also in the Murtipujaka deravasi division of Shvetambar.

Tristutik Gachchha

Tristutik Gachchha was an origin of the Tapa Gachchha of the Svetambara sect of Jainism. It was established in 1194 A.D. (Vikram Samvat 1250). It was known as Agama Gachchha in ancient times.

The 'Tristutik' Gachchha was reformed by Acharya Rajendrasuri. As in the Tristutik' way of worship, there is only devotion to Jain Tirthankar, they do not believe in worshiping other gods known as "devi-devata" like Padmavati, Bharava, Gantakarna, Manibhadra etc during the rituals like Pratikraman, Samayik, Bhaavanusthans. They respect them as extraordinary living beings and do remember and honour in special rituals of Derasar Pratistha, Big Pujas etc.

This sect of Jainism is also in the Murtipujaka deravasi division of Shvetambar.

Terapanth

Terapanth (or Tera Panth) the name given to two independent Jain sects:

- Digambar Terapanth: A sect of the Digambara tradition, that introduced several reforms in 1664 AD, but worship idols. It is not an organized sect, rather a philosophy regarding some of the rituals. The Kanji Swami sect regards itself to represent the Terapanth. It was influenced by Atyadhma movement which arose in 1626 AD.
- Swetembar Terapanth: An organized sect of Swetambar Jainism founded in 1760 AD, which does not have temples or idols. Terapanth is a dharma sangh (religious group) comprising of over 1000 saints and nuns in a very organised structure under Acharya Mahapragya.

Taran Panth, also a Digambar jain sect, should not be confused with Terapanth.

Yapaniya

Yapaniya was a Jain order in western Karnataka which is now extinct. The first inscription that mentions them by Mrigesavarman (AD 475-490) a Kadamba king of Palasika who donated for a Jain temple, and made a grant to the sects of Yapaniyas, Nirgranthas (identifiable as Digambaras), and the Kurchakas (not identified).

The last inscription which mentioned the Yapaniyas was found in the Tuluva region southwest Karnataka, dated Saka 1316 (AD 1394). According to Darshana-Sara, they were a branch of the Svetambara sect, however they were regarded to be Digambara by Swetambar authors. The Yapaniya monks remained naked but followed some Svetamabar views. They also possessed their own versions of texts that have been preserved in the Svetambar tradition.

The great grammarian Shakatayana, who was a contemporary of the Rashtrakuta king Amoghavarsha (c. 817-877), was a Yapaniya, as mentioned by Malayagira in his commentary on the Nandi Sutra.

Jain Symbolism

The *fylfot* (swastika) is among the holiest of Jain symbols. Worshippers use rice grains to create a *fylfot* around the temple altar.

The holiest symbol is a simple swastika. A Jain swastika is normally associated with the three dots on the top accompanied with a crest and a dot. Another important symbol incorporates a wheel on the palm of a hand, symbolizing *Ahimsa*. Other major Jain symbols include:

- 24 *Lanchhanas* (symbols) of the Tirthankaras
- *Triratna* and *Shrivatsa* symbols
- A Tirthankar's or Chakravarti's mother dreams
- *Dharmacakra* and *Siddha-chakra*
- Eight auspicious symbols (The *Asta Mangalas*). Their names are.
    1. *Swastika*-Signifies peace and well-being

2. *Shrivatsa*-A mark manifested on the centre of the Jina's chest, signifying a pure soul.
3. *Nandyavartya*-Large swastika with nine corners
4. *Vardhamanaka*-A shallow earthen dish used for lamps, suggests an increase in wealth, fame and merit due to a Jina's grace.
5. *Bhadrasana*-Throne, considered auspicious because it is sanctified by the blessed Jina's feet.
6. *Kalasha*-Pot filled with pure water signifying wisdom and completeness
7. *Minayugala*-A fish couple. It signifies Cupid's banners coming to worship the Jina after defeating the God of Love
8. *Darpana*-The mirror reflects one's true self because of its clarity.

Culture

Jain Contributions to Indian Culture

While Jains represent less than 1% of the Indian population, their contributions to culture and society in India are considerable. Jainism had a major influence in developing a system of philosophy and ethics that had a major impact on all aspects of Indian culture in all ages. Scholarly research and evidences have shown that philosophical concepts considered typically Indian – Karma, Ahimsa, Moksa, reincarnation and like-either originate in the sramana school of thought or were propagated and developed by Jaina teachers.

Jains have also wielded great influence on the culture and language of the south Indian state Karnataka, India and Gujarat most significantly.In the early period and beginning of the medieval period, between the 9th and 13th centuries, kannada writers were predominantly of the Jain and Veerashaiva faiths. Jains were the earliest known cultivators of Kannada literature, which they dominated until the 12th century. Jain authors wrote about Jain Tirthankars and other aspects of the Jain religion.

Pampa, also known as Adikavi Pampa, is one of the greatest Kannada poets of all time. He was born either in Annigeri or Banavasi, in modern Karnataka state, and was the court poet of Chalukya King Arikesari, a Rashtrakuta feudatory. The works of

Jain writers Adikavi Pampa, Sri Ponna and Ranna, collectively called the "three gems of Kannada literature", heralded the age of classical Kannada in the 10th century. The earliest known Gujarati text, Bharat-Bahubali Ras, was written by a Jain monk. Some important people in Gujarat's Jain history were Acharya Hemacandra Suri and his pupil, the Chalukya ruler Kumarapala.

Jains are among the wealthiest Indians. They run numerous schools, colleges and hospitals and are important patrons of the Somapuras, the traditional temple architects in Gujarat. Jains have greatly influenced Gujarati cuisine. Gujarat is predominantly vegetarian, and its food is mild as onions and garlic are omitted. Jains encourage their monks to do research and obtain higher education. Jain monks and nuns, particularly in Rajasthan, have published numerous research monographs. This is unique among Indian religious groups and parallels Christian clergy. The 2001 census states that Jains are India's most literate community and that India's oldest libraries at Patan and Jaisalmer are preserved by Jain institutions.

Jain Contribution to Art and Architecture

The Jainas have been amongst the foremost in contributing to the field of art and architecture since early days. The images of Tirthankara Risabhadeva and the figures of standing or sealed nude Yogins found inscribed on some terracotta seats, relics of the prehistoric Indus Valley Civilization, discovered at Mohenjodaro, as well as nude Harrappan red stone statue are almost equally old. The latter is remarkably akin to the polished stone torso of a Jana image from Lohanipur (Patna), which is ascribed to the Mauryan times (4th c. B.C.) King Kharavel of Kalinga, as the Hathigumpha inscriptions speaks, reinstalled the Jain image which had been taken away by Nanda to Magadha in (4th c. B.C.) During the Satavahana period (60 B.C. to 225 A.D.) Mathura and Saurastra were the main centres. The earliest Mathura sculpture represented by Kankalitila where from Ayagaptta, Stupa, images, and other Jain cultural material are recovered. Gandhara art and Mathura art belong to Kusana period (First B.C. to 2nd A.D.) in which Jainism flourished to Mathura and the Ardhaphalaka sect, Yapaniya Sangha and Nagara art came into existence.

Gupta period (4th to 7th C.A.D.) is said to be the golden period of ancient Indian Culture. Harigupta, Siddhasena, Harisena,

Ravikirti, Pujyapada, Patrakesari, Udyotanasuri and other Jainacaryas have been in existence during the period. Karnataka, Mathura, Hastinapur, Saurastra, Avanti, Ahicchatra, Bhinnamala, Kausambi, Devagumpha, Vidisa, Sravasti, Varanasi, Vaisali, Pataliputra, Rajagraha, Campa etc. were the main Jain centres of art and architecture. After the Gupta period, Kakkula, Vatsaraja, and Mahendrapala were the Jain kings in the Pratihara dynasty. King Mona, Navasahasanka and Bhoja were followers of Jainism. Dhanapala, Amitagati, Manikyanandi, Prabhacandra, Asadhara, Dhananjaya etc. had contributed to the literary field during the same period. Chittod was the capital of Paramaras where Kalakacarya and Haribhadra devoted their lives for he development of Jain art and architecture. During Candela dynasty, Khajuraho, Devagadh, Mahoba, Madanapur, Canderi, Ahar, Papora, and Gwaliar became famous for their Jain art. Some important inscriptions, Toranas, images and other sculptural material are found in Tripuri.

As mentioned earlier, Bihar has been a prominent state since very early days with regard to Jain culture. It is the Parinirvanabhumi of so many Tirthankaras and is enriched through Jain statues, relics, sculpture etc. at Radiograph, Melinda, Parsvanatha hill, Simbhabhumi, Barabar hill, Patna, Pavapuri etc. The earliest Jain images are recovered in Bengal from Surohar and Mandoil of Mathura style. The images of Jain Tirthankaras found in Udisa at Udaigiri-Khandagiri, and some other places such as Keonjhar, Mayurabhanja, Jaipur, Cuttack are very beautiful from artistic point or view.

Gujarat and Rajasthan have been strongholds of Jainism since an early time. Satrunjaya, Girinar, are Siddhaksetras of Jainism. Rastrakutas and Calukyas, Pratiharas, Paramaras, Cauhan and other dynasties patronized Jainism and its art and architecture. Hemacandracarya was a court poet of Jayasimha and Kumarapala. Vastupala and Tejapala who were ministers of Baghelas of Solanki branch built a large number of Jain temples at Girinar, Abu, Satrunjaya, etc. They are also found in large number at Ranakapur, Udaipur, Sirohi, Jaisalmer, Jodhpur, Jaipur, Alwar and so many places. The existence of Jainism in Punjab and Sindh can traced out long before the Christian era, from the sites of Mohanjodaro, Harappa, Taksasila, Simhapur, Sindhudesh, Lahore etc. The inscriptional history of Jainism in Maharashtra starts with the

Parle inscription of first c. A.D. that commences with "Namo Arihantanam". Keljher, Pavanar, Nagpur, Bhandara, Remtek, Akola, Karanja, Achalpur, Latur, Bhadravati etc. are main Jain ancient sites with archaeological remains. Sirpur is famous for its artistic decoration. Malakhed was found inhabitant when Padaliptacarya visited in about 1st c. A.D., Jain caves are found at Ellora, Nasik, Dharasiva, (Osmanabad) etc. Pratishthanpur, Belgaon, Kolhapur, Ehol, Alaktakanagara, Kunthalgiri, Ardhapur, Kandhar Karanataka (Karad), Mahimagiri, Vatapi, Meghuni etc. have been main centres of Jainism where huge and magnificent Jain temples idols and inscriptions are found. Mrgesavarvarman's in inscription (450-478 A.D.) states that a huge donation was made to Digambaras, Svetambaras, Kurcakas and Yapaniyas. Belagaon and Kolhapur were also ruled over by Silaharas of Konkana who built their huge Jain temples like Adataraditya, Satyavakya, Candraprabha, Ratta, etc. Vatapi, Ehol, Meguli were also Jain centres of this period when Pulakesi First, Kirtivarman, and Ravikirti constructed Jain temples.

Andhra Pradesa has been a stronghold center of Jainism. Acarya Kundakunda (1st c. A.D.), the spiritual leader of the time hails from Kondakunda situated on the boarder of Andhrapradesha. King Vishnuvardhan of Calukyas, Akalavarsa, Amoghavarsa, and Krashnaraja of Rashtrakutas, Bhima, Ganga Vijayaditya, Durgaraj etc. of Vengis, Tailapa, Vikramaditya of Badami Calukyas, some kings of Velanatichoda period patronized Jainism by way of constructing temples, Vasadis and Vidyapeethas. Some of them, afterwards, were occupied by Virasaivaitas and Lingayatas, who have been great destructors of Jain monuments and the community as well.

Jainism in Karnataka goes back at least to Bhadrabahu and Candragupta Maurya who migrated to South India via Ujjain with twelve thousand disciples due to severe calamity and famine into he North. Simhanandin, the Jainacarya, established Gangavadi dynasty. Jainism was its state religion for about seven hundred years during which hundreds of Jain monuments were erected by the kings. Pujyapada, Prabhacandra, Jinasena, Gunanandi, Patrakesari, Puspadanta, Vidyanada, Anantavirya, Joindu etc. get the patronage of the dynasty.

Of the kings the name of Racamalla Satyavakya may be specially mentioned under whose reign Camundaraya, his great minister erected the colossal statue of Gomatesvara Bahubali, the unparallel statue in the world. After Rashtrakutas Jainism got set back. One Vasava murdered his master Vijjala, the Kalacuri Jain king and perished Jainism and its adherents. He established an independent sect named Lingayata and persecuted the Jainas. From Jain archaeological standpoint, the main sites are Mangal, Nandidurga, panditarahalli, Candrasala vasadi, Aarapur, Arkettar, Sarangipattam, Halebid, Kelasaur, Aihole, Marol, Honwad, Honnur, Kalholi, Mulguna, Lakkundi, Nagire, Billigi are the main places where the Jain monuments are richly available.

Jainism entered in Tamilnadu most probably from Kalinga in about 4th c. B.C. Visakhacarya proceeds to Cola and Pandya countries with the entire Munisangha. It can be supported by the caverns containing beds carved out in the rock found in hills and mountains around the Pudukottai, Madura and Tinnevelly and rock-cut sculptures and inscriptions in the hills of the north Arcot district which indicate the existence of Jainism in Tamil Nadu in 3rd c. B.C. Kanci was one of the important seat of learning in South India. It was the capital of Pallvas who were mostly Jainas in early centuries.

The inscriptions of Jinakanchi refers to some prominent Jainacaryas of the city like Kundakunda, Samantabhadra, Jinacandra, Pujyapada, Akalanka, Anantavirya, Bhavanand, mallisena etc. The North and South Arcot region is very rich from Jain archaeological standpoint. Pancapandava, Trirumalai, Vallimalai, Vidal, Villipuram, Chinglaput may be specially mentioned. Sittanavasal, Narttamalai, Tenimalai, Bommamalai, Malamala, Samanar Kudagu, etc. have been the Jain centres since last two thousand years. Most of these places have paintings, and sculptures of Sittanavasala tradition, which may be compared with Ajanta and Sigirya. Some of the rock-cut temples like Samanar Kudagu have been converted into Visnu temples.

Madura was the capital of Pandyas who took their favorable attitude towards Jainism. Its neighboring hills Annaimalai, Nagamalai, Alagarmalai, Muttupatti, Eruvadi, etc. are very rich from Jain sculptural and painting standpoint. It is a land of origin of Samgama literature. Tirukurala, Tolkappiyam, Naladiyara, Cintamani, Silakppadikaram, Nilakesi, Manimekhalai, Kurala etc. are the Jain epics of early period. Pujyapada, Vajranandi, Aryanandi, Patrakesari etc. were the prominent Jainacaryas of the period. Afterwards Jainism was patronized by the Kadamba kings. In

Tinnevelly region the Kalugumallai, Tiruchcharanattumalai, Nagarajaswami temple belonged to Jainas but they are under the control of Vedicas.

Thus the survey of Jainism in South India gives and apparent picture of its position that it was there popular during the period of Tirthankara Mahavira or even earlier to him. The popularity augmented gradually and Digambara sect became the prominent one. During about 11th c. A.D., Vaisnavism, Alawara and Lingayatas came into existence and stood against Jainism that caused a serious blow to its propagation. The devotees of Sambandara, Tirunavukkarasata, Appara, Mukkanti, Tirumalasai, Tirumangai Vira-Saivas committed heavy atrocities on Jain society, temples, sculptures and Vasadis. Their massacres took place and the Jain centres were converted into Saiva or Vaisnava temples. Some places like Pillaiyarapatti and Kunnakkundi, Arittayatti, Nartamallai, and Kulugamalai, Tiruccirapalli, Virasikhamani, Kudumiyamalai, Dalavaura, Siyamangalam and Mamamdura can be cited in this respect. All this can be evaluated as follows.

Jain images, Ayagapttas, Stambhas, Toranas, Vedicas etc. were excavatd from Kankalitila in Mathura belonging to Kusana period. The Stupa made of bricks is called Devanirmita Stupa. The symbols are not traceable on these images, the Sarvatobhadra Pratimas. The names of Kaniska, Ruviska and Vasudeva are inscribed on these images. The unique Jain image of Sarasvati may also be mentioned in this context. The Chausa bronzes, in some Jain images in Lucknow and Patana museums, the Jain remains at Vaibhara hill Rajagiri and the bronzes of the Akota hoard are also belonging to this period. Some auspicious symbols like Phana, Srivats, a Purnaganata, Svastika, Vardhmanaka, Matsya, Nandyavarta etc. are also inscribed on one of the Parsva images. The image of Jivantasvami may also be referred to the period. Then the crystallized forms of the iconography were transferred to rocks on hills like Vaibhara hill, Udaigiri hills in Sanchi and Udaigiri, Kalagumalai in South. Afterwards, the iconography became fixed.

In other words it can be said that the Jain iconography was developed during the Gupta period in 4th century A.D. Decoration on Padpitha, Dharmacakera, Paramesthis, Gandharva Yugala, Navagrahs, Triratnas, Bhamandala, and Astapratiharys were included as the symbols of Jain images. However, all the symbols could not be decided in the early Gupta period. The images of the period can be viewed in Mathura museum, Vesanagar, Budhicanderi, Deogarha, Rajagiri, Kumarahara, Vaisali and other places. Some more images of the Gupta period are found in Udaigiri, Vesanagara, Nacana (Patana) etc. with somewhat more decorated forms. Some of the bronzes of the Akota hoara, particularly the image of Jivantasvami in Kayotsarga pose bearing a crown, Bhujabandha, Kundala, Kangana, and the image of Ambika decorated with ornaments and Yaksa-Yaksis are the representative images of the period. Sasanadevatas, Drum-player, a pair of elephants etc. were also included in the symbols.

In late Gupta period these symbols were more developed and in about 8th-9th c. A.D. all the symbols, Yaksa-Yaksis, Sasnadevidevatas, were fixed. Afterwards, Ksetrapalas, Dikpalas, Navgrahas, and Vidyadharas were also placed around the Jana images. Tantrism entered into Jain iconography in about tenth century A.D. and as a result, the Yaksa-Yaksis etc. got their due place on the pedestal or around the Jain images with more decorative sculptural surroundings. Sandy stone is widely used in about twelfth century along with black and white marble. The bronze images are also popularly available of the period. In the fourteenth century the development of Jain iconography stagnated and the decline started. This can be understood through perspective of iconographical peculiarities of Tirthankaras and their associates.

Temple art is of three types, Nagara, Vesara and Dravid. In Niagara style, the Garvagraha is quadrangular and its summit (Sikhara) is circular with Kalasa. It is used in Punjab, Himalaya, Rajasthan, Madhyapradesa, Udisa and Bengal. The Sikhara becomes flat in Vesar style, which is found in Madhyabharat, and the temple gets the form of pillar in Dravidian style. The earliest Jain temple is found at Lohanipur (Patna) of Maurya period. Then the temple art is available from the seventh century onwards. Painting has also been one of the best methods for expressing the ideas.

6

Jain Texts

Purvas

The Fourteen Purvas, translated as ancient or prior knowledge, are a large body of scriptures that was preached by all Tirthankaras encompassing the entire gamut of knowledge available in this universe. The persons having the knowledge of purvas were given an exalted status of srut-kevali or "scripturally omniscient persons". Both the Jain traditions, Svetambara and Digambara hold that all the fourteen purvas have been lost.

According to tradition, the Purvas were part of canonical literature and deposited in the third section of Drstivada. Knowledge of Purvas became fairly vulnerable after Lord Mahaviras nirvana on account of effects of famine, such that, eventually only one person – Bhadrabahu Svami had a command over it. In accordance with the prophecy of Mahavira, knowledge of Purvas died within 1000 years of his nirvana and eventually, the whole of Drstivada disappeared as well. However, a detailed table of contents of the Drstivada and the Purvas has survived in the fourth Anga, Samavayanga and Nandisutra. Furthermore, certain portions of Drstivada and Purvas is said to have survived in Satkhandagama and Kasayaprabhrta especially the doctrine of Karma.

Subject Matter of Purvas

Following were the fourteen Purvas containing various descriptions and details :

1. Utpaad Purva – Living (Jiv), non-living (Ajiv), and its modes (Paryaya);

2. Agrayaniya Purva – Nine realities (Navtattva), six substances (Shad-dravya), etc.;
3. Viryapravada Purva – Relating to energy of soul, non-living, etc.;
4. Asti Nasti Pravada Purva – Multiplicity of views (Anekantvad), Saptabhangi, etc.;
5. Jnana Pravada Purva – Five types of knowledge and three types of ignorance, etc.;
6. Satya Pravada Purva – Relating to truth, restraint, silence (Maun), speech, etc.;
7. Atma pavada Purva – Analysis of soul from different view points (naya);
8. Karma Pravada Purva – Theory of karma, its bondage, influx, its nature, fruition, shedding;
9. Pratyakhyana Purva – Giving up (Pachchhakhan), restraint, vows, detachment, etc;
10. Vidya Pravada Purva – Expertise (Vidya), exceptional abilities, practice,;
11. Kalyana Pravada Purva – Spiritual alertness (Apramad) and laziness (Pramad);
12. Prana Pravada Purva – Ten types of life substances or vitalities (Pran), life span, etc.;
13. Kriya Visala Purva – Skills, 64 arts of women, 84 arts of men, etc.;
14. Lokbindus a Purva – Three parts of universe including heavens and hells, mathematics, etc.

The contents of the Purvas was so vast, that the tradition holds that, the first one is written by the volume of the ink that is equivalent to the size of one elephant. Second one is two times larger, and third one is two times larger than second one and so on. It was said that, all efforts to describe the knowledge of Purva in words were in vain. It provided detailed information about six kinds of reals or substances, all kinds of living creatures, the things which were to exist for eternal time, those which were to come into existence for a transient time and their time of extinction, five kinds of knowledge, truth, soul, karma, mantra, benefits of austerities, the lifestyle of ascetics and householders, birth, death and a detailed description of the whole universe. It also contained various knowledge on attainment of exceptional abilities including attainment of various magical powers.

The Srutakevalis

The persons having the knowledge of purvas were known as srut-kevali or "scripturally omniscient persons". They were one step away from attaining enlightened or Kevala Jnana. The following persons had the knowledge of Purvas after Lord Mahavira:

1. Ganadhara Gautama Svami
2. Ganadhara Sudharma Svami
3. Jambu Svami.

These three persons also attained Kevala Jnana or enlightenment and were subsequently liberated. After Jambu Svami, the following Heads of the Jaina Order had knowledge of the entire 14 Purvas:

1. Prabhava
2. Sayyambhava
3. Yashobhadra
4. Sambhutavijaya
5. Bhadrabahu
6. Sthulibhadra – Although he is said to have had knowledge of all 14 purvas, the meaning of the last four purvas was not revealed to him.

Loss of the Purvas

The Indologist Hermann Jacobi is of the opinion that there is an element of truth in the existence of Purvas or ancient knowledge; however, he held a view that Drstivada contained an abstract of the Purvas, rather than the entire text of the Purvas itself. According to him, it is no coincidence that the knowledge of Purvas started fading away simultaneously with the redaction of the new canon. He is of the opinion that the Drstivada containing a disputation of the views of heretical traditions may no longer have served a purpose, once the rival traditions became extinct.

On the other hand, Acarya Hemacandra's Parishishtaparva, also known as Sthaviravali (stories on the lives of elders or Jain patriarchs), contains detailed information as to how the knowledge of the Purvas was lost. Bhadrabahu Svami was the last person to have the knowledge of the entire 14 Purvas. He refused to teach the last four Purvas to his chief disciple Sthulibhadra, who had used his knowledge of the Purvas to display magical powers. Bhadrabahu, foreseeing the loss of the Purvas and a decline of morality and conduct, ultimately agreed to teach Sthulabhadra the rest of the Purvas, on the condition that he should not hand down the last four Purvas to anybody else. Hence, Sthulabhadra, in turn, taught his disciples Mahagiri and Suhastin only ten Purvas, for he was forbidden to teach the last four Purvas to anybody. Gradually, with the growth of schisms and the inability of monks to commit the scriptures to memory, the knowledge of the Purvas and of the Dristivada became extinct.

Agamas

Agamas are canonical texts of Jainism based on Mahavira's teachings. Mahavira's preaching were orally compiled by his disciples into various Sutras (texts) which were collectively called Jain canonical or Agamic literature. Traditionally these sutras were orally passed on from teachers (acaryas or gurus) to the disciples for several centuries. The scholars date the composition of Jain Agamas at around 6th to 3rd century BCE.

History of Agamas

While some authors date the composition of Jain Agamas starting from 6th Century BCE, noted indologist Hermann Jacobi holds that the the composition of the Jaina canon would fall somewhere about the end of the fourth or the beginning of the third century B.C.E The general consensus amongst scholars is that the earliest portions of Jain canons were composed around 4th or 3rd century BCE. This is also in agreement with Jain tradition according to which the agamic literature and the Purvas were passed from one heads of the order to his disciples for around 170 years after the Nirvana (Jainism) of Mahavira. However with time, it became difficult to keep the entire Jain literature committed to memory. According to tradition, there occurred a twelve years of famine around 350 BC where it was extremely difficult for the Jain ascetics to survive during this time. Under such circumstances they could not preserve the entire canonical literature. The Purvas or the ancient texts were were already forgotten and lost after the famine. According to Svetambara tradition, the Agamas were collected on the basis of collective memory of the ascetics in the first council of Pataliputra under the stewardship of Acarya Sthulibhadra in around to 463–367 BCE. However, the Digambara Jain sect maintains that after the famine, the entire Jain canonical literature became extinct.

Acaranga Sutra

The Acaranga Sutra (or Acharanga) is the first of the eleven Angas, part of the Agamas (religious texts) which were compiled based on the teachings of Lord Mahavira.

The Acaranga Sutra discusses the conduct of a Jain monk. In antiquity, *Acaranga* was the first text that was studied by the Jain monks.

The existing text of the Acaranga Sutra which is used by the Svetambara sect of Jainism was recompiled and edited by Kshama Shraman Devardhigani, who headed the council held at Valabhi 980 years after Lord Mahavir's Nirvana. The Digambaras do not recognize the existing text, and regard the original text as having been lost in its original form. The Digambara Mulachara text includes the Digambara tradition derived from Acharanga.

Introduction

The Acaranga Sutra is the oldest agam, from a linguistic point of view, written in Ardhamagadhi Prakrit. The Acaranga Sutra contains two books, or Srutaskandhas. The first book is the older part, to which other treatises were later added. It describes the conduct and behavior of ascetic life: the mode of begging for food, bowl, clothes, conduct while walking and speaking and regulation of possessions by ascetics. It also describes the penance of Mahavira, the Great Hero. The second book is divided into four sections called Kulas. There were originally five Kulas, but the fifth, the Nisihiyagghana, is now reckoned as a separate work. The first and second parts lay down rules for conduct of ascetics.

Sutrakrtanga

Sutrakritanga Sutra is the second Agama of the 12 main agnas of the Jain canons. According to the Svetambara tradition it was written by Gandhara Sudharmasvami in Ardhamagadhi Prakrit.

It is written using techniques including narration and questions and answers, and the chapters start with Sudharmasvami explaining the various doctrines to his chief disciple Jambusvami and answering his questions.

This Agama describes nonviolence, Jain metaphysics, and the refutation of other religious theories such as Kriyavada, Akriyavada, Ajnanavada, and Vinayavada. Sanskrit commentary ihas been done by Silanka lived in the second half of the ninth century A. D. The Agama is divided into two parts consisting of 16 lectures and 7 lectures respectively. Following are the diverse topics covered –

- Jain doctrine – Causes of bondage, description of hells, destruction of karmas etc.
- Conduct of Monks – Injunctions and prohibitions, difficulties faced, avoiding temptation of women etc.
- Heretical Doctrines and errors – Materialists, Buddhists, vedics, Fatalists and other wrong beliefs.

Sthananga

As per the Uvetambara belief, Sthananga Sutra forms part of the first eleven Angas of the Jaina Canon which have survived despite the bad effects of this Hundavasarpini kala. This is the reason why, under the leadership of Devardhigani Ksamasramana, the eleven Angas of the Svetambara canon were formalised and reduced to writing. This took place at Valabhi 993 years after Mahavira's nirvana. (466 CE). In the vacana held at Valabhi, in Gujarat, the Sthananga Sutra was finalised and redacted. The language used is Ardhamagadhi Prakrit. The mula sutras of the Sthananga Sutra are difficult to understand without the help of a commentary or tika. Hence, in the 11th century CE, Abhayadevasuri wrote a comprehensive Sanskrit gloss on the Sthananga Sutra.

Description

The Sthanangasutra is known in Prakrit as the Thanam. The word thanam denotes quantum. Hence, the style of the Sthananga Sutra is unique. It is divided into ten chapters, and each chapter enumerates certain topics according to their numbers. Each chapter is titled as a Thana. (Sanskrit: Sthana) This Agama defines and catalogues the main substances of the Jain metaphysics. Diverse topics such as the Dharmakathanuyoga, Carananuyoga, Karananuyoga and Dravyanuyoga are covered. While the focus is on Karananuyoga, this unique Agama serves as a huge anthology to all branches of Jaina knowledge.

Because all topics, terms and things are thought of as fitting well with number one, number two, and so on, up to number ten, and because they are listed accordingly, the word "Sthana" in the titles of the ten chapters as well as in the title of our work means "place". The Sthanangasutra is an anga-text in which "terms and things" are listed in their "right place". Sthananga maybe considered as a memory aid for an Acarya, so that he might not forget the varied subject matters he wants to teach. With this work he has a kind of guideline for his lessons at hand and can easily reply to questions asked by his disciples. Importance of Sthanangasutra can be gauged from the fact that Vyavahara Chedasutra (10, 20-34) mentions that it is suitable to be studied only by those ascetics, who have at least eight years standing in monkhood. Further more it is stated that only a monk who knows the Sthananga by heart may attain the position of an Acarya, which, entitles him to supervise the monks and nuns in regard to their conduct and study.

Authorship

The first Sutra in the Sthananga goes as follows: *suyam me ausam tenam Bhagavaya evam akkhayam*-"I have heard, o Long-Lived one, that the Venerable (i.e. Mahavira) has said thus." From this it can be gauged that as per the tradition it was recited by ganadhara Sudharman, the fifth direct disciple of Mahavira, to his disciple Jambusvamin.

Contribution to Indian Mathematics

Sthananga Sutra lists the topics which made up the mathematics studied at the ftrom the time of 2nd century BCE onwards. In fact this list of topics sets the scene for the areas of study for a long time to come in the Indian subcontinent. The topics are listed in as.:-the theory of numbers, arithmetical operations, geometry, operations with fractions, simple equations, cubic equations, quartic equations, and permutations and combinations. It also gives classifications of five types of infinities. The topics of mathematics, according to the Sthananga-sutra (Sutra 747) are ten in numbers:

- Parikarma (four fundamental operations),
- Vyavahara (subjects of treatment),
- Rajju (geometry),
- Rashi (mensuration of solid bodies),
- Kalasavarna (fractions),
- Yavat-tavat (simple equation),
- Varga (quadratic equation),
- Ghana (cubic equation),
- Varga-varga (biquadratic equation) and
- Vikalpa (permutation and combination).

However, the historians of mathematics differ in explaining some of the terms from the commentator, Abhayadeva Suri (1050 AD).

Samavayanga

The Samavayanga Sutra is the 4th amongst the 12 Angas of the Jaina canon. The Sutra is believed to have been composed by Gandhara Sudharma Svami. This ancient manuscript is the holy book of the Svetambara sect. This text contains the essence of Jain religion, defined and catalogued systematically. It is believed to be written around the year 300 BC. It is a part of the collection of texts containing Lord Mahavira's teachings, collectively termed as Agama Sutras.

Subject Matter of the Agama

Samavayanga Sutra contains elements of mathematics and astronomy. One of the interesting aspects of this text is its portrayal of Monasticism and spirituality in the terms of numerology.

Mathematics-The Samavayanga Sutra seems to be in continuation of the Sthananga Sutra and follows the numeric method of describing substances from 1 to 1 billion.

Astronomy – It contains discussion on Mount Meru, the jyotishcakra, the Jambudvipa itself, the measurements used in the Jaina canon, the Jaina Loka, the different types of Earth, the 7 Hells, the increase in water levels in the Lavana ocean and like. It also gives information on the subject matter of the 14 Purva and the 12th Anga, Drstivada. Being one of the oldest and most referred texts, it forms the backbone of the Jain literature. There is a description of the life-span of the Gods in the Samavayanga Agama. There is also a mention of the days of their inhalation and exhalation. It further defines and catalogues the main substances of the Jain religion from a different perspective than the Sthananga Sutra. Furthermore, it contains references to the Damili script, an early Tamil script which is also called as Tamil-Brahmi Script by the scholars.

Vyakhyaprajnapti or Bhagavati Sutra

Vyakhyaprajnapti commonly known as *Bhagavati Sutra* is the fifth of the 12 Jain Agamas said to be promulgated by Mahavira himself. Vyakhyaprajnapti translated as "Exposition of Explanations" is said to have been composed by ganadhara Sudharmasvami as per the Evetambara tradition. It is the largest text of the canon said to contain 60000 questions answered by Mahavira. The subject matter of the answers ranges from the Jain Doctrine to rules of ascetic behaviour.

Contents

Briefly, the answers may be categorised under the following categories:

- related to ascetic conduct
- related to the six substances
- related to the Jain Ontology
- related to Reincarnation
- related to Jain Geography
- related to Jain Cosmology
- related to Jain Mathematics
- related to Obstetrics
- brief biographies of famous contemporaries of Mahavira
- miscellaneous subjects.

The Bhagavati Sutra is divided into 41 sections known as Shatakas. It follows question and answer pattern. The questions are raised by Gautama, Makandiputra, Roha, Agnibhuti & Vayubhuti, Skandaka, Jayanti, etc. It is written in Ardhamagadhi Prakrit.

Jnatrdharmakathah

Jnatrdharmakathah is the sixth of the 12 Jain Agamas said to be promulgated by Mahavira himself. Jnatrdharmakathah translated as "Stories of Knowledge and Righteousness" is said to have been composed by Ganadhara Sudharmasvami as per the evetambara tradition.

Subject Matter of the Agama

It contains a series of narratives, from which morals about results of following the religious path are drawn. The Eighth Chapter gives the story of Lord Mallinath the nineteenth Tirthankara.

Upasakadauah

Upasakadauah is the seventh of the 12 Jain Agamas said to be promulgated by Mahavira himself. Upasakadauah translated as "Ten Chapters on Lay Attenders" is said to have been composed by Ganadhara Sudharmasvami as per the Evetambara tradition.

Subject Matter

It contains stories describing the piety of the advanced laymen and their fortitude in face of demonic attacks.

Antakrddaauah

Antakrddaauah is the eighth of the 12 Jain Agamas said to be promulgated by Mahavira himself. Antakrddaauah translated as "Ten Chapters on End-Makers" is said to have been composed by Ganadhara Sudharmasvami as per the Evetambara tradition.

Subject Matter of the Agama

It contains stories describing those who succeeded in destroying all their karmas and succeeded in attaining Moksa and putting an end to the re-births.

Anuttaraupapatikadauah

Anuttaraupapatikadauah is the ninth of the 12 Jain Agamas said to be promulgated by Mahavira himself. Anuttaraupapatikadauah translated as "Ten Chapters about the arisers in the Highest Heavens" is said to have been composed by Ganadhara Sudharmasvami as per the Evetambara tradition.

Subject Matter of the Agama

It contains stories describing those who succeeded accumulating pious karmas and succeeded in attaining the highest heavens being reborn as devas on account of good deeds.

Praunavyakaranani

Praunavyakaranani is the tenth of the 12 Jain Agamas as per Evetambara tradition said to be promulgated by Mahavira himself and composed by Ganadhara Sudharmasvami. Praunavyakaranani translated as "Questions and Explanations" discusses a variety of doctrinal matters concerning Jainism.

Subject Matter of the Agama

The Agama contains information about the 5 Sins and conversely their Vows in Jainism. Namely Killing, Stealing, Lying, Unchastity (like Sexual Misconduct) and Possessiveness or Greed.

It talks about Killing and the results of Killing, the results (karma results) of Stealing, Lying, Unchastity and Possessiveness or Greed.

It then talks about Non-Killing, Non-Stealing, Non-Lying, Chastity and Non-Possessiveness or Non-Greed.

Vipakauruta

Vipakauruta is the eleventh of the 12 Jain Agamas as per Evetambara tradition said to be promulgated by Mahavira himself and composed by Ganadhara Sudharmasvami. Vipakauruta translated as "The Scripture about Ripening" contains stories describing those who experience result about karmas.

Subject Matter of the Agama

It contains 10 stories of people who experience the fruit of bad karma and 10 stories of people who experience the fruit of good karma.

These people however simply do not just experience there fruit, but it is explained what they did in the past that brought about the fruit that they experience.

Drstivada (Now Extinct)

Drstivada is the last of the 12 Jain Agamas as per Evetambara tradition said to be promulgated by Mahavira himself and composed by Ganadhara Sudharmasvami. Drstivada translated as "Disputation about views" was said to contain entire knowledge of 14 Purvas or prior knowledge that is now considered to be totally lost. In fact, the tradition holds that Drstivada is also completely lost. However, its contents have been referred and explained in Nandi and *Samavayanga Sutra.*

Subject Matter of the Agama

Dristivada was divided into five parts :-

1. Parikarma
2. Sutra
3. Purvanayoga
4. Purvgata
5. Chulika.

Parikarma contained Jaina calculatory science and the Sutra included discussions about creeds and doctrines. Purvagata contained fourteen subdivisions and contained discussions about Jaina doctrines and principles. As the name suggests, Purvas contain the knowledge prior to Mahavira which was preserved only in oral form. Purvanayoga contained Puranic narratives, religious biographies as well as illustrative tales.

- Twelve *Upanga Agamas* (Texts that provide further explanation of Angas).
    - o *Aupapatika*
    - o *Rajaprauniya*
    - o *Jivajivabhigama*
    - o *Prajnapana*
    - o *Sûryaprajnapti*
    - o *Jambudvipaprajnapt*
    - o *Candraprajnapti*
    - o *Nirayarvali*
    - o *Kalpavatamsikah*
    - o *Puspikah*
    - o *Puspaculikah*
    - o *Vrasnidauah.*

- Six *Chedasutras* (Texts relating to the conduct and behaviour of monks and nuns).
    - o *Acaradauah*
    - o *Brhatkalpa*
    - o *Vyavahara*
    - o *Niuitha*
    - o *Mahaniuitha*
    - o *Jîtakalpa*
- Four *Mulasutras* (Scriptures which provide a base in the earlier stages of the monkhood).
    - o *Dauavaikalika*
    - o *Uttaradhyayana*
    - o *Avauyaka*
    - o *Pindaniryukyti.*
- Ten *Prakirnaka sutras* (Texts on Independent or miscellaneous subjects).
    - o *Catuharana*
    - o *Aturapratyakhyana*
    - o *Bhaktaparijana*
    - o *Samstaraka*
    - o *Tandulavaicarika*
    - o *Candravedhyaka*
    - o *Devendrastava*
    - o *Ganividya*
    - o *Mahapratyakhyana*
    - o *Vîrastava.*
- Two *Culikasutras* (The scriptures which further enhance or decorate the meaning of Angas).
    - o *Nandi-Sutra*
    - o *Anuyogadvara-Sutra.*

Languages of Agamas and Literature

The Jain literature includes both religious texts and books on generally secular topics such as sciences, history, and grammar.

The Jains have used several languages at different times and in different regions of India.

- Prakrit: Prakrit literature includes the Agamas, Agama-tulya texts, and Siddhanta texts. Composition in Prakrits ceased around 10th cent AD.
- Sanskrit: Writing in Sanskrit became common after about 1st cent. CE., starting with Tatvartha Sutra of Uma Swati. Jain Sanskrit literature includes Puranas, Koshas, Shravakacharas, Mathematics, and Nighantus.
- Apabhramsha: Produced from about 10th to 15th cent CE, these texts include Kahas, rasas, and grammars. Most of the known Apabhramsha texts are of Jain origin.
- Tamil: Some of the early Tamil classics such as Tirukural, Cilappatikaram and Jivakachintamani are Jain works.
- Hindi: In the past 8-9 centuries numerous Jain texts in Hindi have been written, which include Ardha-kathanaka, Chhah-dhala, and Mokshamarga Prakashaka.
- Kannada: The earliest texts in Kannada, such as Vaddaradhane are works of Jain authors.
- Gujarati: Bharata-Bahubali Ras, the first Gujarati book, was by a Jain author.

Jainism puts great value on learning. Jains have been prolific authors and avid readers for centuries. India's oldest manuscript libraries have been preserved in Jaisalmer and Patan by Jain scholars. According to the 2001 census, the Jains are the most literate community in India

Kalpasutra (Jainism)

Kalpasutra is a Jain ancient text containing the biographies of the last two Jain Tirthankaras, Parshvanath and Mahavira. It contains detailed life histories with illustrations. Adinath (or RishabhDev) and Neminath are two other Tirthankaras briefly mentioned in the text, with Adinath depicted in some of the illustrations. The book is considered to be written by Bhadrabahu I, and it is considered written about 150 years after Nirvana of Mahavira.

Importance of the Text

The book is read and illustrated in an eight day long festival of Paryushan by Jain monks for general people. Only Monks can read this scriptures. Ordinary people are not suppose to read the Scripture.

Origin of Illustrations

The Kalpasutra art has its origin acclaimedly in the 5th century. It is claimed that the Kalpasutras, though on a different medium, were part of the same sectarian art tradition as the ancient murals of Ajanta, Bagh and other monasteries. However, the earliest known Kalpasutras do not go beyond the 10th century and the number from the period from the 10th to 13th centuries is very small. The greater bulk of Kalpasutra paintings emerges from 14th to mid-16th centuries. These Kalpasutras are mostly from Western India, Gujarat, Rajasthan and the western region of Malwa. The Mandu (Malwa, now in Madhya Pradesh) Kalpasutras of 1439 and some of their contemporary renderings from Gujarat and western Rajasthan, Mewar and Marwar, are all masterpieces of Indian miniature art.

Tattvartha Sutra

Tattvartha Sutra (also known as Tattvarth-adhigama-Sutra or Moksh-Shastra) is a Jaina text written by Acharya Umaswati or Umasvami. It was an attempt to bring together the different elements of the Jain Path, epistemological, metaphysical, cosmological, ethical and practical, otherwise unorganized around the scriptures in an unsystematic format. It is the first Jain text in Sutra (aphoristic) form. The term Tattvartha is made of the Sanskrit words: *Tattva* (things or realities) and *artha* (true nature). Umaswati is accepted by all the sects of Jains and is said to have lived around the 2nd century BC.

The Tattvartha Sutra is regarded as the most authoritative book on Jainism. It has the largest number of commentaries in different Indian languages from the fifth century onward. The first verse, "Samyag darshan jnana charitrani moksha margah" summarizes Jainism by saying that right knowledge, right faith and right conduct collectively only are the path to liberation or *moksha*. The first chapter deals with the process of cognition and details about different types of knowledge. The next three chapters deal with the Soul. The fifth chapter discusses Non-soul (*Ajiva*). The next three chapters deal with the karmas and their manifestations and the inflow and the bondage of the karmas. The ninth chapter describes the blocking and shading of the karmas. The final chapter discusses liberation of the soul or the *moksha*.

Jains have contributed to India's classical and popular literature. For example, almost all early Kannada literature and many Tamil works were written by Jains.

- Some of the oldest known books in Hindi and Gujarati were written by Jain scholars. The first autobiography in Hindi, Ardha-Kathanaka was written by a Jain, Banarasidasa, an ardent follower of Acarya Kundakunda who lived in Agra.
- Several Tamil classics are written by Jains or with Jain beliefs and values as the core subject.
- Practically all the known texts in the Apabhramsha language are Jain works.

The oldest Jain literature is in Shauraseni and Ardha-Magadhi Prakrit (Agamas, Agama-Tulya, Siddhanta texts, etc). Many classical texts are in Sanskrit (Tatvartha Sutra, Puranas, Kosh, Sravakacara, mathematics, Nighantus etc). "Abhidhana Rajendra Kosha" written by Acharya Rajendrasuri, is only one available Jain encyclopedia or Jain dictionary to understand the Jain Prakrit, Sanskrit, and Ardha-Magadhi and other Jain languages, words, their use and references with in oldest Jain literature. Later Jain literature was written in Apabhramsha (Kahas, rasas, and grammars), Hindi (Chhahadhala, Mokshamarga Prakashaka, and others), Tamil (Jivakacintamani and others), and Kannada (Vaddaradhane and various other texts). Jain versions of Ramayana and Mahabharata are found in Sanskrit, Prakrit, Apabhramsha and Kannada.

Jainism and other Religions

Jains are not a part of the Vedic Religion (Hinduism). Ancient India had two philosophical streams of thought: The Shramana philosophical schools, represented by Jainism, and the Brahmana/ Vedic/Puranic schools represented by Vedanta, Vaishnava and other movements. Both streams are subsets of the Dharmic family of faith and have existed side by side for many thousands of years, influencing each other.

The Hindu scholar, Lokmanya Tilak credited Jainism with influencing Hinduism and thus leading to the cessation of animal sacrifice in Vedic rituals. Bal Gangadhar Tilak has described Jainism as the originator of Ahimsa and wrote in a letter printed in Bombay Samachar, Mumbai:10 December, 1904: "In ancient times, innumerable animals were butchered in sacrifices. Evidence in support of this is found in various poetic compositions such as the Meghaduta. Swami Vivekananda also credited Jainism as influencing force behind the Indian culture.

"What could have saved Indian society from the ponderous burden of omnifarious ritualistic ceremonialism, with its animal and other sacrifices, which all but crushed the very life of it, except the Jain revolution which took its strong stand exclusively on chaste morals and philosophical truths? These [same] ascetic ideas prevailed at that time. These Jains were the first great ascetics; but they did some great work. "Don't injure any and do good to all that you can, and that is all the morality and ethics, and that is all the work there is, and the rest is all nonsense — the Brahmins created that. Throw it all away." And then they went to work and elaborated this one principle all through, and it is a most wonderful ideal: how all that we call ethics they simply bring out from that one great principle of non-injury and doing good."

- Relationship between Jainism and Hinduism-According to the Encyclopædia Britannica Article on Hinduism,"...With Jainism which always remained an Indian religion, Hinduism has so much in common, especially in social institutions and ritual life, that nowadays Hindus tend to consider it a Hindu sect. Many Jains also are inclined to fraternization..."
- Independent Religion-From the Encyclopædia Britannica Article on Jainism: "...Along with Hinduism and Buddhism, it is one of the three most ancient Indian religious traditions still in existence....While often employing concepts shared with Hinduism and Buddhism, the result of a common cultural and linguistic background, the Jain tradition must be regarded as an independent phenomenon. It is an integral part of South Asian religious belief and practice, but it is not a Hindu sect or Buddhist heresy, as earlier scholars believed." The author Koenraad Elst in his book, *Who is a Hindu?*, summarises on the similarities between Jains and the mainstream Hindu society.

- Monier Williams, in his article of Jainism, mentions that Jains outdo every other Indian sect in carrying the prohibition of himsa to the most prosperous extremes.

Languages used in Jain Literature

Jain literature exists in Prakrit, Sanskrit, Tamil, Apabhramsha, Rajasthani, Hindi, Marathi, Gujarati, Kutchi, Kannada, Tulu, Telugu, Dhundhari (Old Marwari), English, German, French, Spanish, Italian, Portuguese, Urdu and Russian.

7

Other Heterodox Ideas

Many non-vedic ideas were prevalent in this period. They later developed into small sects. Among them the Ajivika sect had a considerable number of followers with a recognised organisation.

Ajivika

Ajivika was an ancient philosophical and ascetic movement of the Indian subcontinent. The Ajivikas were contemporaries of the early Buddhists and historical Jains; the Ajivika movement may have preceded both of these groups. The Ajivikas may have been a more loosely organized group of wandering ascetics (Shramanas or sanyasins). The Ajivikas believed that transmigration of the human soul was determined by a precise and non-personal cosmic principle called Niyati (destiny or fate) and was completely independent of the person's actions. They are believed to have been strict fatalists, who did not believe in karma or the possibility of free will. The belief is currently considered extinct, and what information is known about its followers is primarily from historical evidence left behind.

Several rock-cut caves belonging to this sect, built during the times of Mauryan Emperor, Ashoka (r. 273 BC to 232 BC), have been found at Barabar Caves, Jehanabad District, Bihar.

History

Very little that is concrete is known about the Ajivikas. Their scriptures and history were not preserved directly — instead, fragments of Ajivika doctrine were preserved in Buddhist and Jain sources, and they are mentioned in several inscriptions from the Mauryan empire. As a result, it is unknown to what degree the available sources reflect the actual beliefs and practices of the Ajivikas. Because most of what is known about them was recorded in the literature of rival groups, it is quite possible that accidental distortions or intentional criticism was introduced into the records. Even the name 'Ajivika' may have only been used by observers from outside the tradition.

Some regard Makkhali Gosala (Pali; Sanskrit: Goshala Maskariputra) (c. 484 BCE) as the founder of the Ajivika faith; other sources state that Gosala was a leader of a large Ajivika congregation, but not himself the founder of the movement. Gosala is believed to have been a friend of Mahavira, the 24th Tirthankara of Jainism. The Jain Bhagavati Sutra depicts Gosala as having been a disciple of Mahavira's for a period of six years, after which the two had a falling out and parted ways. Purana Kassapa was another leader of the Ajivikas.

The emperor Ashoka's father, Bindusara, was a believer of this philosophy, that reached its peak of popularity during Asoka's lifetime, and then declined into obscurity. The Ajivikasa may have continued to exist in India until as late as the 14th Century CE, but the extent to which the tradition survived is unclear. Inscriptions from southern India make reference to the 'Ajivikas' as late as the 13th Century CE, but by this point in history the term Ajivika may have been used to refer to ascetics from other traditions rather than followers of the Ajivika tradition that existed during earlier centuries.

It is interesting that not only Chanakya the founder of the Mauryan Dynasty but also the preceptor of Asoka's mother (or Bindusara's chief queen) Subhadrangi was an Ajivika.

Beliefs and Practices

Along with the history of the Ajivika movement, the practices and beliefs of the Ajivikas are difficult to reconstruct, because they were only preserved in external, often hostile sources. Ajivikas seem to have been exponents of a philosophy of absolute determinism, in which human actions and choices are unable to overcome the forces of fate. Ajivika adherents followed a strict regimen of asceticism, similar in many ways to practices undertaken by the Jains — extreme fasting, indifference to physical discomfort and living exposed to the elements. Makkhala Gosala was often described as having lived without clothing, as are some other senior Ajivika adherents. It is not clear if all Ajivikas lived as naked wanderers, or if this was a practice that was only undertaken by the extremely devout. They were also strongly against the caste system and, much like their Jain and Buddhist counterparts, were mainly non-theistic. Ajivika leaders were sometimes depicted as ending their lives voluntarily when they felt that their bodies or minds were beginning to decline — either by fasting to death, or, in the case of Purana Kassapa, by drowning.

Ajivikas and Theism

Although most Ajivikas were atheistic there were many important theistic figures as well. For example, Goshala Mahakali was a devotee of Shiva and Chanakya (a.k.a. Vishnu Gupt) was a devotee of Vishnu. Only Shiva and Vishnu however appear to the be gods of the Ajivikas. Bhattotpala, in 950 A.D. identified them with the "Ekandandins" (*One-staff men*) writes that they are devotees of Narayana (Vishnu), although Shilanka speaking of the Ekandandins in another connection identifies them as Shaivas. Scholar James Hastings identifies the name "Mankhaliputta" or "Mankhali" with the *bamboo staff*. Scholar Jitendra N. Banerjea compares them to the Pasupatas Shaivas.

It is believed by scholar Charpentier that the Ajivikas before Makkhali Goshala worshiped Shiva.

Chanakya wrote in his text *Chanakya Niti*, "Humbly bowing down before the almighty Lord Sri Vishnu, the Lord of the three worlds, I recite maxims of the science of political ethics (niti) selected from the various satras (scriptures)"

Scriptures

The Ajivika are believed to have possessed a collection of scripture, based on references made to such a collection in Jaina sources. Of these scriptures, the only portions possibly surviving are scattered selections of verse in Buddhist and Jain sources that seem to represent quotations from the Ajivika scriptures. The Ajivika scriptures are not known to have ever been committed to writing, and their contents are unknown outside of these fragmentary quotations and a few hints provided by lists of titles recorded in non-Ajivika sources.

One such list collected by a Jaina commentator identifies the eight primary collections of texts as being grouped as follows:

- Divyam (of the divine)
- Autpatam (of portents)
- Bhaumam (of the earth)
- Angam (of the body)
- Svaram (of sound)
- Lakanam (of characteristics)
- Vyanjanam (of indications).

An alternative listing substitutes Suvine (dreams) for Divyam, and indicates that all of these collections were used for purposes of fortune telling, an activity in which Ajivika mendicants are described as engaging in several sources.

Makkhali Gosala

Makkhali Gosala (Pali; BHS: Maskarin Gouala; Jain Prakrit sources: Gosala Mankhaliputta) was an ascetic teacher of ancient India, often identified as the founder of the Ajivika movement. He was a contemporary of Siddhartha Gautama, the founder of Buddhism, and of Mahavira, the last and 24th Tirthankara of Jainism.

Sources

Details about Gosala's life are sparse. All of the available information about Gosala and about the Ajivika movement generally comes from Buddhist and Jain sources. As Gosala's teachings appear to have been rivals of those of the Buddhist and Jain leaders of his day, this information is regarded by most scholars as being overtly influenced and coloured by sectarian hostilities.

Two primary sources describe Gosala's life and teaching: the Jain Bhagavati Sutra, and Buddhaghosa's commentary on the Buddhist Sammannaphala Sutta. The Bhagavati Sutra goes into detail about the career of Makkhali Gosala and his relationship with Mahavira; the Sammannaphala Sutra itself mentions Makkhali in passing as one of six leading teachers of philosophy of the Buddha's day, and Buddhaghosa's commentary provides additional details about his life and teaching.

Early Life

According to the *Bhagavati Sutra,* Gosala was born in the cowshed of a Brahmin named Gobahula, who was a Kosalan determinist, in the village of Saravana, a name meaning 'thicket of reeds'. This may indicate that Gosala was claimed by his followers to have been born or found in a patch of reeds-like a number of figures from Indian mythology-and the report was later distorted and forgotten, and the patch of reeds transformed into the name of a village. His mother's name is given as 'Bhadda', a name used in many Jaina sources to refer to the unknown mother of some mythological figure, while his father's name is given as Mankhali. Gosala's father was said to be employed as a *mankha*, a somewhat obscure class of mendicant or ascetic that seems to have been occupied with carrying an image of a god or goddess; and with singing religious songs.

The name 'Gosala' literally means 'cow shed', and both the Bhagavati Sutra and Buddhaghosa claim that Gosala was so named because he was born in a cow shed, his parents being unable to find more suitable lodgings in the village of Saravana. The Bhagavati Sutra reports that Gosala went on to follow his father's profession, becoming a *mankha*. Meanwhile, Buddhaghosa claims that Gosala was born into slavery, and became a naked ascetic after fleeing from his irate master, who managed to grab hold of Gosala's garment and disrobe him as he fled. While it is possible that the broad outlines of Gosala's birth story or early life are correct-that he was born into poverty in a cowshed-it may be equally likely that these versions of his early life were concocted by Buddhist and Jain partisans to bring a rival teacher into disrepute.

Makkhali Gosala and Mahavira

The Bhagavati Sutra states that Gosala became Mahavira's disciple three years after the start of Mahavira's asceticism, and travelled with him for the next six years. A commentary to the Jain Avasyaka Sutra provides details of these six years of association, many of them reflecting poorly on Gosala-another likely indication of sectarian bias. Several incidents in the narrative show Mahavira making predictions that then come true, despite Gosala's repeated attempts to foil them. These incidents were likely included in the narrative to provide motivation for Gosala's later belief in the inevitability of fate. Some of these incidents may in fact have been adapted from Ajivika sources but recast by Jaina chroniclers.

Another possible adaptation of an Ajivika story is found in Mahavira's explanation of the end of the association between himself and Gosala, recorded in the Bhagavati Sutra. On coming to a plant by the roadside, Gosala asked Mahavira what the fate of the plant and its seeds would be. Mahavira stated that the plant would grow to fruition, and the seed pods would grow into new plants. Determined to foil his master's prediction, Gosala returned to the plant at night and uprooted it. Later, a sudden rain shower caused the plant to revive and re-root itself. Upon approaching the plant again later, Gosala claimed to Mahavira that he would find his prophecy to have been foiled. Instead, it was found that the plant and its seeds had developed exactly as predicted by Mahavira.

Gosala was so impressed by the reanimation of the plant that he became convinced that all living things were capable of such reanimation. The terms used in the story of the Bhagavati Sutra for reanimation mimic a technical term for reanimation of the dead that is also found elsewhere in Ajivika doctrine. Mahavira disagreed with this thesis, and this seems to have been the cause of the separation of the two ascetics. Mahavira is, however, later depicted as having rescued Gosala from an attack by an enraged renunciant using magical powers acquired through the practice of austerities; this is claimed to motivate Gosala's pursuit of the same sort of magical powers.

Other Ideas

The Charvakas believed in complete materialism. They held that an individual's body is formed of matter and finally would end in matter. Therefore, the aim of human life should be to enjoy all the material pleasures of life.

Purana Kassapa preached the doctrine of Akriya or non-action. He was a Brahman teacher whose main doctrine was that action did not lead to either merit or demerit. According to him, even if a man killed all the creatures on earth he would no: incur any sin. Similarly, he would not e m any merit through a good deed or even by standing on the bank of Ganges. Similarly self-control, gifts and truthfulness would not e m him any credit. Ajita Kesakambalin preached that everything ended with death and there is no further life after death.-He did no believe in the fruits of good or bad acts or persons possessing higher or supernatural powers. According to this sect there is nothing wrong in enjoying the pleasures of the world, and there is no sin in killing. Pakudha

Kachchayna preached the doctrine of Asasvatavada. According to it, there are seven elements, which are immutable and do not in any way contribute to pleasure or pain. The body is ultimately dissolved into these seven elements.

Sanjaya Belatthaputta

Sanjaya Belammhaputta (literally, "Sanjaya of the Belattha clan") was an Indian ascetic teacher who lived around the 5th or 4th c. BCE, contemporaneous with Mahavira and the Buddha.

In the Pali literature, Sanjaya's teachings have been characterized as "evasive" or "agnostic." Hecker (1994) contextualizes it as "a kind of dialectical existentialism" in juxtaposition to the popular materialist views of the day (for instance, typified by the ascetic teacher Ajita Kesakambali.) For example, in the Samannaphala Sutta (DN 2), Sanjaya is recorded as saying:

'If you ask me if there exists another world [after death], if I thought that there exists another world, would I declare that to you? I don't think so. I don't think in that way. I don't think otherwise. I don't think not. I don't think not not. If you asked me if there isn't another world... both is and isn't... neither is nor isn't... if there are beings who transmigrate... if there aren't... both are and aren't... neither are nor aren't... if the Tathagata exists after death... doesn't... both... neither exists nor exists after death, would I declare that to you? I don't think so. I don't think in that way. I don't think otherwise. I don't think not. I don't think not not.'

In the Brahmajala Sutta (DN 1), Sanjaya's views are deemed to be *amaravikkhepavad*, "a theory of eel-wrigglers."

Sanjaya was the first teacher of the future Buddha's future two great disciples, Maha-Moggallana and Sariputta. These two future arahants ultimately left Sanjaya's tutelage as it did not address their unresolved desire to end ultimate suffering.

In Jaina literature, Sanjaya is identified as a Jaina sage (Skt., *muni*). It is believed that he was influenced by Jaina doctrine although Jaina philosophers were critical of Sanjaya.

Purana Kassapa

Purana Kassapa was an Indian ascetic teacher who lived around the 5th or 4th c. BCE, contemporaneous with Mahavira and the

Buddha. Purana taught a theory of "non-action" (Pali, Skt.: *akiriyavada*) whereby the body acts independent of the soul, merit or demerit. In the Pali Canon, Purana (along with the ascetic Makkhali Gosala) is identified as an *ahetuvadin*, "denier of a cause" (of merit).

As an example of Purana's beliefs, in the Samannaphala Sutta (DN 2) it is reported that Purana said:

"...[I]n acting or getting others to act, in mutilating or getting others to mutilate, in torturing or getting others to torture, in inflicting sorrow or in getting others to inflict sorrow, in tormenting or getting others to torment, in intimidating or getting others to intimidate, in taking life, taking what is not given, breaking into houses, plundering wealth, committing burglary, ambushing highways, committing adultery, speaking falsehood — one does no evil.

If with a razor-edged disk one were to turn all the living beings on this earth to a single heap of flesh, a single pile of flesh, there would be no evil from that cause, no coming of evil. Even if one were to go along the right bank of the Ganges, killing and getting others to kill, mutilating and getting others to mutilate, torturing and getting others to torture, there would be no evil from that cause, no coming of evil.

Even if one were to go along the left bank of the Ganges, giving and getting others to give, making sacrifices and getting others to make sacrifices, there would be no merit from that cause, no coming of merit. Through generosity, self-control, restraint, and truthful speech there is no merit from that cause, no coming of merit.'

The Anguttara Nikaya also reports that Purana claimed to be omniscient. The Dhammapada commentary claims that Purana committed suicide by drowning.

Ajita Kesakambali

Ajita Kesakambali(n), was an ancient Indian philosopher in the 6th century BC. He is considered to be the first known proponent of Indian materialism. He was probably a contemporary of Buddha and Mahavira. It has frequently been noted that the doctrines of the Lokayata school were considerably drawn from Ajita's teachings. Like those of Lokayatins, nothing survives of his teachings in script, except some scattered references made by his opponents for the sake of refutation.

Thus, due to the nature of these references, the basic framework of Ajita's philosophy has to be derived by filtering out obscure legends associated with him. For instance, according to a Buddhist legend, he wore a blanket of human hair (*Kesakambali* in Sanskrit means "with the hair blanket"), "which is described as being the most miserable garment.

It was cold in cold weather, and hot in the hot, foul smelling and uncouth". Renowned historian DD Kosambi, who elsewhere calls Ajita a proto-materialist, notes that he "preached a thoroughgoing materialist doctrine: good deeds and charity gained a man nothing in the end. His body dissolved into the primary elements at death, no matter what he had or had not done. Nothing remained. Good and evil, charity and compassion were all irrelevant to a man's fate." According to an early Buddhist source, Ajita Kesakambali argued that:

There is no such thing as alms or sacrifice or offering. There is neither fruit nor result of good or evil deeds...A human being is built up of four elements. When he dies the earthly in him returns and relaapses to the earth, the fluid to the water, the heat to the fire, the wind to the air, and his faculties pass into space. The four bearers, on the bier as a fifth, take his dead body away; till they reach the burning, ground men utter forth eulogies, but there his bones are bleached, and his offerings end in ashes. It is a doctrine of fools, this talk of gifts. It is an empty lie, mere idle talk, when men say there is profit herein. Fools and wise alike, on the dissolution of the body, are cut off, annihilated, and after death they are not.

According to Brahmajala Sutta, Ajita propounded *Ucchedavada* (the Doctrine of Annihilation after death) and *Tam-Jivam-tam-sariram-vada* (the doctrine of identity of the soul and body), which denied the separate existence of eternal soul.. The extent to which these doctrines, which were evidently inherited by Lokayata, were found contemptible and necessary to be refuted in the idealist, theist and religious literature of the time is a possible evidence of their popularity and, perhaps also, their philosophical sophistication.

Pakudha Kaccayana

Pakudha Kaccyana was an Indian Brahmin ascetic teacher who lived around the 5th or 4th c. BCE, contemporaneous with Mahavira and the Buddha.

According to Pakudha, there are seven eternal "elements": Earth, Water, Fire, Air, Joy, Sorrow and Life. Pakudha further asserted that these elements do not *interact* with one another.

The Samannaphala Sutta (DN 2) represents Pakudha's views as follows:

"'...[T]here are these seven substances — unmade, irreducible, uncreated, without a creator, barren, stable as a mountain-peak, standing firm like a pillar — that do not alter, do not change, do not interfere with one another, are incapable of causing one another pleasure, pain, or both pleasure and pain.

Which seven? The earth-substance, the liquid-substance, the fire-substance, the wind-substance, pleasure, pain, and the soul as the seventh. These are the seven substances — unmade, irreducible, uncreated, without a creator, barren, stable as a mountain-peak, standing firm like a pillar — that do not alter, do not change, do not interfere with one another, and are incapable of causing one another pleasure, pain, or both pleasure and pain.

"'And among them there is no killer nor one who causes killing, no hearer nor one who causes hearing, no cognizer nor one who causes cognition. When one cuts off [another person's] head, there is no one taking anyone's life. It is simply between the seven substances that the sword passes.'" In the Brahmajala Sutta (DN 1), theories such as Pakudha's are labelled as "non-action" and "eternalism" (*sassatavd*).

Carvaka

Carvaka is a system of Indian philosophy that assumes various forms of philosophical skepticism and religious indifference. It is also known as Lokyata. It is named after its founder, Crvka, author of the Brhaspatya-sktras. In overviews of Indian philosophy, Carvaka is classified as a "heterodox" (*nastika*) system, the same classification as is given to Buddhism and Jainism. It is characterized as a materialistic and atheistic school of thought. While this branch of Indian philosophy is not considered to be part of the six orthodox schools of Hindu philosophy, it is noteworthy as evidence of a materialistic movement within Hinduism.

Name and Origins

The name Lokyata can be traced to Kautilya's *Arthashastra,* which refers to three *nvikcikis* (logical philosophies), Yoga, Samkhya and Lokayata. Lokayata here still refers to logical debate (*disputatio,* "criticism") in general and not to a materialist doctrine in particular. Similarly, Saddaniti and Buddhaghosa in the 5th century connect the "Lokayatas" with the Vitandas (sophists).

Only from about the 6th century is the term restricted to the school of the *Lokytikas.* The name *Crvka* is first used in the 7th century by the philosopher Purandara, who refers to his fellow materialists as "the Carvakas", and it is used by the 8th century philosophers Kamala and Haribhadra. Shankara, on the other hand, always uses *Lokyata,* not *Crvka.* The etymological meaning of the word *Crvka* is 'a person who is clever in speech and is extremely fond of wrangling (debate)'.

E. W. Hopkins, in his *The Ethics of India* (1924) assumes that Carvaka philosophy is coeval with Buddhism, mentioning "the old Carvaka or materialist of the 6th century BC"; Rhys Davids assumes that *Lokayata* in ca. 500 BC came to mean "scepticism" in general without yet being organized as a philosophical school, and that the name of a villain of the Mahabharata, *Carvaka,* was attached to the position in order to disparage it. The earliest positive statement of skepticism is preserved from the epic period, in the *Ramayana.*

regard only that which is an object of perception, and cast behind your back whatever is beyond the reach of your senses (2.108)

The Carvaka school thus appears to have gradually grown out of generic skepticism in the Mauryan period, but its existence as an organized body cannot be ascertained for times predating the 6th century. The Barhaspatya sutras were likely also composed in Mauryan times, predating 150 BC, based on a reference in the Mahabhasya of Patanjali (7.3.45).

Loss of Original Works

Chatterjee and Datta explain that our understanding of Carvaka philosophy is fragmentary, based largely on criticism of the ideas by other schools, and that it is not a living tradition: "Though materialism in some form or other has always been present in India, and occasional references are found in the Vedas, the Buddhistic literature, the Epics, as well as in the later philosophical works we do not find any systematic work on materialism, nor any organised school of followers as the other philosophical schools possess. But almost every work of the other schools states, for refutation, the materialistic views. Our knowledge of Indian materialism is chiefly based on these."

Available evidence suggests that Carvaka philosophy was set out in the *Barhaspatya sutras*, probably in Mauryan times. Neither this text nor any other original text of the Carvaka school of philosophy has been preserved. Its principal works are known only from fragments cited by its Hindu and Buddhist opponents. Carvaka philosophy appears to have died out some time in the 15th century.

Countering the argument that the Carvakas opposed all that was good in the Vedic tradition, Dale Riepe says, "It may be said from the available material that Carvakas hold truth, integrity, consistency, and freedom of thought in the highest esteem."

Tattvopaplavasimha of Jayaraasi Bhatta

Jayar Bhamm, a was an 8th or 9th century Indian philosopher (dated to ca. 770-830 by Franco 1994), author of the *Tattvopaplavasimha* (*tattva-upa. plava-simha* "The Lion that Devours All Categories"/"The Upsetting of All Principles"). The manuscript of this work was discovered in 1926 and published in 1940 (eds. Sanghavi and Parikh).

The text is often regarded as belonging to the Carvaka school, which would make it the only extant authentic text from that school. Werner (1995) is sceptical of that attribution, while accepting that the text is an important secondary source for Carvaka.

The *Tattvopaplavasimha* examines epistemology, where he considers the pramana (sources of knowledge) accepted in establishing conclusions (perception, inference, and testimony), and proves that none of them are sufficient for establishing knowledge. Inference relies on inductive reasoning, which cannot be shown to be universal premises. Testimony requires the reliability of the witness, which must be established by another of the pramana.

Even direct perception cannot establish truth, because it requires that the perception not be erroneous or illusory, which also cannot be established. Therefore, Jayarasi argues that none of the sources of knowledge are valid, and nothing can be known for certain.

Jayarasi challenged the astika establishment's belief in supernatural beings by attacking their epistemology. Since none of the sources of knowledge are valid, how can anything be said about these beings?

Therefore, he argued for the reasonability of atheism, and that happiness in one's life is the most reasonable goal.

Jayarasi represented extreme skepticism of the Carvaka school, claiming no school of philosophy can claim its view of reality as knowledge, including the Carvaka itself; however, because Carvaka philosophy represents common sense, it could be used as a guide.

Beliefs

The Carvaka school of philosophy had a variety of atheistic and naturalistic beliefs.

No Life after Death

The Carvaka believed there was no afterlife, no life after death

Springing forth from these elements itself.

solid knowledge is destroyed.

when they are destroyed

after death no intelligence remains.

Naturalism

The Carvaka believed in a form of naturalism, that is that all things happen by nature, and come from nature (not from any deity or Supreme Being).

Fire is hot, water cold, refreshingly cool is the breeze of morning;

By whom came this variety?

They were born of their own nature.

Sensual Indulgence

Unlike many of the Indian philosophies of the time, The Carvaka believed there was nothing wrong with sensual indulgence, and that it was the only enjoyment to be pursued.

That the pleasure arising to man from contact with sensible objects, is to be relinquished because accompanied by pain— such is the reasoning of fools.

The kernels of the paddy, rich with finest white grains, What man, seeking his own true interest, would fling them away because of a covering of husk and dust? While life remains, let a man live happily, let him feed on butter though he runs in debt; When once the body becomes ashes, how can it ever return again?

Religion is Invented by Man

The Carvaka believed that religion was invented and made up by men. The three authors of the Vedas were buffoons, knaves, and demons.

All the well-known formulae of the pandits, jarphari, turphari, etc. and all the obscene rites for the queen commanded in Aswamedha, these were invented by buffoons, and so all the various kinds of presents to the priests, while the eating of flesh was similarly commanded by night-prowling demons.

Madhavacharya and Carvaka

Madhavacharya, the 13th & 14th-century Vedantic philosopher from South India starts his famous work *The Sarva-darsana-sangraha* with a chapter on the Carvaka system with the intention of refuting it. After invoking, in the Prologue of the book, the Hindu gods Shiva and Vishnu, ("by whom the earth and rest were produced"), Madhavacharya asks, in the first chapter:

...but how can we attribute to the Divine Being the giving of supreme felicity, when such a notion has been utterly abolished by Charvaka, the crest-gem of the atheistic school, the follower of the doctrine of Brihaspati? The efforts of Charvaka are indeed hard to be eradicated, for the majority of living beings hold by the current refrain:

While life is yours, live joyously;

None can escape Death's searching eye:

When once this frame of ours they burn,
How shall it e'er again return?

Quotations Attributed to Carvaka from Sarva-Darsana-Sangraha

The Agnihotra, the three Vedas, the ascetic's three staves, and smearing oneself with ashes –

Brihaspati says, these are but means of livelihood for those who have no manliness nor sense.

In this school there are four elements, earth, water, fire and air; and from these four elements alone is intelligence produced – just like the intoxicating power from kinwa &c, mixed together; since in "I am fat", "I am lean", these attributes abide in the same subject, and since fatness, &c, reside only in the body, it alone is the soul and no other, and such phrases as "my body" are only significant metaphorically.

If a beast slain in the Jyothishtoma rite will itself go to heaven, why then does not the sacrificer forthwith offer his own father?

If the Sraddha produces gratification to beings who are dead, then why not give food down below to those who are standing on the house-top?

If he who departs from the body goes to another world, how is it that he come not back again, restless for love of his kindred?

Hence it is only as a means of livelihood that Brahmans have established here all these ceremonies for the dead, – there is no other fruit anywhere.

The three authors of the Vedas were buffoons, knaves, and demons.

All the well-known formulae of the pandits, jarphari, turphari, etc. and all the obscene rites for the queen commanded in Aswamedha, these were invented by buffoons, and so all the various kinds of presents to the priests, while the eating of flesh was similarly commanded by night-prowling demons.

Those parts which survive indicate a strong anti-clerical bias, accusing Brahmins of fostering religious beliefs only so they could obtain a livelihood. The proper aim of a Charvakan or Charvaka, according to these sources, was to live a prosperous, happy, and productive life in this world.

Astika Schools, Buddhism, and Jainism Versus Carvaka

Carvakas cultivated a philosophy wherein theology and what they called "speculative metaphysics" were to be avoided. The Carvakas accepted direct perception as the surest method to prove the truth of anything. Though their opponents tried to caricature the Lokayatikas' arguments, the latter did not completely reject the method of inference. Debiprasad Chattopadhyaya quotes S. N. Dasgupta:

"Purandara (a Lokayata philosopher) admits the usefulness of inference in determining the nature of all worldly things where perceptual experience is available; but inference cannot be employed for establishing any dogma regarding the transcendental world, or life after death or the law of karma which cannot be available to ordinary perceptual experience."

While a Carvaka's thought is characterized by an insistence on joyful living on one hand and Jainism is known to emphasize penance on the other, Buddhism is said to stand for a "middle way", avoiding indulgence in sensual pleasures and penance alike. Temperance-the enjoyment of life's pleasures in a moderate manner, rather than total abstinence-was the Carvakas' primary *modus operandi.* In this respect, they much resemble the Epicureans of Greece.

The Carvakas did not deny the difference between the dead and the living and recognized both as realities. A person lives, the same person dies: that is a perceived, and hence the only provable, fact. In this regard, the Carvakas found themselves at odds with all the other religions of the time. Of the five fundamental elements, the *Panchamahaabhutas,* Prithvi (earth or solidity), *jal* (water or liquidity), *agni* (fire or fieriness or brightness), *vaayu* (wind or movement), and *aakaasha* (lit.space-aether or emptiness), the Carvakas recognised the validity of only the first four and thought that a combination of these four elements produced a certain vitality called life.

Rejection of the soul as separate from the body led the Carvakas to confine their thinking to this world only. This does not mean that they denied the cause-effect relationship. They accepted the "like causes like result" (*Karmavipaaka*) rule, restricted it to this life and this world and admitted exceptions to that rule.

Whereas most systems of Astika philosophy advocated a caste system, the Carvakas denounced the caste system, calling it artificial, unreal and hence unacceptable. "What is this senseless humbug about the castes and the high and low among them when the organs like the mouth, etc in the human body are the same?"

Abul Fazl on Lokayata

Ain-i-Akbari, written by Abul Fazl, the famous historian of Akbar's court, mentions a symposium of philosophers of all faiths held in 1578 at Akbar's insistence. Some Carvaka thinkers are said to have participated in this symposium.

Under the heading "Nastika," Abul Fazl has referred to the good work, judicious administration, and welfare schemes that were emphasized by the Carvaka lawmakers. Somadeva has also mentioned the Carvaka method of defeating the enemies of the nation. Contrary to popular opinion, these so-called "peasant religions(or opinions)"-the direct translation of the word "Lokayata"-never demanded that the practitioner give up happiness; all they said was that that the means of happiness is giving up that which contradicts Carvaka, who claimed that (material) pleasures suffice to give happiness to the (material) body.

Impact of the New Religious Movements

The rise and development *of* the new religious ideas had brought some significant changes in the contemporary social life. Following are some of the important changes.

i) The idea of social equality was popularised in this period. The Buddhists and Jains did not give any importance to the caste system. They accepted members of different castes in their religious order. This was a great threat to the age long domination of the Brahmanas in the society. Acceptance of women in the Buddhist order also had an important impact in the society because this gave women equal status with men in the society.

ii) Brahmanical texts had assigned an inferior position to traders. Sea voyages were also condemned. But as Buddhists and Jains did not give any importance to caste and did not look down upon sea voyages so the trading community was very much encouraged by these new religious ideas. Moreover the emphasis on 'karma' by this new religious ideas for future life also indirectly favoured the activities of the trading community.

iii) The new religions gave importance to languages like Prakrit, Pali and Ardha Magadhi. Buddhist and Jaina philosophies were discussed in these languages and later, canons were written in the local language. This paved the way for the development of vernacular literature. Thus the Jains, tor the first time, gave a literary shape to the mixed dialect, Ardha Magadhi, by writing their i.anons in this dialect.

8

Period of Mahajanpadas

Formation of States (Mahajanpadas)

In the later Vedic period the tribal organizations changed its identity and gradually shifted to the territorial identity. This territorial identity was gradually strengthened in the 600 BC with the rise of large states. The formation of bigger kingdoms made the king or the chief more powerful. Tribal authority became territorial and towns became the seat of the power. Instead of copper weapons the kings started using iron weapons and horse drawn chriots. Therefore from the 6th century BC the widespread use of iron in eastern UP and western Bihar led to the formation of large territorial states.

The new agricultural tools and implements enabled the peasants to produce a good amount of surplus which not only met the military needs but also the administrative requirements. The people became content with these material advantages and started settling permanently in their land. Towns came into existence as centres of industry and trade. People owed their allegiance to the territory to which they belonged and not to the Jana or the tribe to which they belonged.

These areas of settlements were now regarded as janapadas or states. In transition from tribe to monarchy, janapadas lost the essential democratic pattern of the tribe but retained the idea of government through an assembly representing the tribes. These states consisted of either a single tribe such as Shakyas, Koliyas, Mallas etc. or a confederacy of tribes such as Vrijis, Yadavas, Panchalas etc. Each janapada or state tried to dominate and subjugate other janapada to become mahajanapadas

Mahajanapadas, literally "Great realms," (from *Maha*, "great", and *Janapada* "foothold of a tribe", "country") were Ancient Indian kingdoms or countries. Ancient Buddhist texts like Anguttara Nikaya make frequent reference to sixteen great kingdoms and republics (*Solas Mahajanapadas*) which had evolved and flourished in the northern/north-western parts of the Indian subcontinent prior to the rise of Buddhism in India.

Overview

The end of the Vedic Age (1500 BC-600 BC) was followed by the rise of small kingdoms and republics in the northern parts of India and especially in the Gangetic plains of Bihar. These small states later paved the way for large empires. The entrenchment of the caste system, which divided the society be-tween the rulers and the ruled, also facilitated the rise of these states.

The earlier Aryan societies in India were tribal in context. Tribal chiefs, whose office was not hereditary, ruled these tribes. The criterion of selection was the number of cattle (cows in particular) a person owned. Clans often fought with each other over the control of herds of cattle. As the population of the tribes grew, their needs and aspirations also began to rise. In the course of time, the erstwhile small settlements grew into large settlements and managing large tracts of land became a problem. Soon these societies saw the rise of a ruling class, which belonged to the Kshatriya (warrior class) caste.

The strength of the early Aryan tribes was derived from the Jana (people) and not the Janapada (land). During the latter part of the Later Vedic Age (1000 BC-600 BC), all this changed with the rising influence of the Kshatriya (warrior class) caste and the Brahmin caste (priestly class), which took the reigns of the society in their hands and marginalized the other castes. The Kshatriyas and Brahmins worked in tandem and began to exploit the people belonging to the lower castes.

However, there was also a rift between the Kshatriyas on one hand and the Brahmins on the other hand. The rising influence of the Brahmins began to collide with the rule of the Kshatriyas, who formed the ruling class of each kingdom or republic. The Kshatriyas were alarmed by the rising power of the Brahmins, but they could not do much as they required the services of the Brahmins in all religious rituals and state occasions. The rise of

Buddhism and Jainism during this period was a natural outcome to counter the threat of the Brahmanical Hindu order, as the founders of these religions were themselves Kshatriyas or warriors.

The First Kingdoms

In the course of time, small settlements grew into small kingdoms and republics. A republic is that form of government where the power is held by the people or a group of elected people or elected chief. The concept of hereditary kingship is not present in republics. The main ruling class, which held the power of these republics, was the Kshatriya. Non-Kshatriyas were not a part of the ruling class in these republics. In the 6th century BC, 16 small territorial states or Mahajanapadas were formed. Of these 16 states, Magadh, Kosala, Vatsa, and Avanti were powerful. These various states constantly fought with each other for over a century to prove their supremacy

The political structure of the ancient Indians appears to have started with semi-nomadic tribal units called *Jana* (meaning subjects). Early Vedic texts attest several Janas or tribes of the Aryans, living in semi-nomadic tribal state, fighting among themselves and with other Non-Aryan tribes for cows, sheep and green pastures. These early Vedic Janas later coalesced into Janapadas of the Epic Age.

The term "Janapada" literally means the *foothold of a tribe*. The fact that *Janapada* is derived from *Jana* points to an early stage of land-taking by the Jana tribe for a settled way of life. This process of first settlement on land had completed its final stage prior to the times of Buddha and Panini. The Pre-Buddhist North-west region of Indian sub-continent was divided into several Janapadas demarcated from each other by boundaries. In Panini, *Janapada* stands for country and *Janapadin* for its citizenry. Each of these Janapadas was named after the Kshatriya tribe (or the Kshatriya Jana) who had settled there-in. The Buddhist and other texts only incidentally refer to sixteen great nations (*Solasa Mahajanapadas*) which were in existence before the time of Buddha. They do not give any connected history except in the case of Magadha.

The Buddhist Anguttara Nikaya, at several places, gives a list of sixteen great nations:

1. Kasi
2. Kosala

3. Anga
4. Magadha
5. Vajji (or Vriji)
6. Malla
7. Chedi
8. Vatsa (or Vamsa)
9. Kuru
10. Panchala
11. Machcha (or Matsya)
12. Surasena
13. Assaka
14. Avanti
15. Gandhara
16. Kamboja.

Another Buddhist text Digha Nikaya mentions only first twelve Mahajanapadas and omits the last four in the above list.

Chulla-Niddesa, another ancient text of the Buddhist canon, adds Kalinga to the list and substitutes Yona for Gandhara, thus listing the Kamboja and the Yona as the only Mahajanapadas from Uttarapatha.

The Jaina Bhagvati Sutra gives slightly different list of sixteen Mahajanapadas viz: Anga, Banga (Vanga), Magadha, Malaya, Malavaka, Accha, Vaccha, Kochcha (Kachcha?), Padha, Ladha (Lata), Bajji (Vajji), Moli (Malla), Kasi, Kosala, Avaha and Sambhuttara.

Obviously, the author of Bhagvati has a focus on the countries of Madhydesa and of far east and south only. He omits the nations from Uttarapatha like the Kamboja and Gandhara. The more extended horizon of the *Bhagvati* and the omission of all countries from Uttarapatha "clearly shows that the Bhagvati list is of later origin and therefore less reliable."

The main idea in the minds of those who drew up the Janapada lists was basically more tribal than geographical, since the lists include names of the people and not the countries. As the Buddhist and Jaina texts only casually refer to the Mahajanapadas with no details on history, the following few isolated facts, at best, are gleaned from them and other ancient texts about these ancient nations.

Kasi

The Kasis were Aryan people who had settled in the region around Varanasi (modern Banaras). The *capital* of Kasi was at Varanasi. The city was bounded by rivers Varuna and Asi on north and south which gave Varanasi its name. Before Buddha, Kasi was the most powerful of the sixteen Mahajanapadas. Several Jatakas bear witness to the superiority of its capital over other cities of India and speaks high of its prosperity and opulence. The Jatakas speak of long rivalry of Kasi with Kosala, Anga and Magadha. A struggle for supremacy went on among them for a time. King Brihadratha of Kasi had conquered Kosala but Kasi was later incorporated into Kosala by King Kansa during Buddha's time. The Kasis along with the Kosalas and Videhans find mention in Vedic texts and appear to have been a closely allied people. Matsya Purana and Alberuni read Kasi as *Kausika* and *Kaushaka* respectively. All other ancient texts read Kasi.

It was a holy place even during epic times. Lord Siva was worshipped here with great devotion. Sumitra the third wife of Kosala king Dasaratha was from Kasi. Lakshmana and Sathrughna were her twin sons. Lakshmana built the city of Lakshmanapura (Lucknow) not far from Kasi. Kuru king Vichitravirya's wives Ambika and Ambalika were from Kasi, who were abducted by the Kuru warrior Bhishma along with their elder sister Amba. Kuru king Dhritarashtra was son of Ambika and Pandu the son of Ambalika.

References in Mahabharata

Brides from Kasi

Janamejaya's Queen from Kasi

- (Mahabharata, Book 1, Chapter 44): Janamejaya, the eldest son of the Kuru King Parikshit, that bull amongst the Kurus, ruled the kingdom like his heroic great-grandfather (Yudhishthira). And the ministers of the youthful monarch, beholding that he could now keep his enemies in check, went to Suvarnavarman, the king of Kasi, and asked him his daughter Vapushtama for a bride. And the king of

Kasi, bestowed with ordained rites, his daughter Vapushtama to Janamejaya.

Bharata's Queen from Kasi

- (Mahabharata, Book 1, Chapter 95) : The son of Sakuntala and Puru King Dushyanta came to be called Bharata (the supported). And Bharata married Sunanda, the daughter of Sarvasena, the king of Kasi, and begat upon her the son named Bhumanyu.

Vichitravirya's Queens from Kasi

- (Mahabharata, Book 1, Chapter 95).

The Ssecond Pandava, Bhima's Wife from Kasi

- (Mahabharata, Book 1, Chapter 95) : Bhima obtaining for a wife Valandhara, the daughter of the king of Kasi, offered his own prowess as dower and begat upon her a son named Sarvaga.

Magadha King Vrihadratha's Queens from Kasi

- (Mahabharata, Book 2, Chapter 17) : There was a mighty king of the name of Vrihadratha (father of Jarasandha), the lord of the Magadhas. Proud in battle, he had three Akshauhinis of troops. That monarch married two twin daughters of the king of Kasi, both endued with the wealth of beauty.

Yuyutsu took a Bride from Kasi

- (Mahabharata, Book 7, Chapter 10) : That tiger among men, viz., Yuyutsu, whom many wrathful kings battling together for six months at Varanavata from desire of slaying him could not vanquish, and who in battle at Varanasi overthrew with a broad-headed arrow that mighty car-warrior, viz., the prince of Kasi, desirous of seizing (at a Swayamvara) a maiden for wife.

Yudhisthira's Rajasuya Sacrifice

- (Mahabharata, Book 2, Chapter 29) : For bathing Yudhishthira at the conclusion of the Rajasuya Sacrifice, many kings with the greatest alacrity, themselves brought there in a state of purity many excellent jars containing water. King Vahlika brought there a car decked with pure gold. And king Sudakshina himself yoked thereto four white horses of Kamboja breed....... king Ekalavya, with the shoes; the king of Avanti, with diverse kinds of water for the final bath; king Chekitana, with the quiver; the king of Kasi, with the bow; and Salya; with a sword.

Holy Places in Kasi

- (Mahabharata, Book 3, Chapter 83) : Having bathed in the tirtha of Kasiswara, one becometh freed from all diseases and is adored in the abode of Brahma. There, in that tirtha, is another called Matri. One that bathes in Matri tirtha hath a large progeny and obtaineth, great prosperity.

Kasi and Mahadeva (Siva)

- (Mahabharata, Book 13, Chapter 165) :....the spot sacred to Visweswara or Mahadeva, viz., Kasi...

Military Campaigns through Kasi

Pandu's Military Campaign

- (Mahabharata, Book 1, Chapter 113) : Pandu led his army against Kasi, Sumbha, and Pundra, and by the strength and prowess of his arms spread the fame of the Kurus.

Bhima's Military Ccampaign

- (Mahabharata, Book 2, Chapter 29) : Bhima of terrible prowess and long arms, vanquishing in battle the unretreating Suvahu the king of Kasi, brought him under complete sway.

Karna's Military Campaign

- (Mahabharata, Book 8, Chapter 8) : Karna had subjugated many invincible and mighty foes—the Gandharas, the Madrakas, the Matsyas, the Trigartas, the Tanganas, the Khasas, the Pancalas, the Videhas, the Kulindas, the Kasi-kosalas, the Suhmas, the Angas, the Nishadhas, the Pundras, the Kichakas, the Vatsas, the Kalingas, the Taralas, the Asmakas, and the Rishikas.

Vasudeva Krishna's Military Campaigns

- (Mahabharata, Book 7, Chapter 11) : The Angas, the Vangas, the Kalingas, the Magadhas, the Kasis, the Kosalas, the Vatsyas, the Çargyas, the Karushas and the Paundras,— all these Krishna vanquished in battle.

- (Mahabharata, Book 16, Chapter 6) : *Reflections of Arjuna seeing the destruction of Dwaraka.*

How is it that Krishna, the slayer of Madhu, who had put forth his prowess for achieving the destruction of Kesin and Kansa, and Chaidya swelling with pride, and Ekalavya, the son of the ruler of the Nishadas, and the Kalingas and the Magadhas, and the Gandharas and the king of Kasi, and many rulers assembled together in the midst of the desert, many heroes belonging to the East and the South, and many kings of the mountainous regionsalas, how could he remain indifferent to such a calamity?

Arjuna's Post-War Military Campaign

- (Mahabharata, Book 14, Chapter 83) : Turning round in course of his wanderings at will, the mighty steed came upon the beautiful city of the Chedis called after the oyster. Sarabha, the son of Sisupala, endued with great strength, first encountered Arjuna in battle and then worshipped him with due honours. Worshipped by him that best of steeds then proceeded to the realms of the Kasis, the Angas, the Kosalas, the Kiratas, and the Tanganas.

Kushan Attack on Kashi

During pre Gupta period, the Kushans attacked and occupied Varanasi and surrounding areas. The erstwhile ruler of Kashi sought the help of powerful Bhaarshiva rulers of Padmavati. Bhaarshiva warriors drove-off the Kushan tribals from the land of Ganges. After their victory, they took bath in Holy Ganges and performed Ashwamegha Yajnas (Horse sacrifices made by kshatriyas in ancient times). The ghat where the Bhaarshiva kshatriyas took bath in River Ganges and performed Ashwamegha yajnas is still known as Dashahwamegha ghat.

Kashi Kings

A Kasi King who was Devoted to Krishna

- (Mahabharata, Book 5, Chapter 28) : Vabhru, the king of Kasi, having obtained Krishna, that fructifier of wishes, as his brother, and upon whom Krishna showers all the blessings of life, hath attained the highest prosperity, so great is this Krishna.

Mention about a Kasi King who also Ruled Karusha Kingdom

- (Mahabharata, Book 3, Chapter 25) : *Sage Markandeya tells to Yudhisthira:-*The virtuous and truthful king of Kasi and Karusha was called a mad dog for having renounced his territories and riches.

Yayati as the Ruler of Kasi

Yayati, the father of Puru, who founded the Puru Dynasty, seems to be a ruler of Kasi Kingdom as per the following extracts from Mahabharata:-

- (Mahabharata, Book 5, Chapter 114) : There is a king born in the lunar race. That royal sage is known by the name of Yayati, and he is the son of Nahusha. Garuda and Galava (also known as Tarkshya) together went to king Yayati, who was then in his capital called Pratisthana.
- (Mahabharata, Book 5, Chapter 115) : That performer of thousand sacrifices, that foremost of givers, that liberal ruler of all the Kasis, the lord Yayati, in view particularly of the fact that those two came to him having passed over all the kings of the Solar race, said to Garuda and Gavala, who came to solicit wealth from him, thus:-Blessed is my life, my race and my province. There is one thing, however, O friend, I am not so rich now as thou thinkest.

Divodasa as the Ruler of Kasi

- (Mahabharata, Book 5, Chapter 117) : The ruler of the Kasis is an illustrious king known by the name of Divodasa. He is the son of Bhimasena, is endued with great prowess, and is a mighty sovereign..... And unto king Divodasa, that sporting with and taking delight in her, Madhavi bore a son named Pratardana.

Pratardana as the Ruler of Kasi

- (Mahabharata, Book 12, Chapter 233) : Pratardana, the ruler of Kasi, having given away his very eyes to a Brahmana, obtained great fame both here and hereafter.

Sivi (Vrishadharbha), the King of Kasi

- (Mahabharata, Book 13, Chapter 32) : King Vrishadarbha to a pegion who sought protection from a chasing hawk:- I shall for thy sake, give up today the very kingdom of the Kasi.

The royal sage Sivi alias Vrishadharbha, that ruler of the kingdom of Kasi, became celebrated over the three worlds for his deeds of righteousness.

Kasi in the List of Provinces in Bharata Varsha (Ancient India)

- (Mahabharata, Book 6, Chapter 9) : *The names of the provinces as Sanjaya mentions them.*

They are the Kuru-Panchalas, the Salwas, the Madreyas, the Jangalas, the Surasena, the Kalingas, the Vodhas, the Malas, the Matsyas, the Sauvalyas, the Kuntalas, the Kasi-kosalas, the Chedis, the Karushas, the Bhojas,..............

Abhimanyu's Marriage with Virata Princess Uttara

- (Mahabharata, Book 4, Chapter 72) : After the expiry of the 13th year, the five Pandavas took up their abode in one of King Virata's towns called Upaplavya. Arjuna, brought over Abhimanyu and Janardana, and also many people of the Dasarha race from the Anarta country. And the king of Kasi, and also Saivya, being very friendly to Yudhishthira, arrived there, each accompanied by an Akshauhini of troops. And the mighty Drupada, also with the heroic sons of Draupadi and the unvanquished Sikhandin, the invincible Dhrishtadyumna came there with another Akshauhini of troops.

Kasi, the Principal Ally of the Pandavas

- (Mahabharata, Book 5, Chapter 72) : Having the Kasis, the Panchalas, the Chedis, and the Matsyas, for my allies and with thee, O Krishna, for my protector, I prayed for only five villages, viz. Avishthala, Vrikasthala, Makandi, Varanavata, with any other, as the fifth; Grant us, we said, five villages or towns, where we five may dwell in union, for we do not desire the destruction of the Bharatas. The wicked-minded son of Dhritarashtra (Duryodhana, however, doth not agree to even that.

Kasi in Kurukshetra War

Careful examination of Mahabharata, suggests that the Kasis took part in the war, siding with the Pandavas. However there seems to be two exceptions, which suggest that at least a portion of the Kasis, or another Kasi king, sided with Duryodhana.

On Duryodhana's Side

The Son of the King of Kasi

- (Mahabharata, Book 6, Chapter 51) : And then king Duryodhana advanced cheerfully against the Pandava host. And Bhurisravas, and Sala, and Salya,..... and Kritavarman of Satwata's race, with a very large division of the troops, were, stationed at the rear of the army. And behind them were the rulers of many provinces, and Ketumat, and Vasudana, and the powerful son of the king of Kasi.
- (Mahabharata, Book 9, Chapter 2)

Dhritarashtra's Reflections

Bhagadatta and Kripa and Shalya....... and Vrihadvala and the ruler of the Kasi and Shakuni the son of Subala and many thousands of Mlecchas and Sakas and Yavanas, and Sudakshina the ruler of the Kambojas and the king of the Trigartas......and numerous other kings, O best of monarchs, have taken up arms for Duryodhana's sake

On Pandava's Side

March from Upaplavya to Kurukshetra

- (Mahabharata, Book 5, Chapter 152) : The princes of Kekaya, and Dhrishtaketu, and the son of the king of the Kasis, and Srenimat, and Vasudana, and the invincible Sikhandin, all hale and hearty, cased in armour and armed with weapons and decked with ornaments, marched behind Yudhishthira, towards Kurukshetra.

March Further into the War-front

- (Mahabharata, Book 5, Chapter 199) : Like Duryodhana, king Yudhishthira alsoordered out, O Bharata, his heroic warriors headed by Dhrishtadyumna. Indeed, he ordered that commander of force, that leader of the Chedis, the

Kasis, and the Karushas, viz., Dhrishtaketu, as also Virata, and Drupada, and Yuyudhana, and Sikhandin, and those two mighty bowmen, those two princes of Panchala, viz., Yudhamanyu and Uttamaujas, to set out.

Day 1: The Kings in the War-front

- (Mahabharata, Book 6, Chapter 25) : They are Yuyudhana, and Virata, and that mighty car-warrior Drupada, and Dhrishtaketu, and Chekitana, and the ruler of Kasi endued with great energy; and Purujit, and Kuntibhoja, and Saivya that bull among men; and Yudhamanyu of great prowess, and Uttamaujas of great energy......

Other References

- (Mahabharata, Book 6, Chapter 47) The palmyra standard of Bhishma was seen to glide continually through the Chedis, the Kasis, the Karushas, and the Panchalas.
- (Mahabharata, Book 6, Chapter 50) The rear (of the Krauncharuma-a military formation-of the Pandavas on Day 2) was protected by Virata aided by the Kekayas, and the ruler of Kasi and the king of the Chedis, with 30,000 cars.
- (Mahabharata, Book 7, Chapter 8) Bhimasena and Dhananjaya and the grandson of Sini, and the sons of Drupada, and the ruler of Kasi, viz., the son of Saivya, and Sivi himself, cheerfully and with loud roars covered Drona with their arrows.
- (Mahabharata, Book 8, Chapter 6) Abhibhu the ruler of Kasis, at the head of many of his followers, hath been obliged by Vasudana's son to lay down his life in battle.
- (Mahabharata, Book 8, Chapter 47) Kripa and Kritavarma, and Shakuni the son of Subala, those heroes difficult of defeat in battle, accompanied by troops that were all cheerful, themselves filled with rage, and capable of smiting down thick ranks of cars, fought with the Koshalas, the Kasis, the Matsyas, the Karusas, the Kaikayas, and the Surasenas.
- (Mahabharata, Book 8, Chapter 49) Satyaki and Chekitana and Yuyutsu and Shikhandi and the sons of Draupadi and the Prabhadrakas, and the twins (Nakula and Sahadeva)

and Bhimasena and Shishupala and the Karushas, Matsyas, the Suras, the Kaikayas, the Kasis and the Kosalas, all these brave heroes, endued with great activity, assailed Vasusena (Karna).

A Hunter in the Kingdom of Kasi

- (Mahabharata, Book 13, Chapter 5) : In the territories of the king of Kasi, a fowler, having poisoned arrows with him went out of his village on a hunting excursion in search of antelopes.

Rivalry of Kasi Kings and the Haihayas

- (Mahabharata, Book 13, Chapter 30) : In Kasi also, there was a king who was the grandfather of Divodasa, known by the name of Haryyaswa. The sons of Haihaya king Vitahavya, invaded the kingdom of Kasi and advancing to the country that lies between the rivers Ganga and Yamuna, fought a battle with king Haryyaswa and also slew him They then went back to their own city in the country of the Vatsas (*It seems the Haihayas migrated from Vatsa Kingdom on the banks of Ganga to the Heheya Kingdom on the banks of Narmada, in the later periods*). Meanwhile Haryyaswa's son Sudeva was installed on the throne of Kasi. As he ruled his kingdom for sometime, the hundred sons of Vitahavya once more invaded his dominions and defeated him in battle. After that Divodasa, the son of Sudeva, became installed on the throne of Kasi as its ruler. Realising the prowess the sons of Vitahavya, king Divodasa rebuilt and fortified the city of Baranasi at the command of Indra. The territories of Divodasa were full of Brahmanas and Kshatriyas, and abounded with Vaisyas and Sudras. And they teemed with articles and provisions of every kind, and were adorned with shops and marts swelling with prosperity. Those territories stretched northwards from the banks of Ganga to the southern banks of Gomati, and resembled a second Amaravati (the city of Indra). The Haihayas once again, O Bharata, attacked. The mighty king Divodasa gave them battle. King Divodasa fought the enemy for a thousand days at the end of which, having lost a number of followers and animals, he became exceedingly distressed. King Divodasa having lost his army and seeing his treasury exhausted, left his capital and fled away.

Divodasa sought protection of his priest Bharadwaja, the son of Vrihaspati. Unto Divodasa was born a son named Pratarddana. Divodasa then installed his son Pratarddana as Yuvaraja. Pratarddana speedily crossed the Ganga and proceeded against the city of the Vitahavyas. He killed all the sons of Vitahavya. Then Vitahavya sought protection of his priest Bhrigu. In order to save Vitahavya from Pratarddana, Bhrigu converted Vitahavya into a Brahmana.

Kosala

Kosala was an ancient Indian region, corresponding roughly in area with the region of Oudh in the present day Uttar Pradesh state. According to the Buddhist text *Anguttara Nikaya* and the Jaina text, the *Bhagavati Sutra,* Kosala was one of the *Solasa* (sixteen) Mahajanapadas (powerful realms) in 6th century BCE and its cultural and political strength earned it the status of great power. However, it was later weakened by a series of wars with the neighboring kingdom of Magadha and, in the 4th century BCE, was finally absorbed by it. The Kosala region had three major cities, Ayodhya, Saket and Shravasti and a number of minor towns as Setavya, Ukattha, Dandakappa, Nalakapana and Pankadha. According to the Puranas, Ayodhya was the capital of Kosala during the reign of Ikshvaku and his descendants. Shravasti was the capital of Kosala between 6th century BCE and 6th century CE.

The Kosala Kingdom

In the Ramayana, Mahabharata and the Puranas the ruling family of the Kosala kingdom was descended from king Ikshvaku. The Puranas give lists of kings of the Aikhsvaka dynasty (the dynasty founded by Ikshvaku) from Ikshvaku to Presenajit (Pasenadi). A Buddhist text, the *Majjhima Nikaya* mentions Buddha as a Kosalan and Mahavira, the 24th Tirthankara of Jainism taught in Kosala. In the time of king Mahakosala, Kashi was an integral part of the kingdom.. Mahakosala was succeeded by his son Pasenadi (Prasenajit). He was a follower of Buddha. During his absence from the capital, his minister Digha Charayana raised his son Vidudabha to the throne.. Kosala kingdom was absorbed not much later into Magadha kingdom.

Kosala Proper or Uttara Kosala is the kingdom of the celebrated personality of Treta Yuga, Raghava Rama. Ayodhya was its capital, presently in Faizabad district, Uttar Pradesh. Rama's sons Lava and Kusa inherited parts of this kingdom. Lava ruled from the city called Sravasti and Kusa from the city called Kusavati. A colony of Kosala kings existed in Madhya Pradesh. It was called Dakshina Kosala. Rama's mother Kausalya was from this kingdom. King Rama extended his influence up to the island-kingdom of Lanka situated in the southern ocean. He had friendly relations with the southern kingdom of *forest dwellers* (Vanaras) called Kishkindha.

Rama's brother Bharata, colonized the Gandhara kingdom and founded the city of Takshasila there. Gandhara lies close to Kekeya Kingdom, the native kingdom of Bharata's mother, Kaikeyi. Rama's second brother Lakshmana founded the city of Lakshmanapura near river Ganga which is now known as Lucknow. He colonized the Vanga kingdom and founded the city of Chandrakanta there. Rama's youngest brother Satrughna destroyed the forest called Madhu and founded the city of Mathura which later became the capital of the Surasena Kingdom.

Nishadha king Nala's friend *Rituparna* was a ruler of Kosala. *Brihadbala* another ruler of Kosala during Dwapara Yuga, took part in Mahabharata war and was killed by Abhimanyu, the son of Arjuna.

Kosala Kingdom Through the Ages

Era of Treta Yuga

The Indian epic Ramayana is the window to this era.

Kosala Proper and Dakshina(Southern) Kosala

During the period of the forefathers of Raghava Rama, there was only one Kosala kingdom. It had its capital at Ayodhya, identified as the Ayodhya town near Faizabad in Uttar Pradesh state of India. During the reign of Dasaratha, the father of Rama, Dakshina Kosala came into prominence. It was situated in the Orissa state of India. Dasaratha married his eldest wife Kausalya from this kingdom.

Kosala Proper Splits into Two

Raghava Rama's son's Lava and Kusa, inherited each half of

the Kosala kingdom, with Ayodhya as its capital. Thus, this Kosala split into two parts; one ruled by Lava, with capital at Sravasti, to the north of Ayodhya and the other by Kusa at Kusavati, believed to be towards the east of Ayodhya.

Era of Dwapara Yuga

The Indian epic Mahabharata is the window to this era.

During the time of Kurukshetra War, and the reign of Pandavas and Kauravas, we find mention of numerous kingdoms with the name, Kosala (as per the references in Mahabharata).

Kingdoms that Sprang from Kosala Proper

Raghava Rama's Kosala (Kosala Proper) was already split into two, owing to his two sons attaining kingship after his reign. During the era of Kurukshetra War it was split into five kingdoms.

Eastern Kosala

This was, probably the kingdom ruled by Kusa, with Kusavati as its capital. They were described as fleeing to the southern country of Kuntis due to Magadha king Jarasandha. The route taken by Bhima, Arjuna and Krishna from Kuru Kingdom to Magadha Kingdom was through this Eastern Kosala.

Northern Kosala

This was, probably the kingdom ruled by Lava with Sravasti as its capital. This kingdom was defeated by the Pandava general Bhima, in his military campaign to the east.

Kosala Kingdom of Vrihadvala to the South of Ayodhya

Vriahadvala was a Kosala king mentioned as a general under Duryodhana, in the Kurukshetra War. (MBh. 5.277, 5.198).This kingdom was defeated by the Pandava general Bhima, in his military campaign to the east. (MBh 2.29). It seems that this Kosala had its power extended to the neighbouring kingdom of Kasi to the south of it, because Vrihadvala sometimes commanded the troops from Kasi also in Kurukshetra War. This probably was the reason to consider Kasi-Kosala as a single kingdom. For a period of time in the past, Kasi would have been a vassal state of Kosala kingdom. The grandmothers of Kauravas and Pandavas were called sometimes as princesses of Kasi and some times as princesses of Kosala, attesting to this fact.

Kosala with Ayodhya as its capital or Central Kosala

This was the original Kosala ruled by king Raghava Rama. This was ruled by Dirghayaghna, during this era. This kingdom was defeated by the Pandava general Bhima, in his military campaign to the east.

Kingdoms that Sprang from the Sothern Kosala

The native kingdom of Raghava Rama's mother Kausalya, considered as Dakshina Kosala Kingdom split *at least* into two during the era of Kurukshetra War. This became evident if we follow the passage in Mahabharata, describing the military campaign of the Pandava general Sahadeva, who led his troops to the southern direction.

Western Kosala in Central India

This kingdom was close to the Vidarbha Kingdom ruled by Bhishmaka, probably to the east of it. Sahadeva defeated this kingdom first and moved to the Eastern Kosala.

Eastern Kosala in Central India

After defeating the other Kosala kingdom Sahadeva defeated numerous kings in the Eastern Kosala, indicating that there were many kingdoms, and not one, however collectively known as Eastern Kosalas.

References in Mahabharata

The Mothers of Dhritarashtra and Pandu

- Mahabharata, Book 1, Chapter 114 : *The mothers of Dhritarashtra and Pandu, viz Ambika and Ambalika, where described to be Kosala princesses. They were some times described as princesses from Kasi Kingdom, Kasi and Kosala being a single kingdom (often denoted as Kasi-Kosalas) during the time of Mahabharata.*

Then Satyavati and Bhishma and the Kosala princesses were all gratified with the presents Pandu made out of the acquisitions of his prowess. And Ambalika in particular, upon embracing her son of incomparable prowess, became very glad.

The Self-Choice Event of Panchali

- Mahabharata, Book 1, Chapter 188 : *Kosala king was present in this event*..........the highly intelligent Vatsaraja, the king of Kosala, Sisupala and the powerful Jarasandha, these and many other great kings—all Kshatriyas celebrated throughout the world—have come, O blessed one (Panchali), for thee.

The Impact of Magadha King on Kosala

- Mahabharata, Book 2, Chapter 14 : The eighteen tribes of the Bhojas, from fear of (Magadha King) Jarasandha, have all fled towards the west; so also have the Surasenas, the Bhadrakas, the Vodhas, the Salwas, the Patachchavas, the Susthalas, the Mukuttas, and the Kulindas, along with the Kuntis. And the king of the Salwayana tribe with their brethren and followers; and the southern Panchalas and the eastern Kosalas have all fled to the country of the Kuntis. So also the Matsyas and the Sannyastapadas, overcome with fear, leaving their dominions in the north, have fled into the southern country. And so all the Panchalas, alarmed at the power of Jarasandha, have left their own kingdom and fled in all directions.

The Trip from Kuru Kingdom to Magadha Kingdom

- Mahabharata, Book 2, Chapter 21 : *The following was a route taken by Krishna, Arjuna and Bhima to reach Magadha Kingdom. It passes through the Eastern Kosala Kingdom.*

Having set out from the country of the Kurus, they passed through Kuru-jangala and arrived at the charming lake of lotuses. Passing over the hills of Kalakuta, they then went on crossing the Gandaki, the Sadanira (Karatoya), and the Sarkaravarta and the other rivers taking their rise in the same mountains. They then crossed the delightful Sarayu and saw the country of Eastern Kosala. Passing over that country they went to Mithila and then crossing the Mala and Charamanvati, the three heroes crossed the Ganges and the Sone and went on towards the east. At last those heroes of unfaded glory arrived at Magadha in the heart of (the country of) Kushamva. Reaching then the hills of Goratha, they saw the city of Magadha.

Bhima's Military Campaign

- Mahabharata, Book 2, Chapter 29 : Bhima then vanquished king Srenimat of the country of Kumara, and then

Vrihadvala, the king of Kosala. Then the foremost of the sons of Pandu, by performing feats excelling in fierceness, defeated the virtuous and mighty king Dirghayaghna of Ayodhya. And the exalted one then subjugated the country of Gopalakaksha and the northern Kosalas and also the king of Mallas.

Sahadeva's Military Campaign

- Mahabharata, Book 2, Chapter 30 : Sahadeva, vanquishing the invincible Bhismaka, then defeated in battle the king of Kosala and the ruler of the territories lying on the banks of the Venwa, as also the Kantarakas and the kings of the eastern Kosalas.

Conversation of Nala and Damayanti

- Mahabharata, Book 3, Chapter 61 : These many roads lead to the southern country, passing by (the city of) Avanti and the Rikshavat mountains. This is that mighty mountain called Vindhya; yon, the river Payasvini running sea-wards, and yonder are the asylums of the ascetics, furnished with various fruit and roots. This road leadeth to the country of the Vidarbhas—and that, to the country of the Kosalas. Beyond these roads to the south is the southern country.

Rituparna, King of Kosala Visiting Vidharbha Kingdom

- Mahabharata, Book 3, Chapter 73 : The ruler of the Vidarbhas, approaching Rituparna, said, 'Welcome! What is the occasion of this thy visit?' And king Bhima asked this without knowing that Rituparna had come to obtain the hand of his daughter. And king Rituparna, saw that there were no other kings or princes. Nor did he hear any talk relating to the Swayamvara, nor saw any concourse of Brahmanas. And at this, the king of Kosala reflected a while and at length said, 'I have come here to pay my respects to thee.' And the king Bhima was struck with astonishment, and reflected upon the (probable) cause of Rituparna's coming, having passed over a hundred yojanas.

Sacred Places in Kosala Kingdom

- Mahabharata, Book 3, Chapter 85 : Sojourning next to the tirtha called Rishabha in Kosala and fasting there for three nights one earneth the merit of the Vajapeya sacrifice, and of the gift of a thousand kine, and also delivereth his race. Arriving at 'Kosala, a man should bathe in the tirtha named Kala.

Karna's Military Campaign

- Mahabharata, Book 3, Chapter 252 : Having conquered the eastern quarter Karna then presented himself before Batsa-bhumi. And having taken Batsa-bhumi, he reduced Kevali, and Mrittikavati, and Mohana and Patrana, and Tripura, and Kosala,—and compelled all these to pay tribute.

Ramayana inside Mahabharata

- Mahabharata, Book 3, Chapter 277 : Behold my plight! The loss of thy kingdom, and then the death of our father, and then the abduction of Sita, and finally this disaster that hath overwhelmed me! Alas, I shall not behold thee return with the princess of Videha to Kosala and seated on thy ancestral throne as the ruler of the entire Earth! They only that are fortunate will behold thy face, like unto the moon emerged from the clouds, after thy coronation bath in water sanctified with Kusa grass and fried paddy and black peas!' And the intelligent Lakshmana uttered those and other lamentations in the same strain.
- Mahabharata, Book 3, Chapter 282 : That descendant of Raghu, who ruleth at Kosala and whose renown hath spread over the whole world, sayeth unto thee these words suited to the occasion. Accept thou that message and act according to it.

Vrihadvala the Ruler of Kosala

- Mahabharata, Book 5, Chapter 277 : *Bhishma rates the battle skills of every king who were to take part in the Kurukshetra War.* Endued with great impetus and prowess, king Vrihadvala, the ruler of the Kosalas, is, in my judgment, equal to one Ratha (a grade of battle-skill).

Kosala King Supported Duryodhana in the War

- Mahabharata, Book 5, Chapter 198 : *King Vrihadvala of Kosala, supported Duryodhana in the Kurukshetra War.* Then came Kritavarman at the head of his troops, and that mighty car-warrior, viz., the ruler of the Trigartas, and the king Duryodhana surrounded by his brothers, and Sala, and Bhurisravas, and Salya, and Vrihadratha, the ruler of the Kosalas.

- Mahabharata, Book 6, Chapter 16 : And Suvala's son Sakuni, and Salya, Jayadratha and the two princes of Avanti named Vinda and Anuvinda, and the Kekeya brothers, and Sudakshina the ruler of the Kamvojas and Srutayudha the ruler of the Kalingas, and king Jayatsena, and Vrihadvala the ruler of the Kosalas, and Kritavarman of Satwata's race,—these ten tigers among men, stood each at the head of an Akshauhini of troops. These and many other kings and princes, mighty car-warriors conversant with policy, obedient to the commands of Duryodhana, all cased in mail, were seen stationed in their respective divisions.
- Mahabharata, Book 6, Chapter 45 : The mighty bowman Abhimanyu battled with Vrihadvala. Soon, however, in that encounter, O king, the ruler of Kosala cut off the standard and overthrew the charioteer of Subhadra's son. The son of Subhadra then upon the overthrow of his charioteer, was filled with wrath and pierced Vrihadvala

Abhimanyu Slays Vrihadvala the King of Kosala

- Mahabharata, Book 7, Chapter 45 : The ruler of the Kosala struck Abhimanyu, in the chest with a barbed arrow. Abhimanyu, however, quickly felled on the earth his antagonist's steeds and standard and bow and charioteer. The ruler of the Kosalas, then, thus deprived of his car, took up a sword and wished to sever from Abhimanyu's trunk his beautiful head, decked with ear-rings. Abhimanyu then pierced king Vrihadvala, the ruler of the Kosalas, in the chest, with a strong arrow. The latter then, with riven heart, fell down. Beholding this, ten thousand illustrious kings broke and fled. Those kings, armed with swords and bows, fled away, uttering words inimical (to king Duryodhana's Interest). Having slain Vrihadvala thus, the son of Subhadra careered it battle.

Connection with Saraswati Civilization

- Mahabharata, Book 9, Chapter 38 : It was on that sacred region, the northern part of Kosala, that the sacrifice of high-souled Auddalaka was performed. Before Auddalaka began his sacrifice, he had thought of the Sarasvati. That foremost of rivers came to that region for the sake of those Rishis. Worshipped by all those Munis clad in barks and deer-skins she became known by the name of Manorama, as those Rishis mentally called her.

Arjuna's Post War Military Campaign

- Mahabharata, Book 14, Chapter 82 : The sacrificial horse then, equipt with beautiful manes, proceeded at his will along the sea-coast, repairing to the countries of the Bangas, the Pundras, and the Kosalas. In those realms Dhananjaya (Arjuna), with his bow Gandiva, vanquished innumerable Mlechecha armies one after another
- Mahabharata, Book 14, Chapter 83 : That best of steeds then proceeded to the realms of the Kasis, the Angas, the Kosalas, the Kiratas, and the Tanganas.

Other References in Mahabharata

- Mahabharata, Book 12, Chapter 18 : *Mention of a Janaka king of Videha, with a wife from Kosala*
- Mahabharata, Book 12, Chapter 67 : There was a king of Kosala possessed of great intelligence, named Vasumanas.
- Mahabharata, Book 12, Chapter 81 : It hath been heard by us that once on a time the sage Kalakavrikshiya came to Kshemadarsin who had ascended the throne of the kingdom of Kosala.
- Mahabharata, Book 13, Chapter 6 : Saudasa, the king of Kosala, though dignified by the performance of Ashwamedha and other sacrifices, obtained the status of a man-eating Rakshasa, through the curse of a great Rishi.

Kosala under Mauryan Rule

It may be presumed that during the Mauryan reign, Kosala was administratively under the viceroy at Kaushambi. The Sohgaura copper plate inscription, probably issued during the reign of Chandragupta Maurya deals with a famine in Shravasti and the relief measures to be adopted by the officials. The Yuga Purana section of the Garga Samhita mentions about the *Yavana* (Indo-Greek) invasion and subsequent occupation of Saket during the reign of the last Maurya ruler Brihadratha.

Kosala in Post-Mauryan Period

The names of a number of rulers of Kosala of the post-Maurya period are known from the square copper coins issued by them. The rulers are: Muladeva, Vayudeva, Vishakhadeva, Dhanadeva, Naradatta, Jyesthadatta and Shivadatta. There is no way to know whether king Muladeva of the coins is identifiable with Muladeva, murderer of the Sunga ruler Vasumitra or not (though a historian, Jagannath has tried to do so). King Dhanadeva of the coins is identified with king Dhanadeva (1st century BCE) of Ayodhya inscription. In this Sanskrit inscription, King Kaushikiputra Dhanadeva mentions about setting a *ketana* (flag-staff) in memory of his father, Phalgudeva. In this inscription he claimed himself as the sixth in descent from Pusyamitra Sunga. Dhanadeva issued both cast and die-struck coins and both the types have a bull on obverse.

Anga

The earliest reference to Angas occurs in the Atharava Veda (V.22.14) where they find mention along with the *Magadhas, Gandharis* and the *Mujavatas*, all apparently as a despised people.

The Jain *Prajnapana* ranks the *Angas* and the *Vangas* in the first group of Aryan peoples.

According to Buddhist texts like the Anguttara Nikaya, Anga was one of the sixteen great nations (solas Mahajanapadas) which had flourished on the eastern Indian subcontinent in the 6th century BC.

Anga also finds mention in the Jain *Bhagvati-Sutra*'s list of ancient Janapadas.

Location

The Puranic texts like the *Garuda Purana, Vishnu-Dharmottara,* and the *Markendeya Purana* divide the ancient Janpada horizon into nine divisions and place the Janapadas of the Angas, Kalingas, Vangas, Pundras or Pundra Kingdom (now some part of Eastern

Bihar i.e. Purnea, West Bengal and Bangladesh), Vidarbhas, and Vindhya-vasis in the *Purva-Dakshina* division.

Based on Mahabharata evidence, the kingdom of the Angas roughly corresponded to the region of Bhagalpur, Banka and Monghyr in Bihar and parts of Bengal; later extended to include most of Bengal. The River Champa (modern Chandan) formed the boundaries between the Magadha in the west and Anga in the east. Anga was bounded by river Koshi on the north. According to the Mahabharata, Duryodhana had named Karna the King of Anga.

Sabhaparava of Mahabharata (II.44.9) mentions Anga and Vanga as forming one country. The *Katha-Sarit-Sagara* also attests that Vitankapur, a city of Anga was situated on the shores of the sea. Thus the boundaries of Anga may have extended to the sea in the east.

The capital of Anga was Champa. According to Mahabharata and Harivamsa, Champa was formerly known as Malini. Champa was located on the right bank of river Ganga near its junction with river Champa. It was a very flourishing city and is referred to as one of six principal cities of ancient India (Digha Nikaya). In the Jataka stories, the city of Champa is also referred to as *Kala-Champa*. *Maha-Janaka Jataka* states that the city was located about sixty yojanas (*one yojana* = 16.4 km) from Mithila. The relics of actual site of ancient Champa are stated to still exist near Bhagalpur in Bihar in the names of two villages called *Champanagara* and *Champapura*.

Champa was noted for its wealth and commerce. It was also a great center of trade and commerce and its merchants regularly sailed to distant Suvarnabhumi for trading purposes. The ancient name of region and kingdom of Champa of central Vietnam (Lin-yi in Chinese records) apparently has its origin in this east Indian Champa.

Other important cities of Anga are said to be *Assapura* and *Bhadrika*.

Origin of Name

Mahabharata (I.104.53-54) and Puranic literature (Matsya Purana: 48.19) attest that the name *Anga* had originated *eponymously* from the name of *Prince Anga*, the founder of the kingdom. Matsya Purana describes the father of this eponymous hero as the chief among the demons (*Danavarshabhah*). Ramayana (1.23.14) narrates the origin of name *Anga* as the place where Kamadeva was burnt to death by Siva and where his body parts(*angas*) are scattered.

History

Bodhayana Dharma Sutra groups the Angas with people of *mixed origin* and Mahbharata brands an Anga prince (*not Karana of the Mahabharata*) as a mlechcha and barbarian.

The Puranas list several early kings of Anga. The *Mahagovinda Suttanta* refers to king Dhatarattha of Anga. Jain texts refer to Dhadhivahana, as a ruler of the Angas. Puranas and Harivamsa represent him as the son and immediate successor of *Anga*, the eponymous founder of the kingdom. Jain traditions place him at the beginning of sixth century BCE.

Between the Vatsas and the realm of Anga, lived the Magadhas, who initially were comparatively a weak people. A great struggle went on between the Angas and its eastern neighbors. The *Vidhura Pandita Jataka* describes Rajagriha (the Magadhan Capital) as the city of Anga and Mahabharata also refers to a sacrifice performed by the king of Anga at *Mount Vishnupada* (at Gaya). This indicates that Anga had initially succeeded in annexing the Magadhas, and thus its borders extended to the kingdom of Matsya country.

This success of Angas did not last long. About the middle of 6th century BC, Bimbisara, the crown prince of Magadha had killed Brahmadatta, the last independent king of Anga and seized Champa. Bimbisara made it as his head-quarters and ruled over it as his father's Viceroy. Thenceforth, Anga became an integral part of growing Magadha empire (PHAI, 1996).

Magadha

The first reference to the Magadhas occurs in the Atharva-Veda where they are found listed along with the Angas, Gandharis and the Mujavats as a despised people. The bards of Magadha are, however, referred to in early Vedic literature and are spoken of in terms of contempt.

Rigveda mentions a king *Pramaganda* as a ruler of Kikata. Yasaka declares that Kikata was a non-Aryan country. Later literature refers to Kikata as synonym of Magadha. With the exception of the Rigvedic Pramaganda, whose connection with

Magadha is very speculative, no other king of Magadha is mentioned in Vedic literature. According to the Mahabharata and the Puranas, the earliest ruling dynasty of Magadha was founded by king *Brihadratha*, but Magadha came into prominence only under king Bimbisara and his son Ajatasatru. In the war of supremacy which went on for long between the nations of Majjhimadesa, kingdom of Magadha finally emerged victorious and became a predominant empire in Mid India.

The kingdom of the Magadhas roughly corresponded to the modern districts of Patna and Gaya in southern Bihar, and parts of Bengal in the east. It was bounded on the north by river Ganga, on the east by the river Champa, on the south by Vindhya mountains and on the west by river Sona.

During Buddha's time, its boundaries included Anga. Its earliest capital was Girivraja or Rajagriha modern Rajgir in Patna district of Bihar. The other names for the city were Magadhapura, Brihadrathapura, Vasumati, Kushagrapura and Bimbisarapuri. It was an active center of Jainism in ancient times. The first Buddhist Council was held in Rajagriha in the Vaibhara Hills. Later on, Pataliputra became the capital of Magadha.

Vajji or Vriji

Vajji or Vrijji was one of the principal mahajanapadas of ancient India. Both the Buddhist text *Anguttara Nikaya* and the Jaina text *Bhagavati Sutra* (*Saya* xv *Uddesa* I) included Vajji in their lists of *solasa* (sixteen) mahajanapadas. The name of this mahajanapada was derived from one of its ruling clans, the Vrjis. This clan is mentioned by Panini, Kautilya and Xuanzang.

The Territory

The territory of the Vajji mahajanapada was located on the north of the Ganga River and extended up to the Terai region of Nepal. On the west, the Gandak River was probably the boundary between it and the Malla mahajanapada and possibly also separated it with the Kosala mahajanapada.

On the east, its territory was probably extended up to the forests along the banks of the rivers, Koshi and Mahananda. The capital of this Mahajanapada was Vaishali. Other important towns and villages were Kundapura or Kundagrama (a suburb of Vaishali), Bhoganagara and Hatthigama.

Ruling Clans

The rulers of this mahajanapada were a confederacy of the eight clans (*atthakula*) of whom the*Vrijis*, the *Lichchavis*, the *Jnatrikass* and the *Videhas* were the most important. The identities of the other four clans are not certain. However, in a passage of the *Sutrakritanga*, the *Ugras*, the *Bhogas*, the *Kauravas* and the *Aikshvakas* are associated with the *Jnatris* and *Licchavis* as the subjects of the same ruler and the members of the same assmebly.

Vajji Administration

It was known as *Vajji Sangha* (Vajji confederation), which consisted of several *janapadas*, *gramas* (villages), *gosthas* (groups). The eminent people were chosen from each *khandas* (districts) to represent on their behalf in *Vajji gana parishad* (people's council of Vajji). These represetatives were called *gana mukhyas*. The chairman of the council was called *Ganapramukh* (head of the state), but often he was addressed as the king, though his post was not dynastic. The other executives were *Mahabaladhrikrit* (equivalent to the minister of internal security), *binishchayamatya* (chief justice), *dandadhikrit* (other justices) etc.

Vajji's capital was Vaishali. It was a prosperous city. In the introductory portion of the *Ekapanna Jataka*, the Vaishali was described as encompassed by a triple wall with the three gates with watch-towers. The main gosthas were Lichchhavis, Mallas and Œakyas. In around 600 BCE, the Lichchhavis were disciples of Lord Mahavira, but later they shifted to *Buddha Marga* (Buddhism). During his life time Lord Buddha visited Vaishali several times, the *vihara* where he used to stay in Vaishali was called *Kuthagarshala*. It was gifted to him by a *Ganapramukh*, Chetaka.

Licchavi (Clan)

The Licchavis were the most famous clan amongst the ruling confederate clans of the Vajji mahajanapada of ancient India. Vaishali, the capital of the Licchavis was the capital of the Vajji mahajanapada also. It was later occupied by Ajatashatru, who annexed the Vajji territory into his kingdom..

Buddhaghola in his Paramatthajotik, traced the origin of the Licchavis to Benaras. The date of the establishment of the Licchavi domination over the area consisting of present day north Bihar and terai region of Nepal is not known. By the time of Mahavira and Gautama Buddha this clan was already well settled in the area around their capital Vaill+. Buddhist tradition has preserved the names of a number of eminent Licchavis, which include prince Abhyaya, Ommhaddha (Mahli), generals, Sha and Ajita, Dummukha and Sunakkhata. The Kalpasktra of Bhadravhu refers to the nine Licchavi gagarjas (chieftains) who along with the nine Malla ganarjas and the eighteen Koala ganarjas formed a league against Magadha. The leader of this alliance was Chemaka, whose sister Trial was the mother of Mahavira..

Licchavi Administration

Only scattered reports of the Licchavi government system survive. The introductory portions of the Cullakalinga Jtaka and the Ekapanna Jtaka mention the Licchavi as having 7,707 Rjs. The number is one of convention, and unlikely to have been exact. It does demonstrate that Licchavi, unlike most of its neighbours, was not an absolute monarchy. Ultimate authority rested with the 7,707 *raja* who met each year to elect one of their member as ruler and a council of nine to assist him. It was far from a democracy as only a small portion of the Licchavi population qualified to vote. Those with *raja* status were only the male heads of households who belonged to the kshatriya varna.

The seat of the Licchavi administration was in Vaill+, the capital of the Vajjiian confederacy. The Rj was the highest executive and judicial authority.

The Executive

The Ammhakath mentions about the three chief functionaries of the Licchavi administration, the Rj (the ruling chief), the Uparj (the deputy chief) and the Senpati (the chief of the army). The introductory portion of the Ekapanna Jtaka adds one more with it, the BhGgrika (the chancellor of exchequer).

The Judiciary

The Vajji or Vrijji Mahajanapada in 600 BCE.

According to the Ammhakath, a criminal was first handed over to a Viniccaya Mahmtta (the inquiring magistrate), who after the investigation and the interrogation of the accused if found guilty took him to the Vohrika (the jurist-judge). He could discharge him if he found him innocent, otherwise he handed over him to the Skttadhra (the master of the sacred code).

The Skttadhra after confirming the guilt of the accused, handed him over to the Ammhakklak (literally, the eight clans, probably a federal court). The Ammhakklakif satisfied of the guilt of the accused made him over to the Senpati, who after satisfying himself about the guilt of the accused made him over to the Uparj. If the Uparj also found him guilty, he handed him over to the Rj. In case, the Rj found him guilty, the convict received the punishment prescribed in the Pave Gipotthaka (the book of precedence) for the offence committed by him.

Licchavis and the Imperial Guptas

The Gupta emperor Chandragupta I married a Licchavi princess Kumaradevi and the legend *Licchavayah* is found along with a figure of goddess Lakshmi on the reverse of the Chandragupta I-Kumaradevi type gold coins of Samudragupta..

In Allahabad Pillar Inscription, Samudragupta was described as the *Licchavidauhitra* (the grandson of the Licchavis from his mother's side). These probably suggest Licchavi occupation of Magadha immediately before the rise of the imperial Guptas, although there is no direct evidence to prove it..

Shakya

Shakya was an ancient janapada (realm) of India in the 1st millennium BCE. In Buddhist texts, the Zkyas are mentioned as a Kshatriya clan of Gotama gotra. The Zkyas formed an independent kingdom at the foothills of the Himlayas. The Zkya capital was Kapilavastu (Pli: Kapilavatthu), currently situated in Nepal.

The most famous Zkya was Shakyamuni Buddha (Gautama Buddha), a member of the ruling Gautama (Pli: Gotama) clan of Lumbini, who is also known as Zkyamuni.

History

The Zkyas were settled in the territory bounded by the Himalayas in the north, The Rohini (the present-day Kobana, a tributory of the Rapti) in the east and the Rapti in the south. The Buddhist texts, Mahavastu, Mahavamsa and Sumangalavilasini give detailed accounts of the Zkyas.

The Accounts of Buddhist Texts

The Zkyas are mentioned in the accounts of the birth of the Buddha (Mahvastu, c. late 2nd century BCE) as a part of the dichchas (solar race) and as descendants of the legendary king Ikcvaku (Pli: Okkka):

There lived once upon a time a king of the Zkya, a scion of the solar race, whose name was Zuddhodana. He was pure in conduct, and beloved of the Okay like the autumn moon. He had a wife, splendid, beautiful, and steadfast, who was called the Great My, from her resemblance to My the Goddess. —*Buddhacarita* of Avaghoca.

The Buddhist text, Mahavamsa (II, 1-24) traces the origin of the *Sakyas* (Zkyas) to king Okkaka (Ikshvaku) and gives their genealogy from Mahasammata, an ancestor of Okkaka. This list comprises the names of a number of prominent kings of the Ikshvaku dynasty, which include Mandhata and Sagara.

According to this text, Okkamukha was the eldest son of Okkaka. Sivisamjaya and Sihassara were the son and grandson of Okkamukha. King Sihassara had eighy-two thousand sons and grandsons, who were together known as the Sakyas.

The youngest son of Sihassara was Jayasena. Jayasena had a son, Sihahanu, and a daughter, Yashodhara, who was married to Devadahasakka. Devadahasakka had two daughters, Anjana and Kaccana.

Sihahanu married Kaccaña, and they had five sons and two daughters, Suddhodana was one of them. Suddhodana had two queens, Maya and Prajapati, both daughters of Anjana. Siddhattha (Gautama Buddha) was the son of Suddhodana and Maya. Rahula was the son of Siddhatta and Bhaddakaccana, daughter of Suppabuddha and grandaughter of Anjana..

Annexation by Kosala

Vikabha, the son of Pasenadi and Vsavakhattiy, the daughter of a Zkya named Mahnma by a slave girl ascended the throne of Kosala after overthrowing his father. As an act of vengeance for cheating Kosala by sending his mother, the daughter of a slave woman for marriage to his father, he invaded the Zkya territory, massacred them and annexed it.

Malla

Mall or Malla was one of the *solasa* (16) mahajanapadas of ancient India mentioned in the *Anguttara Nikaya*. It was named after the ruling clan of the same name. The Mahabharata (VI.9.34) mentions the territory as the *Mallarashtra* (Mall state). The Mall mahajanapada was situated north of Magadha. It was a small mahajanapada. The mahajanapada was divided into two main parts and the river Kakuttha (present day Kuku) was probably the dividing line. The capital of these two parts were Kusavati or Kurinra (modern Kasia near Gorakhpur) and Pv, modern Padrauna, 12 miles from Kasia). Kutinra and Pava are very important in the history of Buddhism since Buddha took his *last meal* and was taken ill at Pava and went to his Mahparinirvna at Kutinra.

The Malls were a powerful clan of eastern India at the time of Gautama Buddha and they are frequently mentioned in Buddhist and Jaina works.

The Mahabharata (II.30.3) mentions that the second Pandava Bhima is said to have conquered the chief of the Mall in course of his expedition to eastern India. The Mahabharata (VI.9.46) mentions Malls along with the Angas, Vangas, and Kalingas as eastern tribes. The Malls were republican people with their dominion consisting of nine territories (Kalpa Sutra; Nirayavali Sutra), one of each of the nine confederated clans.

The Mall, like the Licchavis, are mentioned by Manusmriti as Vratya Kshatriyas. They are called Vasishthas (Vasetthas) in the Mahapparnibbana Suttanta. The Malls originally had a monarchical form of government but later they switched to Samgha (republic) of which the members called themselves *rajas*. The Malls were a brave and warlike people. Jainism and Buddhism found many followers among the Malls. The Malls appeared to have formed alliance with Lichchhavis for self defense. They however, lost their independence not long after Buddha's death and their dominions were annexed to the Magadhan empire.

The two main towns of the mahajanapada were Pv, where the Jain founder Mahavira breathed his last and Kuinara, where Uakyamuni Buddha went to his MahparinirvGa. The *Cullavagga* of the Vinaya Pitaka mentions another town named Anupiya. A fourth town called Uruvelakappa is mentioned in the Anguttara Nikaya.

Chedi or Cheti

Chedi kingdom was one among the many kingdoms ruled during early periods by *Paurava* kings and later by Yadav kings in the central and western India. It falls roughly in the Bundelkhand division of Madhya Pradesh regions to the south of river Yamuna and along river Betwa or Vetravati. The Chedi kingdom was ruled by Sisupala, an ally of Jarasandha of Magadha and Duryodhana of Kuru. He was a rival of Vasudeva Krishna who was his uncle's son. He was killed by Vasudeva Krishna during the Rajasuya sacrifice of the Pandava king Yudhisthira. Bhima's wife was from Chedi. The city called Suktimati is mentioned as the capital of Chedi. Prominent Chedis during Kurukshetra War included Damaghosha, Shishupala, Dhrishtaketu, Suketu, Sarabha, Bhima's wife, Nakula's wife Karenumati, Dhristaketu's sons. Other famous Chedis included King Uparichara Vasu, his children, King Suvahu, King Sahaja.

References in Mahâbhârata

Chedi Mentioned as a Kingdom of Ancient India (Bharata Varsha).

The Kuru-Panchalas, the Salwas, the Madreyas, the Jangalas, the Surasena, the Kalingas, the Vodhas, the Malas, the Matsyas, the Sauvalyas, the Kuntalas, the Kasi-Kosalas, the Chedis, the Karushas, the Bhojas...(6,9).

Chedi was one among the kingdoms chosen for spending the 13th year of exile by the Pandavas.

Surrounding the kingdom of the Kurus, are, many countries beautiful and abounding in corn, such as Panchala, Chedi, Matsya, Surasena, Pattachchara, Dasarna, Navarashtra, Malla, Salva, Yugandhara, Saurashtra, Avanti, and the spacious Kuntirashtra.

King Uparichara Vasu and the Festival of Bamboo Pole

Uparichara Vasu was a king of Chedi belonging to the Puru Dynasty. He was known as the friend of Indra. During his reign, Chedi kingdom contained much mineral wealth. It was abundant in animals and corn. There were many towns and cities in the kingdom. He possessed a very special chariot. He introduced a festival in his kingdom in the honor of Indra. The festival involved planting of a bamboo pole every year, in honor of Indra. The king will then pray for the expansion of his cities and kingdom. After erecting the pole, people decked it with golden cloth and scents and garlands and various ornaments. From Chedi, he ruled a large territory, placing his sons as governors of various provinces. His son Vrihadratha (Maharatha) was installed in Magadha. His other sons, viz Pratyagraha, Kusamva (Manivahana), Mavella and Yadu also became governors at various places. Thus the Chedi king attained the status of an emperor and his kingdom became a vast empire. He diverted the waters of river Suktimati from the locks of the Mountain Kolahala, for irrigating his capital-city which he named Suktimati.

- This beautiful city of the Chedis was called after the Oyster (14,83) : His wife Girika, was from the valley of Kolahala. Girika's brother was installed as the generalissimo of Vasu's army. Apart from his five royal sons, he had a son and a daughter born of a woman of fisherman community. The male child, in due course established the Matsya Kingdom and founded the royal dynasty called *Matsya Dynasty*. The female child lived as a member of fishermen community. Her line established as fishermen on the banks of river Yamuna, in the kingdom of Kurus. The famous Kuru king Santanu's wife Satyavati was from this fishermen community. The author of Mahâbhârata, vis Krishna Dwaipayana Vyasa and the Kuru kings viz Chitrangada and Vichitravirya were the sons of Satyavati. Pandavas and Kauravas where the grandsons of Vichitravirya.
- Another story connects Vasu with non-vegetarianism in ancient India. Filled with doubts respecting the propriety of eating flesh, some sages asked Uparichara Vasu for solving them. King Vasu, knowing that flesh is inedible, he answered that it was edible.
- A similar story connects Vasu with the issue of animal sacrifices. In his opinion sacrifices could be performed with or without the slaughter of animals.

King Sisupala of Chedi

Sisupala was the son of the King Damaghosha (1,189). He had another name viz Sunitha. His mother was a Yadava lady by the name Srutakirti, who was the sister of Kunti, the mother of Pandavas. Both Kunti and Srutakirti were sisters of Vasudeva the father of Vasudeva Krishna. However Sisupala developed enmity with Krishna (2,44), though he was affectionate to the Pandava Bhima. During his military campaign to collect tribute for Pandava king Yudhisthira's Rajasuya sacrifice, Bhima stayed at the palace of Sisupala for a month as a guest. He also accepted Yudhisthira's sway over his kingdom and gave Bhima tribute (2,28). During the midst of Yudhisthira's Rajasuya ceremony, a dispute arose between Sisupala and Vasudeva Krishna. Pandavas tried to mediate. He also rebuked the Pandavas and Kuru grandsire Bhishma along with Krishna. Then Krishna, extremely provoked, slew Sisupala.

Sisupala's hostilities to Krishna were many. He burned the city of Dwaraka, while Krishna was in Pragjyotisha with his army. He attacked king Bhoja, sporting at Raivataka hill close to Dwaraka. He stole the horse of Krishna's father Vasudeva, during his horse-sacrifice. He insulted the wife of Akrura (Vabhru-the friend of Krishna), on her way from Dwaraka to Sauvira Kingdom. He also insulted princess of Visala, viz Bhadra, the fiancé of Karusha king.

- Yudhisthira installed Sisupala's son in the throne of Chedi.
- Sisupala's sister was married to Bhima as per the reference in (15,25).

King Dhristaketu of Chedi

Dhristaketu, the king of Chedi (3,12), was described as the son of king Sisupala (5,50). During the time of Dhristaketu also, Suktimati was the capital of Chedi. Dhristaketu was an army-general in the army of Pandavas in Kurukshetra War. He was the leader of the army of the Chedis, the Kasis, and the Karushas (5,199). He was a Maharatha (a great car-warrior) as per the rating of Bhishma (5,172). One of his sons also took part in the war (5,57). He was slain by Drona (7,128), (11,25). Dhristaketu also was slain in battle by Drona.

- Chedi Princess Karenumati was wedded to the Pandava Nakula, and prince Narimitra was their son. (1,95). It is not clear if she was Dhristaketu's sister. However it was mentioned that his sister was the wife of one of the Pandavas (3,22) (15,1).
- Sarabha, the son of Sisupala became the king of Chedi after the death of Dhristaketu. He was defeated in battle by Arjuna during his military campaign, after the Kurukshetra War. (14,83).

Other Kings of Chedi

- King Suvahu was described as the king of Chedi, during the time of Nishadha king Nala. His wife, Damayanti the princess of Vidarbha, left alone in forest, met a caravan of traders heading towards Chedi. Along with them she reached the Chedi capital and lived as a servant maid of queen, in the palace of Chedi. (3-64,65).
- King Sahaja among the Chedis and Matsyas, were described as an annihilator of his own race (5,74).

Chedis in Kurukshetra War

Chedi King Dhristaketu and his Sons

- The powerful chief of the Chedis, Dhrishtaketu, accompanied by an Akshauhini, came to the sons of Pandu. (5-19,57)
- The assembled kings of the Chedi and the Karusha tribes have all taken the part of the Pandavas with all their resources. (5,22)
- Chedi King Dhrishtaketu employed Kamboja steeds of variegated hue in the battle (7,23)
- Drona slew Dhristaketu and his son (7,122)
- Another Chedi prince was slain by Aswatthaman, the son of Drona (7,198)
- Another son of Sisupala, brother of Dhristaketu, named Suketu also was slain by Drona (8,6).

Chedi Army

Chedi army is mentioned with many other armies fighting on the side of Pandavas:

- The Kasayas, the Chedis, the Matsyas, the Srinjayas (5,57)
- The Kasis, the Panchalas, the Chedis, and the Matsyas (5,72)
- The Chedis, the Panchalas, and the Kekayas (5,144)
- The Pandavas, the Chedis, the Panchalas, and the Yadavas (5,144)
- The Chedis, the Kasis, the Karushas, and the Panchalas (6,47)

- The Chedis, the Kasis, the Karushas, and the Pauravas (6,54)
- The Chedis, the Panchalas, the Kurushas, the Matsyas (6,59)
- The Chedis, the Kasis, and the Karushas (6-107,117)
- The Chedis and the Panchalas (6,116)
- The Matsyas, the Panchalas, and the Chedis (6,119)
- The Kekayas, the Chedis, the Karushas, the Matsyas (7,9)
- The Panchalas, the Kekayas, the Matsyas, the Chedis, the Karushas and the Kosalas (7-21,153,163)
- The Chedis, the Panchalas, and the Pandávas (7,30)
- The Chedis, the Matsyas, and the Srinjayas (7,76)
- The Chedis and Panchalàs and Srinjayas (7,105)
- The Chedis, the Panchalas, the Srinjayas, and the Kekayas (7,111)
- The Chedis, the Srinjayas, the Kasis, and the Kosalas (7,112)
- The Kaikeyas and the Chedis (7,151)
- The Chedis, the Panchalas, and the Somakas (7,157)
- The Prabhadrakas, the Panchalas, the Chedis, and the Kaikeyas (7,191)
- A king named Chediddhaja sided with Kauravas (5,62).

Vamsa or Vatsa

Vatsa (also known as Vamsa, Batsa, or Bansa) was one of the *solasa* (sixteen) Mahajanapadas (great kingdoms) of Uttarapatha of ancient India mentioned in the *Anguttara Nikaya.*

Vatsa's geographical location was near the confluence of the Ganges and Yamuna rivers. Its capital was Kaumb+ (present day Kosam, 35 miles southwest of Allahabad).

The Early Period

The Puranas state that the Vatsa kingdom was named after a Kar+ king, Vatsa. The Ramayana and the Mahabharata attribute the credit of founding its capital Kau [mb+ to a Chedi prince Kula or Kumba. The Puranas state that after the washing away of Hastinapura by the Ganga, the Bhrata king Nicakcu, the great-

great grandson of Janamejaya, abandoned the city and settled in Kaumb+. This is supported by the Svapnavsavadatt and the Pratijna-Yaugandharyaga attributed to Bhsa. Both of them have described the king Udayana as a scion of the Bhrata family (Bhrata-kula). The Puranas provide a list of Nicakcu's successors which ends with king Kcemaka.

Zatn+ka II, Parantapa

The first ruler of the Bhrata dynasty of Vatsa, about whom some definite information available is Zatn+ka II, Parantapa. While the Puranas state his father's name was Vasudna, Bhsa tells it was Sahasrn+ka. Zatn+ka II married a princess of Videha, who was the mother of Udayana. He also married Magavat+, a daughter of the Licchavi chieftain Cemaka. He attacked Camp, the capital of Aega during the rule of Dadhivhana.

Udayana

Udayana, the son of Zatn+ka II by the Videha princess succeeded him. Udayana, the romantic hero of the Svapnavsavadatt, the Pratijna-Yaugandharyaga and many other legends was contemporary of Buddha and of Pradyota, the king of Avanti. The Kathsaritsgara contains a long account of his conquests. The Priyadarnik narrates the event of his victory over the ruler of Kalinga and restoration of Dhavarman to the throne of AEga. The commentary on the Dhammapada describes the story of his marriage with Vsavadatt or Vsuladatt, the daughter of Pradyota, the king of Avanti. It also mentions about his two other consorts, Mgandiy, daughter of a Kuru Brahmin and Smvat+, the adopted daughter of the treasurer Ghosaka. The Milindapañho refers to a peasant girl Gopla-mt who became his wife. The Svapnavsavadatt of Bhsa mentions about another queen named Padmvat+, a sister of king Daraka of Magadha. The Priyadarik tells us about the marriage of Udayana with ranyak, the daughter of Dhavarman, the king of Aega. The Ratnval+ narrates a story of romance between him and Sgarik, an attendant of his chief queen, Vsavadatt. The name of his son by his chief queen is Bodhi.

The Buddha visited Koushambi several times during the reign of Udayana on his effort to spread the dharma, the Eightfold Path and the Four Noble Truths. Udayana was an Upasaka (lay follower) of Buddha. The Chinese translation of the Buddhist canonical text

Ekottara gama states that the first image of Buddha, curved out of sandalwood was made under the instruction of Udayana.

Later Developments

According to the Puranas, the 4 successors of Udayana were Vahinra, Danapni, Niramitra and Kcemaka. Later, the Vatsa kingdom was annexed by the Avanti kingdom. Maniprabha, the great-grandson of Pradyota ruled at Kau [mb+ as a prince of Avanti.

Kuru

Kuru was the name of an Indo-Aryan tribe and their kingdom in the Vedic civilization of India, and later a republican Mahajanapada state. Their kingdom was located in the area of modern Haryana.

They formed the first political center of the Indo-Aryans after the Rigvedic period, and after their emergence from the Punjab, and it was there that the codification and redaction of the Vedic texts began. Archaeologically, they most likely correspond to the black and red ware culture of the 12th to 9th centuries BC. At this time, iron first appears in western India. Iron is still absent from the Rigvedic hymns, and makes its first appearance as "black metal" (*ayama ayas*) in the Atharvaveda.

The Atharvaveda refers to Parikshit as the king of the Kurus. His son Janamejaya figures in Satapatha Brahmana as well as in the Aitareya Brahmana. The Kurus in association with the Panchalas are frequently mentioned in the later Vedic literature.

Geographical Location of Kuru

In the epic times (final centuries BC), the region between the triangle of Thaneshwar, Hissar and Hastinapur was distinguished by three different names: (1) Kuru-Jangala equal to Rohtak, Hansi, Hissar; (2) Kuru-rashtra proper between the Ganges and Yamuna with its capital at Hastinapura and (3) the Kuru-kshetra comprising Thaneshwar, Kaithal and Karnal.

The whole kingdom roughly corresponded to modern Thanesar, Delhi and the greater part of Upper Gangetic Doab.

The rivers Aruna, Ashumati, Hiranvati, Apaya, Kausiki, Sarasvati and Drishadvati or Rakshi washed the lands of Kurus.

Kurus of Buddha's Times

The Kuru kingdom figures in the list of the sixteen great kingdoms, the Mahajanapadas of the early Buddhist Anguttara Nikaya. At the time of Buddha, the Kuru realm was only three hundred leagues in extent. Legendary Buddhist stories-the Jatakas attest that the capital of the Kurus was Indraprastha (Indapatta) near modern Delhi. It extended for seven leagues. The other city in the realm was Hatthinipura i.e Hastinapura. The reigning king *Dhananjaya* is stated as prince from the race of Yudhishtra. But he was merely a titular chieftain (king consul).

During Buddha's time, Ratthapala, son of the Kuru ruler had embraced Buddhism.

The Buddha taught important and profound discourses in the Kurus such as the "Mahasatipammhana Sutta", the Great Discourse on the Foundation of Mindfulness, "Mahanidana Sutta", The Great Discourse on Causation, and "Anenjasappaya Sutta", the Way to the Imperturbable. Other discourses, as recorded in the Pali Canon, taught by the Buddha in the Kurus are MgaGiya Sutta, Rammhapla Sutta, Sammasa Sutta, Dutiya Ariyavasa Sutta.

The Kurus of the Buddhist period did not occupy the same position as they did in the Vedic period but they continued to enjoy their ancient reputation for deep wisdom and sound health. The Kurus had matrimonial relations with Yadavas, the Bhojas and the Panchalas.

Though a well known monarchical people in earlier period, the Kurus are known to have switched to republic form of government during sixth/fifth century BCE. Fourth century BCE Kautiliya's Arthashastra also attests the Kurus as following the *Rajashabdopajivin* (king consul) constitution (11/1/1-4).

Kurus are mentioned by Panini (Astadhyayi 4.1.168-75) as one of the fifteen powerful Kshatriya Janapadas of his times, with Hastinapura as its capital.

Panini refers to the house-holders' way of life as against ascetic way obtaining amongst the Kurus.

Kuru Dharma

In Buddhism, "Kuru Dharma" specifically refers to the Five Precepts of moral restraints which every Buddhist must take along with the Triple Gem. Buddhists trace the origins of the 5 precepts in the "Kuru Dhamma Jataka".

Kurus have frequently been coupled with the Panchalas in later Vedic and Puranic literature. The Kurus were followers of Brahmanical way of life, and the early kingdom in all probability is the location of the codification of the Vedas and the establishment of major schools of Vedic priesthood. They insisted on the purity of family life and cultivation of proper domestic relations and virtues, a way of life and philosophy that are reflected in the basic doctrine of Bhagvadgita expounded at Kurukshetra. In the land of Kurus-Panchalas, the speech is said to have its particular home. The mode of sacrifice among the Kuru-Panchalas is proclaimed to be the best. The Kuru Panchala kings are said to have performed *Rajasuya* sacrifice. There are numerous references to the Brahmanas of Kuru-Panchala country. Kurus were noted for deep wisdom and purity of life.

Speculations on Origins

Kuru-Puru-Bharata Connection

Epic traditions reveal that the kings of Kuru belonged to the *Puru-Bharata* family.

The *Kuru-Puru connection* is suggested by Rigveda (10.33.4) which attests Kuru-Sravana as the descendant of famous Puru king Trasadasyu. (4.38.1, 7.19.3).

A connection of the Bharatas with Kurukshetra is attested by Rigveda 3.23, Shatapatha Brahmana 13.5.4, Aitareya Brahmana 8.23 as well as the Mahabharata 7.66.8. The former Purus, Bharatas and several other minor clans were later fused together and amalgamated into the powerful Kurus who expanded east from the Punjab.

Mahabharata refers to kings *Puru-ravas Aila, Ayu, Yayati Nahushya, Puru-Bharata Dauhshanti Saudyumni, Ajamidha, Riksha, Samavarana, Kuru, Uchchaihsravas Kaupayeya, Prati sutvana, Bahlika Pratipeya, Santnu and Dhritarashtra* in the ancestral line of Parikshit, the grandson of Pandava Arjuna.

Speculations on Origin of Kuru Kingdom and Kurus

Kuru dynesty kings were called med-bhuti or med kshatriyas and Kuru forces were med or mair rajputs from ancient time in

India. According to Bhagvata and Vishnu Puran, Medes or Mair Kshatriyas are one of the oldest warriors. Mair Kshatriyas are originally from Lord Brahama dynesty King Ajmenid, Badmer, Ajmer, Jesalmer are some of ancient cities of old Aryans Medes, mer or mair. After Golden age the Mahabharat fall of the Mairs Empire a power vacuum shortly existed in the region.

The Word Mairbhuti, Kurukshetra War against the Kuruavas which is detailed in the Hindu epic, the Mahabharata. In this war, the Kshatriyas assumed the role of warriors for either side of the battle, after the war of Mahabharat Pandavs had gone for Swargarohan (Battle of heven) with all armies. Dispersal and dissolving of Mairs resulted medes had gone for movment to ancient Median Empires of Indian mair kshatriyas in Iran. The Medes are credited with the foundation of the first Iranian empire, the largest of its day until Cyrus (KURUS) the Great established a unified Iranian empire of the Medes (Indian origin) and Persians, often referred to as the Achaemenid Empire, (KING Ajmenid of India great grandfather of all Medes). by defeating his grandfather and overlord, Astyages the Raja of Media. In present time med kshatriyas of India claims that they are from KURU dynesty and in Iran and rest of the world Kurdish community also claim to related with ancient meds. Kurdish are from Indo-Europian language origin, they can be from ancient Kurukshetra. Mahabharata and the Puranas attest the Kurus as the most important branch of the Ailas i.e descendants of king Puru-ravas Aila.

The princes of Aila lineage are also designated as Karddameyas. This designation connects the *Ailas* to river Karddama, located in Persia. Hence the home of the *Karddameyas* or the *Aila princes* (Kurus) is often identified with Bahlika or Balkh (Bactria) in Iran and not in India proper (Studies in Antiquities, 234).

Puru-ravas Aila, first king in the line of ancestors of the Kurus above, is mentioned in Ramayana stories as the son of a ruler who came, in some remote antiquity, from Bahli (Balkh) in Central Asia to Mid India (Ramayana, VII,103.21-22).

Mahabharata locates the birth place of king *Puru-ravas Aila* on a hill near the source of a river called Ganga (3.90.22-25).

This ancient Ganga is said to be different from the main Ganga and finds reference in ancient Sanskrit texts like Raghuvamsa, where it is found located in the neighborhood of the Kambojas of Pamirs/Badakshan. This river and river Sita (Yarkand) are said to be originating from *Anavtapat Sarovar* (in Pamirs or in Karakoram Jot, somewhere)

Papancha-sudanai also refers to the Kurus, as colonists from trans-Himalayan region known as Uttarakuru (Dr B. C. Law, Ancient Indian Mid-Indian Kshatriya Tribes, p 16)..

The Kurus are associated with the Mahavrishas and the Bahlikas according to Mahabharata (II.63.2-7).

This association of the Kuru, Mahavrishas and the Bahlikas powerfully supports the northern origin of the Kurus. Shatapatha Brahmana also attests one king called *Bahlika* Pratipiya *whom it designates as Koravya i.e one from Kuru lineage.*

We also know that *Bahlika Pratipiya* is an important epic king of the Kurus. He was from the Puru-rava Aila lineage and hence from the line of Kurus of Kurukshetra.

The word *Bahlika* in the name of Kuru king *Bahlika Pratipiya* is his *personal designation* and points to northern (Bahlika or Bactria) origin of the Kurus of *Middle country,* in accordance with ancient naming conventions.

A section of the Kurus, known as *Uttarakurus,* is stated to be living beyond the Himalayan region in the days of Mahabharata and Aitreya Brahmana as we learn from Aitareya Brahmana verse (VIII.14).

It is also to be noted that the Himalaya of the ancient Indian traditions extended from the east occean to the west ocean, and even today is not separated from it.Mahabharata also attests that the ancestors of the Kauravas and Pandavas originally migrated from *Uttarakuru* (MBH 1/187/28).

Buddhaghosa also records a tradition which states that, when Vedic king Mandhata returned to Jambudvipa from his sojourn in the four *Mahadipas,* there were, in his retinue, a large number of the people of *Uttarakuru.* They all settled down in Jambudípa, and their settlement became known as Kururattha (Kuru Rashtra).

Majjhima Commentary also attests that the people of Kururatha had originally belonged to the *Uttarakuru.*

The above several references would indicate that the ancestors of the Kurus of *Middle India* had migrated from Bahlika/Uttarakuru which was a region stated to be to the north of Himalaya / Hindukush.

But Przyluski has also shown that Bahlika or Balkh was the original home the Madra peoples known as the Uttaramadras. This shows that *Uttarakuru,* the original home of the Kurus, was not precisely located in Bahlika, but probably in some nearby region, north of Bahlika in Central Asia, possibly bordering with it. We know that on the east side of Bahlika i.e. the Uttaramadra, was located the Parama-Kamboja (say *Uttara-Kambojas*) branch of the Kambojas. Thus it appears likely that the Uttarakurus as immediate neighbors to the Uttaramadras/Bahlikas were located to north-east of Uttaramadras and to north of Parama-Kambojas (Badakshan/Pamir).

By the way, if Bahlika is to be insisted upon to be same as Uttarakuru, then one can assume that the Madras and Kurus in the remote antiquity were one people.

Later, the Kurus of the Middle country became known as *Kuru* proper or the *Dakshina Kuru* (MBH I, 109-10).

None of the above sources claim knowledge or information from any of the four Vedas, nor do they cite references. Therefore they must understood in a presumptive manner rather than as facts.

Puranic View of Kuru Origin

The Puranas trace the lineage of the *Pauravas,* the line of kings who are related to the Kuru-Panchalas, to king *Puru-rava Aila,* who is stated to be king of *Pratishthana.* (This Pratishthana is near modern Allahabad and is not to be confused with the western Indian one, now called Paithan). It is stated that Kuru was the son of king Samvarna and Tapti. He had given his name to Kurukshetra. At Kurukshetra, he had performed *tapasya* (penance) and pleased Indra. Kuru's descendants became known as Kauravas.

This Puranic view, in view of the evidence presented before, is not considered reliable.

Panchala

Panchala is an ancient region of northern India, which corresponds to the geographical area around the Ganges River and Yamuna River, the upper Gangetic plain in particular. This would encompass the modern-day states of Uttarakhand and Uttar Pradesh. During the ancient times, it was home to a confederacy, the Panchalas and in c. 6th century BCE, it was considered as one of the *solasa* (sixteen) mahajanapadas.

Geographical Extent

The Panchalas occupied the country to the east of the Kurus, between the upper Himalayas and the river Ganga. It roughly corresponded to modern Budaun, Farrukhabad and the adjoining districts of Uttar Pradesh. The country was divided into Uttara-Panchala and Dakshina-Panchala. The northern Panchala had its capital at Ahichatra, (also known as Adhichhatra and Chhatravati, near present-day Ramnagar village in Aonla tehsil of Bareilly district, while southern Panchala had it capital at Kampilya or Kampil in Farrukhabad district. The famous city of Kanyakubja or Kannauj was situated in the kingdom of Panchala.

Panchala During the Vedic Period

Panchala was the second "urban" center of Vedic civilization, as its focus moved east from the Punjab, after the focus of power had been with the Kurus in the early Iron Age. This period is associated with the Painted Grey Ware culture, arising beginning around 1100 BCE, and declining from 600 BCE, with the end of the Vedic period. The Shaunaka and Taittiriya Vedic schools were located in the area of Panchala.

The ruling confederacy, the Panchalas, as their name suggests, probably consisted of five clans-the Krivis, the Turvashas, The Keshins, the Srinjayas and the Somakas. Each of these clans is known to be associated with one or more princes mentioned in the Vedic texts-the Krivis with Kravya Panchala, the Turvashas with Sona Satrasaha, the Keshins with Keshin Dalavya, the Srinjayas with Sahadeva Sarnjaya and the Somakas with Somaka Sahadevya. The names of the last two clans, the Somakas and the Srinjayas are also mentioned in the Mahabharata and the Puranas. King Drupada, whose daughter Draupadi was married to the Pandavas belonged to the Somaka clan. However, the Mahabharata and the Puranas consider the ruling clan of the northern Panchala as an offshoot of the Bharata clan and Divodasa, Sudas, Srinjaya, Somaka and Drupada (also called Yajnasena) were the most notable rulers of this clan.

Panchala under Magadhan Rule

Originally a monarchical clan, the Panchalas appear to have switched to republican corporation around 500 BCE. The Buddhist text, Anguttara Nikaya mentions Panchala as one of the sixteen mahajanapadas of the c. 6th century BCE. The 4th century BCE Arthashastra also attests the Panchalas as following the *Rajashabdopajivin* (king consul) constitution. Panchala was annexed into the Magadha empire during the reign of Mahapadma Nanda.

The Yuga Purana section of the Gargi Samhita informs us that Panchala was invaded and occupied by the *Yavana* (Greco-Bactrian) army led by King Dhamamita (Demetrius) during Brihadratha's reign But soon they had to leave to Bactria to fight a fierce battle (probably between Eucratides and Demetrius).

Panchala During Post-Mauryan Period

Numismatic evidence reveals the existence of the independent rulers of Panchala during the post-Mauryan period. Most of the coins issued by them are found at Ahichatra and adjoining areas. All coins are round, made of a copper alloy and have a set pattern on the obverse-a deeply incised square punch consisting of a row of three symbols and the ruler's name placed in a single line below them. The reverse bears depiction of the deities or sometimes their attributes, whose names form as a component of the issuers' names (like coins of Agnimitra bear the depiction of Agni).

The names of the rulers found from these coins are Vangapala, Yajnapala, Damagupta, Rudragupta, Jayagupta, Suryamitra, Phalgunimitra, Bhanumitra, Bhumimitra, Dhruvamitra, Agnimitra, Indramitra, Vishnumitra, Jayamitra, Prajapatimitra, Varunamitra, Anamitra, Bhadraghosha and Yugasena (reverse of the coins of Varunamitra, Yugasena and Anamitra do not exhibit any deity). Shaunakayaniputra Vangapala, ruler of Ahichatra, whom Vaidehiputra Ashadhasena refers as his grandfather in his Pabhosa inscription, is identified with king Vangapala, known from his coins. The name of Damagupta is also found on a clay sealing. Probably, the last independent ruler of Ahichatra was Achyuta, who was defeated by Samudragupta and Panchala was annexed into the Gupta Empire. The coins of Achyuta found from Ahichatra have a wheel of eight spokes on the reverse and the legend *Achyu* on the obverse.

Machcha or Matsya

Country of Matsya or Machcha tribe lied to south of the Kurus and west of the Yamuna which separated them from the Panchalas, It roughly corresponded to former state of Jaipur in Rajasthan, and included the whole of Alwar with portions of Bharatpur. The capital of Matsya was at *Viratanagara* (modern Bairat) which is said to have been named after its founder king Virata. In Pali literature, the Matsyas are usually associated with the Surasenas. The western Matsya was the hill tract on the north bank of Chambal. A branch of Matsya is also found in later days in Vizagapatam region. The Matsyas had not much political importance of their own during the times of Buddha. King Sujata ruled over both the Chedis and Matsyas thus showing that Matsya once formed a part of Chedi kingdom.

Surasena

Country of the Surasenas lied to south-west of Matsya and west of Yamuna. It had its capital at Madhura or Mathura. Avantiputra, the king of Surasena was the first among the chief disciples of Buddha through whose help, Buddhism gained ground in Mathura country. The Andhakas and Vrishnis of Mathura/ Surasena are referred to in the Ashtadhyayi of Panini. In Kautiliya's Arthashastra, the Vrishnis are described as Samgha or republic. The Vrishnis, Andhakas and other allied tribes of the Yadavas formed a Samgha and Vasudeva (Krishna) is described as the *Samgha-mukhya*. Mathura, the capital of Surasena was also known at the time of Megasthenes as the centre of Krishna worship. The Surasena kingdom had lost its independence on annexation by Magadhan empire.

Assaka or Ashmaka

The Country of Assaka or Ashmaka tribe was located in *Dakshinapatha* or southern India. In Buddha's time, Assakas were located on the banks of river Godavari (south of Vindhya mountains). The capital of Assakas was Potana or Potali which corresponds to Paudanya of Mahabharata. The Ashmakas are also mentioned by Panini. They are placed in the north-west in the *Markendeya Purana* and the *Brhat Samhita*. River Godavari separated the country of Assakas from that of the Mulakas (or Alakas). The commentator of Kautiliya's Arthashastra identifies Ashmaka with

Maharashtra. The country of Assaka lay outside the pale of Madhyadesa. It was located on a southern high road, the *Dakshinapatha*. At one time, Assaka included Mulaka and their country abutted with Avanti (Dr Bhandarkaar).

Avanti

Avanti was an ancient Indian janapada (realm), roughly corresponded to the present day Malwa region. According to the Buddhist text, the *Anguttara Nikaya,* Avanti was one of the *solasa mahajanapadas* (sixteen great realms) of the 6th century BCE. The *janapada* was divided into two parts by the Vindhyas, the northern part had its capital at Ujjayini and the southern part had its centre at Mahishmati.

The Haihayas of Mahishmati

According to the Puranic accounts, the Haihayas were the earliest rulers of Avanti, who captured the region from the Nagas. Initially, they ruled from Mahishmati. Later the whole janapada was divided into two parts with the capitals at Mahishmati and Ujjayini. The Haihayas were a confederation of five clans, the Vitihotras, the Bhojas, the Avantis, the Tundikeras and the Sharyatas. Ripunjaya, the last Vitihotra ruler of Ujjayini was overthrown by his *amatya* (minister) Pulika, who placed his son, Pradyota on the throne.

Pradyota Dynasty

Pradyota was contemporary to Gautama Buddha. He was also known as *Chandapradyota Mahasena.* Pradyota captured the Vatsa king Udayana but later he married Pradyota's daughter Vasavadatta. The *Mahavagga* described him as cruel and according to the Majjhima Nikaya, Ajatashatru, the king of Magadha fortified Rajagriha to protect it from an invasion led by Pradyota. He also waged war on Pushkarasarin, king of Takshashila Pradyota's chief queen Gopalamata (mother of prince Gopala) was a disciple of Buddhist monk Mahakatyayana and constructed a stupa in Ujjayini.

Prodyota had two sons, Gopala and Palaka. He was succeeded by Palaka. According to Jaina accounts Palaka ascended to the throne on the day of passing away of Mahavira. According to the Kathasaritsagara and the *Avashyaka Kathanaka,* the kingdom of Vatsa was already a part of Avanti during the reign of Palaka and a prince of the royal family was the governor of Kaushambi. In the Mricchakatika, Palaka was described as a tyrant who was overthrown by a popular revolt. This revolt placed Aryaka on the throne of Ujjayini. The Puranas place Nadivardhana or Vartivardhana after Aryaka. But these names are probably corruptions of Avantivardhana, the name of the son of Palaka according to the *Kathasaritsagara* or the son of Gopala according to the Nepali *Brihatkatha*. He was defeated by Shishunaga, the king of Magadha.

Avanti under Magadhan Rule

Avanti was a part of the Magadha empire during the rule of the Shaishunaga and the Nanda dynasties. During the Mauryan dynasty rule, Avanti became the Avantirmmha or the western province of the empire, with its capital at Ujjayini. The Junagarh Rock inscription of Rudradaman I (150 CE) mentions Pushyagupta as the governor of the western province during the reign of Chandragupta Maurya. During the reign of the next ruler Bindusara, prince Ashoka was the provincial governor. After the fall of the Mauryas, at the time of Pusyamitra Sunga, his son Agnimitra was the Magadhan viceroy at Vidisha, but he ruled independent of Magadha for all practical purposes.

Gandhara

The wool of Gandharis is referred to in the Rigveda. The Gandharis, along with the Mujavantas, Angas and the Magadhas, are also mentioned in the Atharvaveda, but apparently as a despised people. Gandharas are included in the Uttarapatha division of Puranic and Buddhistic traditions. Aitareya Brahmana refers to king Naganajit of Gandhara who was contemporary of raja Janaka of Videha. According to Dr Zimmer, Gandharas were settled since the Vedic times on the south bank of river Kubha (Kabol) up to its mouth into Indus itself. Later the Gandharas crossed Indus and expanded into parts of north-west Panjab. Gandharas and their king figure prominently as strong allies of the Kurus against the Pandavas in Mahabharata war. The Gandharas were a furious people, well trained in the art of war.

According to Puranic traditions, this Janapada was founded by *Gandhara*, son of Aruddha, a descendant of Yayati. The princes of this country are said to have come from the line of Druhyu who was a famous king of Rigvedic period. The river Indus watered the lands of Gandhara. Taksashila and Pushkalavati, the two cities of this Mahajanapada, are said to have been named after Taksa and Pushkara, the two sons of Bharata, a prince of Ayodhya. According to Vayu Purana (II.36.107), the Gandharas were destroyed by Pramiti aka Kalika, at the end of Kaliyuga. Panini has mentioned both Vedic form Gandhari as well as the later form Gandhara in his Ashtadhyayi. The Gandhara kingdom sometimes also included Kashmira. Hecataeus of Miletus (549-468) refers to Kaspapyros (Kasyapura i.e Kashmira) as Gandharic city.

According to Gandhara Jataka, at one time, Gandhara formed a part of the kingdom of Kashmir. Jataka also gives another name *Chandahara* for Gandhara. Gandhara Mahajanapada of Buddhist traditions included territories of east Afghanistan, and north-west of the Panjab (modern districts of Peshawar (Purushapura) and Rawalpindi). Its capital was Takshasila (Prakrit Taxila). The Taxila University was a renowned center of learning in ancient times, where scholars from all over the world came to seek higher education. Panini, the Indian genius of grammar and Kautiliya are the world renowned products of Taxila University. King Pukkusati or Pushkarasarin of Gandhara in middle of sixth century BCE was the contemporary of king Bimbisara of Magadha. Gandhara was located on the grand northern high road (Uttarapatha) and was a centre of international commercial activities.

It was an important channel of communication with ancient Iran and Central Asia. According to one school of scholars, the Gandharas and Kambojas were cognate people. It is also contended that the Kurus, Kambojas, Gandharas and Bahlikas were cognate people and all had Iranian affinities. According to Dr T. L. Shah, the Gandhara and Kamboja were nothing but two provinces of one empire and were located coterminously hence influencing each others language. Naturally, they may have once been a cognate people. Gandhara was often linked politically with the neighboring regions of Kashmir and Kamboja.

Kamboja

Kambojas are also included in the Uttarapatha. In ancient literature, the Kamboja is variously associated with the Gandhara, Darada and the Bahlika (Bactria). Ancient Kamboja is known to have comprised regions on either side of the Hindukush. The original Kamboja was located in eastern Oxus country as neighbor to Bahlika, but with time, some clans of Kambojas appear to have crossed Hindukush and planted colonies on its southern side also. These latter Kambojas are associated with the Daradas and Gandharas in Indian literature and also find mention in the Edicts of Ashoka. The evidence in Mahabharata and in Ptolemy's Geography distinctly supports two Kamboja settlements. The cis-Hindukush region from Nurestan up to Rajauri in southwest of Kashmir sharing borders with the Daradas and the Gandharas constituted the *Kamboja* country. The capital of *Kamboja* was probably *Rajapura* (modern Rajori) in south-west of Kashmir. The *Kamboja Mahajanapada* of the Buddhist traditions refers to this cis-Hindukush branch of ancient Kambojas.

The trans-Hindukush region including Pamirs and Badakhshan which shared borders with the Bahlikas (Bactria) in the west and the Lohas and Rishikas of Sogdiana/Fergana in the north, constituted the Parama-Kamboja country.

The trans-Hindukush branch of the Kambojas remained pure Iranian but a large section of the Kambojas of cis-Hindukush appears to have come under Indian cultural influence. The Kambojas are known to have had both Iranian as well as Indian affinities.

The Kambojas were also a well known republican people since Epic times. Mahabharata refers to several Ganah (or Republics) of the Kambojas. Kautiliya's Arthashastra and Ashoka's Edict No. XIII also attest that the Kambojas followed republican constitution. Panini's Sutras, though tend to convey that the Kamboja of Panini was a Kshatriya Monarchy, but "the special rule and the exceptional form of derivative" he gives to denote the ruler of the Kambojas implies that the king of Kamboja was a titular head (*king consul*) only.

According to Buddhist texts, the first fourteen of the above Mahajanapadas belong to Majjhimadesa (*Mid India*) while the last two belong to Uttarapatha or the *north-west* division of Jambudvipa.

In a struggle for supremacy that followed in the sixth/fifth century BCE, the growing state of Magadhas emerged as the most predominant power in ancient India annexing several of the Janapadas of the Majjhimadesa. A bitter line in the Brahmin Puranas laments that Magadhan emperor Mahapadma Nanda exterminated all Kshatriyas, none worthy of the name Kshatrya being left thereafter. This obviously refers to the Kasis, Kosalas, Kurus, Panchalas, Vatsyas and other neo-Vedic tribes of the east Panjab of whom nothing was ever heard except in the legend and poetry.

The Kambojans and Gandharans, however, never came into direct contact with Magadhan state until Chandragupta and Kautiliya arose on the scene. But these nations also fell a prey to the Achaemenids of Persia during the reign of Cyrus (558-530 BCE) or in the first year of Darius. Kamboja and Gandhara formed the twentieth and richest strapy of Achaemenid Empire. Cyrus I is said to have destroyed the famous Kamboja city called Kapisi (modern Begram) in Paropamisade.

Republics

Historians who are interested in democracy often insist it must be understood in context of a unique western tradition of political development beginning with the Greeks. The spread of democratic ideals and practice to other cultures, or their failure to spread, have many times been explained on the assumption that democracy or personal liberty are ideals foreign to the non-Western world – an assumption at least as old as Herodotus. But events since the late 1980s have shown that people both in "Western" and "non-Western" countries have a lively interest in democracy as something relevant to their own situation. The old assumption deserves to be re-examined.

In fact, the supposed differences between "Western" and "non-Western" cultures are in this case, as in so many others, more a matter of ideological faith than of cool, impartial judgment. If we are talking about the history of humanity as a whole, democracy is equally new or equally old everywhere. Fair and effective elections, under adult suffrage and in conditions that allow the free discussion of ideas, are a phenomenon of this century. The history of democracy, properly so called, is just beginning.

The "prehistory" of democracy, however, is scarcely restricted to Europe and Europeanized America and Australasia. A search of world history finds much worth studying. There are no perfect democracies waiting to be discovered, but there is something else: a long history of "government by discussion," in which groups of people having common interests make decisions that affect their lives through debate, consultation, and voting. The vast majority of such groups, it may be objected, are more properly called oligarchies than democracies. But every democracy has been created by widening what was originally a very narrow franchise. The history of government by discussion, which may be called republicanism for brevity's sake, has a claim to the interest of anyone who takes democracy seriously.

This article will examine one important case of government by discussion — the republics of Ancient India. Although they are familiar to Indologists, these republics are hardly known to other historians. They deserve, however, a substantial place in world historiography. The experience of Ancient India with republicanism, if better known, would by itself make democracy seem less of a freakish development, and help dispel the common idea that the very concept of democracy is specifically "Western."

The present article has two goals. First, it will summarize the history of the ancient Indian republics as it is currently known. This survey is restricted to North India and the period before about 400 A.D., when sovereign republics seem to have become extinct.

Second, the article will examine the historiographical evaluations of the Indian republican experience, and suggest that most of them have placed it in too narrow a context. Ancient Indian democratic experiments, it will be argued, are more important than they are usually granted to be. It is well known that the sources of ancient Indian history present considerable difficulties. All the indigenous ancient literature from the subcontinent has been preserved as part of a religious tradition, Brahmanical, Buddhist or Jaina. When the subject is political theory and its implementation, the preselected nature of sources is a distinct handicap to the researcher. The largest and most influential Indian literary tradition, the Brahmanical, is distinctly hostile to anything resembling democracy.

Brahmanical literature gives kingship a central place in political life, and seldom hints that anything else is possible. For moral philosophers and legislators such as Manu (reputed author of the *Manu-Smrti* between 200 B.C.-A.D. 200), the king was a key figure in a social order based on caste (*varna*). Caste divided society into functional classes: the Brahmans had magical powers and priestly duties, the *ksatriyas* were the rulers and warriors, the *vaisyas* cultivators, and the *sudras* the lowest part of society, subservient to the other three. Moral law or *dharma* depended on the observance of these divisions, and the king was the guarantor of *dharma*, and in particular the privileges of the Brahmans. 3 Another tradition is best exemplified by the *Arthasastra* of Kautilya (c. 300 B.C.), which alloted the king a more independent role but likewise emphasized his responsibility for peace, justice and stability.

Both Kautilya's work and the *Manu-Smrti* are considered classic expressions of ancient Indian political and social theory. A reader of these or other Brahmanical treatises finds it very easy to visualize ancient Indian society as one where "monarchy was the normal form of the state."

Until the end of the last century, the only indication that this might not always have been the case came from Greek and Roman accounts of India, mostly histories of India during and just after Alexander the Great's invasion of India in 327-324 B.C. These works spoke of numerous cities and even larger areas being governed as oligarchies and democracies, but they were not always believed by scholars. The Pali Canon is the earliest version of the Buddhist scriptures, and reached its final form between 400-300 B.C.7 It contains the story of Buddha's life and teaching and his rules for monastic communities.

The rules and teachings are presented in the form of anecdotes, explaining the circumstances that called forth the Buddha's authoritative pronouncement. Thus the Pali Canon provides us with many details of life in ancient India, and specifically of the sixth century (the Buddha's lifetime) in the northeast. In 1903, T.W. Rhys Davids, the leading Pali scholar, pointed out in his book *Buddhist India* that the Canon (and the *Jatakas*, a series of Buddhist legends set in the same period but composed much later) depicted a country in which there were many clans, dominating extensive and populous territories, who made their public decisions in assemblies, moots, or parliaments.

Rhys Davids' observation was not made in a vacuum. Throughout the nineteenth century, students of local government in India (many of them British bureaucrats) had been fascinated by popular elements in village life. The analysis of village government was part of a continuous debate on the goals and methods of imperial policy, and the future of India as a self-governing country. Rhys-Davids' book made the ancient institutions of India relevant to this debate. His reconstruction of a republican past for India was taken up by nationalistic Indian scholars of the 1910s. Later generations of Indian scholars have been somewhat embarrassed by the enthusiasm of their elders for early republics and have sought to treat the republics in a more balanced and dispassionate manner.

Nevertheless, their work, like that of the pioneering nationalists, has been extremely productive. Not only the classical sources and the Pali Canon, but also Buddhist works in Sanskrit, Panini's Sanskrit grammar (the *Astadhyayi*), the *Mahabharata*, the Jaina Canon, and even Kautilya's *Arthasastra* have been combed for evidence and insights. Coins and inscriptions have documented the existence of republics and the workings of popular assemblies.

The work of twentieth century scholars has made possible a much different view of ancient political life in India. It has shown us a landscape with kings a-plenty, a culture where the terminology of rule is in the majority of sources relentlessly monarchical, but where, at the same time, the realities of politics are so complex that simply to call them "monarchical" is a grave distortion. Indeed, in ancient India, monarchical thinking was constantly battling with another vision, of self-rule by members of a guild, a village, or an extended kin-group, in other words, any group of equals with a common set of interests. This vision of cooperative self-government often produced republicanism and even democracy comparable to classical Greek democracy.

Though evidence for non-monarchical government goes back to the Vedas, 12 republican polities were most common and vigorous in the Buddhist period, 600 B.C.-A.D. 200. At this time, India was in the throes of urbanization. The Pali Canon gives a picturesque description of the city of Vesali in the fifth century B.C. as possessing 7707 storied buildings, 7707 pinnacled buildings, 7707 parks and lotus ponds, and a multitude of people, including the famous courtesan Ambapali, whose beauty and artistic achievements contributed mightily to the city's prosperity and reputation. The cities of Kapilavatthu and Kusavati were likewise full of traffic and noise. Moving between these cities were great trading caravans of 500 or 1000 carts — figures that convey no precise measurement, but give a true feeling of scale: caravans that stopped for more than four months in a single place, as they often did because of the rainy season, were described as villages.14 Religion, too, was taking to the road. The hereditary Brahman who was also a householder, as in later Vedic tradition, saw his teachings, authority and perquisites threatened by wandering holy men and self-appointed teachers.

There were warlord-kings who sought to control this fluid society, some with a measure of success. But the literature, Pali and Sanskrit, Buddhist and Brahmanical, shows that non-monarchical forms of government were omnipresent. There was a complex vocabulary to describe the different types of groups that ran their own affairs. Some of these were obviously warrior bands; 17 others more peaceful groups with economic goals; some religious brotherhoods. Such an organization, of whatever type, could be designated, almost indifferently, as a *gana* or a *sangha;* and similar though less important bodies were labelled with the terms *sreni, puga,* or *vrata. Gana* and *sangha,* the most important of these terms, originally meant "multitude." By the sixth century B.C., these words meant both a self-governing multitude, in which decisions were made by the members working in common, and the style of government characteristic of such groups. In the case of the strongest of such groups, which acted as sovereign governments, the words are best translated as "republic."

That there were many sovereign republics in India is easily demonstrated from a number of sources. Perhaps it is best to begin with the Greek evidence, even though it is not the earliest, simply because the Greek writers spoke in a political language that is familiar.

Perhaps the most useful Greek account of India is Arrian's *Anabasis of Alexander*, which describes the Macedonian conqueror's campaigns in great detail. The *Anabasis,* which is derived from the eyewitness accounts of Alexander's companions, 18 portrays him as meeting "free and independent" Indian communities at every turn. What "free and independent" meant is illustrated from the case of Nysa, a city on the border of modern Afghanistan and Pakistan that was ruled by a president named Aculphis and a council of 300. After surrendering to Alexander, Aculphis used the city's supposed connection with the god Dionysus to seek lenient terms from the king:

"The Nysaeans beseech thee, O king out of respect for Dionysus, to allow them to remain free and independent; for when Dionysus had subjugated the nation of the Indians...he founded this city from the soldiers who had become unfit for military service...From that time we inhabit Nysa, a free city, and we ourselves are independent, conducting our government with constitutional order."

Nysa was in Greek terms an oligarchy, as further discussion between Alexander and Aculphis reveals, and a single-city state. There were other Indian states that were both larger in area and wider in franchise. It is clear from Arrian that the Mallian republic consisted of a number of cities. Q. Curtius Rufus and Diodorus Siculus in their histories of Alexander mention a people called the Sabarcae or Sambastai among whom "the form of government was democratic and not regal." The Sabarcae/Sambastai, like the Mallians, had a large state. Their army consisted of 60,000 foot, 6000 cavalry, and 500 chariots. Thus Indian republics of the late fourth century could be much larger than the contemporaneous Greek *polis*. And it seems that in the northwestern part of India, republicanism was the norm. Alexander's historians mention a large number of republics, some named, some not, but only a handful of kings. The prevalence of republicanism and its democratic form is explicitly stated by Diodorus Siculus. After describing the mythical monarchs who succeeded the god Dionysus as rulers of India, he says:

At last, however, after many years had gone, most of the cities adopted the democratic form of government, though some retained the kingly until the invasion of the country by Alexander.

What makes this statement particularly interesting is that it seems to derive from a first-hand description of India by a Greek traveller named Megasthenes. Around 300 B.C., about two decades after Alexander's invasion, Megasthenes served as ambassador of the Greek king Seleucus Nicator to the Indian emperor Chandragupta Maurya, and in the course of his duties crossed northern India to the eastern city of Patna, where he lived for a while.

If we turn to the Indian sources, we find that there is nothing far-fetched about this idea. The most useful sources for mapping north India are three: The Pali Canon, which shows us northeastern

India between the Himalayas and the Ganges in the sixth and fifth centuries B.C.; the grammar of Panini, which discusses all of North India, with a focus on the northwest, during the fifth century; and Kautilya's *Arthasastra*, which is a product of the fourth century, roughly contemporaneous with Megasthenes. All three sources enable us to identify numerous *sanghas* and *ganas*, some very minor, others large and powerful.

What were these republican polities like? According to Panini, all the states and regions (*janapadas*) of northern India during his time were based on the settlement or conquest of a given area by an identifiable warrior people who still dominated the political life of that area. Some of these peoples (in Panini's terms *janapadins*) were subject to a king, who was at least in theory of their own blood and was perhaps dependent on their special support. Elsewhere, the *janapadins* ran their affairs in a republican manner. Thus in both kinds of state, the government was dominated by people classified as *ksatriyas*, or, as later ages would put it, members of the warrior caste.

But in many states, perhaps most, political participation was restricted to a subset of all the *ksatriyas*. One needed to be not just a warrior, but a member of a specific royal clan, the *rajanya*. Evidence from a number of sources shows that the enfranchised members of many republics, including the Buddha's own Sakyas and the Licchavis with whom he was very familiar, considered themselves to be of royal descent, even brother-kings. The term *raja*, which in a monarchy certainly meant king, in a state with *gana* or *sangha* constitution could designate someone who held a share in sovereignty. In such places, it seems likely that political power was restricted to the heads of a restricted number of "royal families" (*rajakulas*) among the ruling clans. The heads of these families were consecrated as kings, and thereafter took part in deliberations of state.

Our Indian republics are beginning to sound extremely undemocratic by our modern standards, with real power concentrated in the hands of a few patriarchs representing the leading lineages of one privileged section of the warrior caste. A reader who has formed this impression is not entirely mistaken. No doubt the rulers of most republics thought of their *gana* as a closed club – as did the citizens of Athens, who also defined themselves as a hereditarily privileged group.

First, the closed nature of the ruling class is easy to exaggerate. Republics where only descendants of certain families held power were common; but there was another type in which power was shared by all *ksatriya* families. This may not sound like much of a difference, since the restriction to the warrior caste seems to remain. But this is an anachronistic view of the social conditions of the time. The *varnas* of pre-Christian-era India were not the castes of later periods, with their prohibitions on intermarriage and commensality with other groups. Rather, they were the constructs of theorists, much like the division of three orders (priests, warriors and workers) beloved by European writers of the Early Middle Ages. Such a classification was useful for debating purposes, but was not a fact of daily existence. Those republics that threw open the political process to all *ksatriyas* were not extending the franchise from one clearly defined group to another, albeit a larger one, but to all those who could claim, and justify the claim, to be capable of ruling and fighting.

Other evidence suggests that in some states the enfranchised group was even wider. Such a development is hinted at in Kautilya: according to him, there were two kinds of *janapadas, ayudhiya-praya,* those made up mostly of soldiers, and *sreni-praya,* those comprising guilds of craftsmen, traders, and agriculturalists. The first were political entities where military tradition alone defined those worthy of power, while the second would seem to be communities where wealth derived from peaceful economic activity gave some access to the political process. This interpretation is supported by the fact that *sreni* or guilds based on an economic interest were often both part of the armed force of a state and recognized as having jurisdiction over their own members.

In the Indian republics, as in the Greek *poleis* or the European cities of the High Middle Ages, economic expansion enabled new groups to take up arms and eventually demand a share in sovereignty If it was not granted, one could always form one's own mini-state. Panini's picture of stable, long-established *janapadas* is certainly the illusion of a systematizing grammarian. As Panini's most thorough modern student has put it, there was "a craze for constituting new republics" which "had reached its climax in the *Vahika* country and north-west India where clans constituting of as many as one hundred families only organized themselves as *Ganas.*" Furthermore, power in some republics was vested in a large number of individuals. In a well-known *Jataka* tale we are told that in the Licchavi capital of Vesali, there were 7707 kings (*rajas*), 7707 viceroys, 7707 generals, and 7707 treasurers.

These figures, since they come from about half a millenium after the period they describe, have little evidentiary value, despite the ingenious efforts of scholars to find a core of hard fact. The tale does not give us the number of Licchavi ruling families (*rajakulas*), the size of the Licchavi assembly, or any real clues as to the population of Vesali. Yet the *Jataka* does retain the memory of an undisputed feature of Indian republicanism: the rulers were many. The same memory can be found in other sources, especially in those critical of republicanism. The *Lalitavistara*, in an obvious satirical jab, depicts Vesali as being full of Licchavi *rajans*, each one thinking, "I am king, I am king," and thus a place where piety, age and rank were ignored. The *Santi Parva* section of the *Mahabharata* shows the participation of too many people in the affairs of state as being a great flaw in the republican polity:

> The *gana* leaders should be respected as the worldly affairs (of the *ganas*) depend to a great extent upon them...the spy (department) and the secrecy of counsel (should be left) to the chiefs, for it is not fit that the entire body of the *gana* should hear those secret matters. The chiefs of *gana* should carry out together, in secret, works leading to the prosperity of the *gana*, otherwise the wealth of the *gana* decays and it meets with danger.

A Jaina work again criticizes *gaṇas* for being disorderly: the monks and nuns who frequent them will find themselves bullied, beaten, robbed, or accused of being spies.

The numerous members of a sovereign *gana* or *sangha* interacted with each other as members of an assembly. Details of the working of such assemblies can be found both in Brahmanical and Buddhist literature. By the time of Panini (fifth century B.C.), there was a terminology for the process of corporate decision-making. Panini gives us the terms for vote, decisions reached by voting, and the completion of a quorum. Another cluster of words indicates that the division of assemblies into political parties was well known. Further, Panini and his commentators show that sometimes a smaller select group within a *sangha* had special functions – acting as an executive, or perhaps as a committees for defined purposes.

The Pali Canon gives a much fuller, if somewhat indirect, depiction of democratic institutions in India. This is found in three of the earliest and most revered parts of the canon, the *Maha-parinibbana-suttanta,* the *Mahavagga,* and the *Kullavagga.* These works, taken together, preserve the Buddha's instructions for the proper running of the Buddhist monastic brotherhood – the *sangha* – after his death. They are the best source for voting procedures in a corporate body in the earliest part of the Buddhist period. They also give some insight into the development of democratic ideology.

The rules for conducting the Buddhist *sangha* were, according to the first chapter of the *Maha-parinibbana-suttanta,* based in principle on those commonly found in political *sanghas* or *ganas.* In the case of the Buddhist *sangha,* the key organizational virtue was the full participation of all the monks in the ritual and disciplinary acts of their group. To assure that this would be remembered, detailed rules concerning the voting in monastic assemblies, their membership, and their quorums, were set down in the *Mahavagga* and the *Kullavagga.*

Business could only be transacted legitimately in a full assembly, by a vote of all the members. If, for example, a candidate wanted the *upasampada* ordination, the question (*ñatti*) was put to the *sangha* by a learned and competent member, and the other members asked three times to indicate dissent. If there was none, the *sangha* was taken to be in agreement with the *aatti.* The decision was finalized by the proclamation of the decision of the *sangha.*

In many cases, as in the granting of *upasampada* ordination, unanimity of a full assembly was required. Of course, unanimity was not always possible. The *Kullavagga* provides other techniques that were used in disputes especially dangerous to the unity of the *sangha,* those which concerned interpretation of the monastic rule itself. If such a dispute had degenerated into bitter and confused debate, it could be decided by majority vote, or referred to a jury or committee specially elected by the *sangha* to treat the matter at hand.

It is here that we see a curious combination of well-developed democratic procedure and fear of democracy. The rules for taking votes sanctioned the disallowance by the vote-taker of results that threatened the essential law of the *sangha* or its unity. Yet, if the voting procedure is less than free, the idea that only a free vote could decide contentious issues is strongly present. No decision could be made until some semblance of agreement had been reached. Such manipulations of voting were introduced because Buddhist elders were very concerned about the survival of the religious enterprise: disunity of the membership was the great fear of all Indian republics and corporations. Yet the idea of a free vote could not be repudiated. The *Kullavagga* illustrates a conflict within the Buddhist *sangha* during its earliest centuries between democratic principles and a philosophy that was willing in the name of unity to sacrifice them.

Since the rules of the Buddhist *sangha* are by far the best known from the period we have been discussing, it is tempting to identify them with the rules of political *ganas*, particularly those of the Licchavis (or Vajjians), since the Buddha made a clear connection between the principles applicable to the Licchavi polity and those of his *sangha*. But from early on, scholars have recognized that the Buddhist constitution was not an exact imitation of any other: for instance, sovereign republics had a small, elected executive committee to manage the affairs of the *gana* when the whole membership of the *gana* was unable to be assembled. But neither did the Buddha or his earliest followers invent their complex and carefully formulated parliamentary procedures out of whole cloth. R.C. Majumdar's conclusion, first formulated in 1918, still seems valid: the techniques seen in the Buddhist *sangha* reflect a sophisticated and widespread political culture based on the popular assembly.

Similarly, the value placed on full participation of members in the affairs of their *sangha* must reflect the ideology of those who believed in the *sangha-gana* form of government in the political sphere. The Buddha's commitment to republicanism (or at least the ideal republican virtues) was a strong one, if we are to believe the *Maha-parinibbana-suttanta*, among the oldest of Buddhist texts. As is common in the Buddhist scriptures, a precept is illustrated by a story. Will his attack be a success? Rather than answer directly, the Buddha speaks to Ananda, his closest disciples:

"Have you heard, Ananda, that the Vajjians hold full and frequent public assemblies?"

"Lord, so I have heard," replied he.

"So long, Ananda," rejoined the Blessed One, "as the Vajjians hold these full and frequent public assemblies; so long may they be expected not to decline, but to prosper...

In a series of rhetorical questions to Ananda, the Buddha outlines other requirements for Vajjian prosperity:

"So long, Ananda, as the Vajjians meet together in concord, and rise in concord, and carry out their undertakings in concord...so long as they enact nothing not already established, abrogate nothing that has been already enacted, and act in accordance with the ancient institutions of the Vajjians as established in former days...so long as they honor and esteem and revere and support the Vajjian elders, and hold it a point of duty to hearken to their words...so long as no women or girls belonging to their clans are detained among them by force or abduction...so long as they honor and esteem and revere and support the Vajjian shrines in town or country, and allow not the proper offerings and rites, as formerly given and performed, to fall into desuetude...so long as the rightful protection, defense, and support shall be fully provided for the Arahats among them, so that Arahats from a distance may enter the realm, and the Arahats therein may live at ease — so long may the Vajjians be expected not to decline, but to prosper."

Then the Blessed One addressed Vassakara the Brahman, and said, "When I was once staying, O Brahman, at Vesali at the Sarandada Temple, I taught the Vajjians these conditions of welfare; and so long as those conditions shall continue to exist among the Vajjians, so long as the Vajjians shall be well instructed in those conditions, so long may we expect them not to decline, but to prosper."

The comment of the king's ambassador underlines the point of this advice: "So, Gotama, the Vajjians cannot be overcome by the king of Magadha; that is, not in battle, without diplomacy or breaking up their alliance."

The same story tells us that once the king's envoy had departed, the Buddha and Ananda went to meet the assembly of monks. Buddha told the monks that they too must observe seven conditions if they were to prosper: Full and frequent assemblies, concord, preserving and not abrogating established institutions, honoring elders, falling "not under the influence of that craving which, springing up within them, would give rise to renewed existence," delighting in a life of solitude, and training "their minds that good and holy men shall come to them, and those who have come shall dwell at ease." 57 These precepts, and others that follow in sets of seven, were the main point for the monks who have transmitted the *Maha-parinibbana-suttanta* to us. We, however, may wish to emphasize another point: the Buddha saw the virtues necessary for a righteous and prosperous community, whether secular or monastic, as being much the same. Foremost among those virtues was the holding of "full and frequent assemblies." In this, the Buddha spoke not only for himself, and not only out of his personal view of justice and virtue. He based himself on what may be called the democratic tradition in ancient Indian politics — democratic in that it argued for a wide rather than narrow distribution of political rights, and government by discussion rather than by command and submission.

The Pali Canon gives us our earliest, and perhaps our best, detailed look at Indian republicanism, its workings, and its political philosophy. About no other republics do we know as much as we do about the Buddhist *sangha* and the Licchavis in the time of Buddha — even though we do know that republics survived and were a significant factor until perhaps the fourth century A.D., a period of over 800 years. Scattered inscriptions, a great number of coins, and the occasional notice in Greek sources, the *Jatakas* or other Indian literature give us a few facts. But any history of Indian republicanism is necessarily a rather schematic one.

The theme that has most attracted the attention of scholars is the constant danger to republicanism, and its ultimate failure. Much of what we know about the sovereign *ganas* of India derives from stories of attacks upon them by various conquerors. Yet it is remarkable that for several centuries, the conspicuous successes of monarchs, even the greatest, had only a temporary effect on the sovereign republics and very little effect indeed on the corporate organization of guilds, religious bodies, and villages. The reason is, of course, that Indian kings have seldom been as mighty as they wished to be, or wished to be presented. Conquerors were not in a position to restructure society, to create states as we visualize them today. Rather they were usually content to gain the submission of their neighbors, whether they were other kings or republics. These defeated rivals were often left in control of their own affairs, merely required to pay tribute and provide troops for the conquerors next war. The great emperors of ancient India, including Chandragupta Maurya and Asoka, ran rather precarious realms. Once the center weakened, these unraveled very quickly, and society returned to its preceding complexity. Rival dynasties revived, as did defeated republics.

As Altekar recognized, the mere existence of warlords was not fatal to the republican tradition of politics. Far more important was the slow abandonment of republican ideals by republicans themselves. We have seen that many republics were content even in the earliest days with a very exclusive definition of the political community. In some, ideas of wider participation gained currency and even implementation. But the contrary movement is easier to document. By the third and fourth centuries A.D., states known to be republics in earlier times were subject to hereditary executives. Eventually such republics became monarchies.

An evolution away from republicanism is clearly seen in the literature of politics and religion. If we grant that the society depicted by the Pali Canon is the beginning of a new era, one with an economy and culture quite distinct from the Vedic period, it immediately becomes obvious that the most democratic ideals are the earliest. The Pali Canon, and to some extent the Jaina Canon, show us energetic movements that rejected the hierarchialism and caste ideology seen in the Vedas and Brahmanas in favour of more egalitarian values. Buddhism and Jainism were scarcely exceptional: they are merely the most successful of many contemporary religious movements, and left us records. It is clear from Panini that egalitarianism was an important element in the fifth century B.C.: he preserves a special term for the *gana* where "there was no distinction between high and low."

Such Brahmanical classics as the *Mahabharata,* the writings of Kautilya and the *Manu-Smrti,* works that promoted hierarchy, are manifestations of a later movement (300 B.C.-200 A.D.) away from the degree of egalitarianism that had been achieved. Kautilya, who is traditionally identified with the chief minister of the Mauryan conqueror Chandragupta Maurya (fl. after 300 B.C.), is famous for his advice to monarchs on the best way to tame or destroy *ganas* through subterfuge; perhaps a more important part of his achievement was to formulate a political science in which royalty was normal, even though his own text shows that *ganas* were very important factors in the politics of his time. Similarly, the accomplishment of the *Manu-Smrti* was to formulate a view of society where human equality was non-existent and unthinkable.

Members of *ganas* were encouraged to fit themselves into a hierarchical, monarchical framework by a number of factors. Kings were not the only enemies of the *ganas*. The relationships between competing *ganas* must have been a constant political problem. *Ganas* that claimed sovereignty over certain territory were always faced by the competing claims of other corporate groups. How were these claims to be sorted out, other than by force? The king had an answer to this question: if he were acknowledged as "the only monarch [i.e. *raja*, chief executive] of all the corporations," 65 he would commit himself to preserving the legitimate privileges of each of them, and even protect the lesser members of each *gana* from abuse of power by their leaders. It was a tempting offer, and since the alternative was constant battle, it was slowly accepted, sometimes freely, sometimes under compulsion. The end result was the acceptance of a social order in which many *ganas* and *sanghas* existed, but none were sovereign and none were committed to any general egalitarian view of society. They were committed instead to a hierarchy in which they were promised a secure place. Such a notional hierarchy seems to have been constructed in North India by the fifth century A.D. Even the Buddhist *sangha* accommodated itself to it — which led eventually to the complete victory of the rival Brahmans.

This was not quite the end of republicanism, because "government by discussion" continued within many *ganas* and *sanghas*; but the idea of hierarchy and inequality, of caste, was increasingly dominant. The degree of corporate autonomy in later Indian society, which is considerable and in itself a very important fact, is in this sense a different topic that the one we have been following. A corporation that accepts itself as a subcaste in a great divine hierarchy is different from the more pugnacious *ganas* and *sanghas* of the Pali Canon, Kautilya or even the *Jataka* stories.

What have modern historians made of what we might call the golden age of Indian republicanism? We have already distinguished above between two eras of scholarship on the topic. In the first, patriotic enthusiasm and the simple thrill of discovery of unsuspected material characterized scholars' reactions. The former attitude was especially seen in K.P. Jayaswal's *Hindu Polity*. Published first in article form in 1911-1913, then as a book in 1924,

Jayaswal's work was avowedly aimed to show that his countrymen were worthy of independence from Britain. The history of "Hindu" institutions demonstrated an ancient talent for politics:

> The test of a polity is its capacity to live and develop, and its contribution to the culture and happiness of humanity. Hindu polity judged by this test will come out very successfully...The Golden Age of [the Hindu's] polity lies not in the Past but in the Future... Constitutional or social advancement is not a monopoly of any particular race.

In Jayaswal's book scholarship was sometimes subordinated to his argument. In his discussion of ancient republics (which was not his only subject), the evidence was pushed at least as far as it would go to portray the republics as inspiring examples of early democracy. A similar, though quieter satisfaction can be seen in the contemporary discussions of R.C. Majumdar and D.R. Bhandarkar.

In the second period of scholarship, in the years since independence, a more restrained attitude has been adopted by younger scholars who feel they have nothing to prove. Among these scholars the general tendency has been to emphasize that the republics were not real republics, in the modern usage that implies a universal adult suffrage. The clan-basis and the exclusiveness of the ruling class are much discussed. Sometimes writers have bent over backwards to divorce the Indian republican experience from the history of democracy: thus A.K. Majumdar's judgement that because in a *gana-rajya* "all inhabitants other than the members of the *raja-Kulas* [had] no rights [and] were treated as inferior citizens," people were actually better off in the monarchies, where "if not the general mass, at least the intellectuals and the commercial community enjoyed freedom in a monarchy, which seems to have been lacking in a *gana-rajya*." The contrast drawn here is not backed up by any real argument, and makes one wonder about the how the author defines "freedom."

The reaction has perhaps gone too far. One feels that modern scholars have still not come to grips with the existence of widespread republicanism in a region so long thought to be the home *par excellence* of "Oriental Despotism." Republicanism now has a place in every worthwhile book about ancient India, but it tends to be brushed aside so that one can get back to the main story, which is the development of the surviving Hindu tradition. Historians, in India as elsewhere, seem to feel that anything which could be so thoroughly forgotten must have had grievous flaws to begin with. Most historians still cannot discuss these republics without qualifying using the qualifiers "tribal" or "clan." Long ago Jayaswal rightly protested against the use of these terms: "The evidence does not warrant our calling [republics] 'clans.' Indian republics of the seventh [sic] and sixth centuries B.C...had long passed the tribal stage of society. They were states, *Ganas* and *Samghas*, though many of them likely had a national or tribal basis, as every state, ancient or modern, must necessarily have." He was equally correct when he pointed out that "Every state in ancient Rome and Greece was 'tribal' in the last analysis, but no constitutional historian would think of calling the republics of Rome and Greece mere tribal organizations."

Yet the phrases "clan-" and "tribal-republic" are still routinely used today in the Indian context, and it is difficult to avoid the conclusion that they are being used perjoratively. In both common and scholarly usage, to label a people's institutions or culture as tribal is to dismiss them from serious consideration. "Tribespeople" are historical dead-ends, and their suppression or absorption by more advanced cultures (usually those ruled by centralizing governments) is taken for granted. The terminology of even Indian historians demonstrates the survival of an ancient but inappropriate prejudice in the general evaluation of Indian republicanism.

Once that prejudice is overcome, Indian republicanism gains a strong claim on the attention of historians, especially those with an interest in comparative or world history.

It is especially remarkable that, during the near-millenium between 500 B.C. and 400 A.D., we find republics almost anywhere in India that our sources allow us to examine society in any detail. Unless those sources, not least our Greek sources, are extremely deceptive, the republics of India were very likely more extensive and populous than the *poleis* of the Greeks. One cannot help wondering how in many other parts of Eurasia republican and democratic states may have co-existed with the royal dynasties that are a staple of both ancient and modern chronology and conceptualization. This may well be an unanswerable question, but so far no one has even tried to investigate it. If an investigation is made, we may discover things that are as surprising to us as the republics of India originally were. The existence of Indian republicanism is a discovery of the twentieth century. The implications of this phenomenon have yet to be fully digested, because historians of the past century have been inordinately in love with the virtues of centralized authority and government by experts, and adhered to an evolutionary historicism that has little good to say about either direct or representative democracy. Perhaps the love affair is fading. If so, historians will find, in the Indian past as elsewhere, plenty of raw material for a new history of the development of human government.

According Romila Thapar the republics grew out of monarchies. The more independent Aryans rebelled against the monarchical rule and established republics which were more in keeping with the tribal traditions. While some say republics predated monarchies. In ancient India these republics were given the term gana and sangha. According Panini the term 'Samgha' and 'gana' had the same meaning. The Arthsashtra of Kautilya mentions a number of republics including those of Lichchhavis, the Vrijikas, the Kuru, the Panchalas, the kamboj etc. The most prominent and powerful of these republics was that of the Lichchhavis. It had its capital at Vaisali. Even the Greek writers are of the opinion that a large number of republics existed in India at the time of Alexander's invasion. The Buddhist literature is another source of these republics. It refers to a large number of republics which covered the area to the east of the kingdoms of Kosala and Kausambhi and to the west of Anga, to the north of Magadha and the south of the Himalayas. The republics were basically of two types-the republics comprising a single tribe like those of the Sakyas, the Kolias and the Mallas and the republics comprising a number of tribes or the republics of confederacy like the Vrijjis.

Government of the Republics: The kings in these states had the supreme authority. These republics or sanghs were governed on democratic lines. A chief was elected to act as the president of the administrative council. The administrative and the judicial matters of the republics were carried out in public assembly at which young and old are alike present in the common hall at Kapilavastu. It was called as Santhagara. The assembly of the people could also be called on special occasions. The president of the council was called a Raja. It is not known as to how he was elected and for how long he ruled but it appears that the office was not hereditary. The local administration was carried by local assemblies which played an important role in the administration of the state. In some of these republics villages were organized on professional basis e.g. the potter, smiths of the clan used to have separate villages of their own. The small republics were gradually losing their importance and were being over-shadowed by kingdoms like Vatsa, Avanti, Kosala, Magadha etc. Soon the leadership became hereditary in certain families. The leaders took up the titles of Maharajas and Mahasenapatis in the 4th century. The ancient Indian republics flourished in Mauryan times and survived up to Gupta period.

Kosala and Magadha

The new moral philosophies of the sixth century B.C. that formulated and preached a doctrine beyond the tribe had their political counterpart. There was a parallel move towards a universal government for all society. The basis was identical both in religious and secular movements: the new needs of gahapati, trader, and farmer. Whereas the founders of the great monastic orders had considered tribal patterns of organisation quite suitable and perfectly natural for their own samghas, especially the Jain and the Buddhist, the theoreticians of state policy could think of only one way to break tribal exclusiveness-a dictatorial absolute monarchy. Ancient Greeks would have recognised this as transition from the Homeric basileus to the Peisitratid tyrannos.

A cold, inexorable, grimly calculating, logically formulated and carefully reasoned political theory lay behind the prolonged struggle for absolute power. There was never the least pretence of morality or specious excuse of doing good to others. The theorists of this new polity were as important and as capable thinkers in their own way as the contemporary religious leaders. Their names survive only in one book, a compendium by the greatest and the last of the line, the Arthasastra of Kautalya, which will be considered in the next chapter. The roster is quite impressive: Bharadvija, Kityayana, Parasara, Ushanas, and Brihaspati bear good brahmin names; some of them represent an entire traditional school each, as with the older religious sects of the time.

A 'son of Bahudanti', Kinjalka, Kaunapadanta, Pisuna, Visalaksha, Vatavyadhi, and Dirgha-Carayana were presumably kshatriyas; the main school of importance in the kshatriya line bore the name of Ambhi. The list given here is by no means complete. The full teaching has survived for none, though the views of each are cited and discussed in the Arthasastra where relevant, very much in the analytical manner of a jurist reviewing former enunciations of legal principles. The historical context is never given and is not otherwise known except for 'Long' Carayana. This obscurity is natural.

Where the teachers of religion had to convince the multitude and win over people in all walks of life by open and widely disseminated preaching, advice on state policy could be effective only if kept secret, reserved for the chosen few. The great religious almsmen-teachers of the sixth century were far above the all-too-common parasitic beggars and thick-headed cult leaders of later India, because the former participated vigorously in the formation of a totally new type of society. This is precisely the difference between the tale of war, intrigue, assassination and broken faith that unfolds itself in the sixth century and similar actions in later absolute tyrannies where the throne had no constitutional check. The sixth-century monarchies were the first, an innovation to suit the formation of a completely new social stage; the medieval 'oriental despotisms' were changes at the top without effect upon the social basis, which had long been crystallised.

There had traditionally been sixteen principal janapadas (territories) in the seventh century B.C., perhaps even a century earlier. Of these sixteen only four retained any importance in the final struggle for power that was fought out at the end of the sixth and beginning of the fifth centuries. Two were powerful tribal oligarchies acknowledging no absolute ruler, namely the Licchavi or Vajji ('pastoral nomads', which shows that they settled down rather late) and the Mallas. These two tribes conducted their affairs by tribal assembly and constantly practised military exercises. They had tribal constitutions renowned for justice and equity; but both were developing patrician groups over subordinate agricultural people (not all of whom were members of the tribe) while the oligarchs were beginning to be further divided among themselves by private property.

The Licchavi chief town and meeting-place was Vesali, modern Basarh; the Mallas had several branches of which two were about the small headquarters towns of Pava and Kusinara. Each tribe could put a formidable army into the field at need. They formed a redoubtable aggressive confederacy at the beginning of the fifth century which had either to conquer other territory or to lose its own independence, but could not be ignored. For these two groups blocked the portion of the uttarapatha trade route that ran southwards from the Nepal frontier through Camparan district down to the Ganges and then across the river to the ores that produced iron and copper for everyone. To their north-west lay Kosala; to the south and south-east Magadha, both absolute monarchies.

Kosala and Magadha had been tribes (like the rest of the sixteen janapadas), as shown by the regular use of the plural, 'the Kosalas', 'the Magadhas', to designate the countries. However, nothing is ever recorded of a Kosalan or a Magadhan tribe in any of the Buddhist or Jain records, nor of tribal councils and meetings. The word Magadhan earlier meant 'bard' later 'trader', which shows the development of two special guilds from the original tribe; otherwise the brahmin scriptures refer to the Magadhan as a mixed caste. The word janapada, literally 'foothold of a tribe', is later used for 'country', 'state', or even 'district'; which shows fairly well how the course of development ran in the Gangetic basin.

These Aryan and Aryanised tribes were comparable to Greek tribal states of the sixth century B.C., with one crucial difference. Argives, Boeotians, Lacedaemonians, etc., seem by then to have developed private holdings in their restricted and relatively less fertile lands. Indian tribal lands, always ample in extent and generally under shifting cultivation, remained territory rather than property. A holding was formally subject to reassignment by tribal assembly, even when cultivated by the same family for a long time. In contrast, the very existence of the absolute monarchies depended upon regular taxes from permanently fixed private holdings in steadily cultivated plots.

Of the two great monarchies, Kosala was the older and at the beginning of the sixth century definitely the more powerful. The sixth-century Kosalan capital lay at Savatthi, though the older chief city had been to its south at Saketa, the traditional Ayodhya ('impregnable') city from which the mythical epic hero Rama had set out into voluntary exile through what was then unbroken wilderness. This supposed route of exile later developed or was extended into the southern trade route, the dakshinapatha that gave its name to the modern Deccan. The Bavari narrative shows that Savatthi lay at the junction of the two major routes for sixth-century trade. In addition, Kosala also commanded the Ganges, having annexed Kasi (Banaras) after a long series of battles.

The conquest should lie in the seventh century, for nothing is ever heard of the Kasi tribe. Only some legends of the good 'King Brahmadatta of Kasi' show that the place, whereof the early first-millennium date is now confirmed by archaeology, had some traditional importance. The name of the kingdom was thereafter hyphenated to 'Kasi-Kosala', so important was Banaras as a river port. The cotton, silk (tussore), and other manufactures of Banaras were already famous; its well-known orange-brown dye kashaya gave the first colour for Buddhist robes and retains its popularity even now under much the same name as the famous Banaras kailhai. Already, the most daring navigators could reach the sea from Kasi, sometimes trading even beyond the delta and doubtless relying on salt for their earliest and steadiest item of profitable trade.

Magadha appeared to be rather badly placed on the trade route, beyond the river and towards the end of the track where the route disappeared into trackless forest. But this kingdom, destined to grow into India's first 'universal monarchy' and empire, controlled something much more important than a caravan track, namely the supply of metals. The capital Rajgir (Rajagriha, 'King's House') was the solitary old-Aryan settlement south of the river, for a very good reason.

The hills near Rajgir have the northernmost Dharwar outcrop, a geological formation in which iron is rather handily available. Flakes of iron oxide occur therein as considerable encrustations which can be scraped off the rock with hardly any mining, reduced by charcoal fire, and then hammered out at white heat into tools or utensils. Rajgir has the added convenience of an easily defended perimeter of hills, fortified quite early with cyclopean outer walls twenty-five miles in length, enclosing the inner walled city. This was Rajgir proper, of about one square mile, with a third intermediate circumvallation.

The enclosed area has an excellent water supply from springs both hot and cold, and could hold out indefinitely against a hostile environment, in view of the excellent grazing between the walls. To the south-east lies Gaya, an early Magadhan colony. Beyond Gaya came the primeval forest through which hardy explorers passed to locate copper and iron ores in the hills to the south-east, the richest such deposits in India. The ore was mined and reduced on the spot, the metal brought back to be traded in the central Gangetic basin. The reason is that the hill-land of the ores is not so profitable to cultivate as the riparian alluvium. This, then, was Magadha's great source of power, for that state used the metal systematically to clear land and to bring it under the plough.

The sixteen were by no means all the janapadas and peoples to be taken into account. The virgin forest which covered the greater portion of the land was infested with a thin population of food-gathering savages who still used stone axes (pasana-muggara), and would be increasingly dangerous to trade caravans as time went on. Even on the two main trade routes, this primeval forest separated the janapadas by long distances through which the convoys had to pass with care, generally under heavy escort A minor tribe like the Sakyan is known to us only because it produced a great man.

Others like 'the Bulls of Allakappa' were important enough at the time to claim and receive a share of the Buddha's ashes, but are not known beyond the solitary reference. Mithila was the name of a city and zjanapada, but the tribe was extinct; its last king, Sumitra of the direct Ikshvaku line, died about the time of the Buddha's birth. Whether Mithila had annexed Videha before being taken over by Kosala, or was attached to Videha after the Kosalan conquest of both, neither people had any independent existence towards the middle of the sixth century. Magadha had absorbed the Angis, which lay to the east on both sides of the river. The capital Campa (Bhagalpur), become an inconsiderable village, was donated to a brahmin sacrificial priest by King Bimbisara of Magadha.

More important than ordinary tribesmen were the traders, generally called sathavaha (caravaneers) or Vaidehikas. The latter name means 'men of the Videha tribe'. Though all traders no longer belonged to any one tribe or janapada and the Videha tribe had vanished, the nomenclature shows the origin of the profession as with a particular tribal guild. The groups of merchant-caravaneers extended in a long chain from Taxila to the very end of Magadha. The bolder went beyond any known janapada limits, especially on the Deccan route. The trade was no longer of the primitive type confined to "trade friends", unless perhaps with some of the forest savages who might still retain the institution. Regular collage had come into use before the end of the seventh century, to judge by the coins found.

The eastern standard of weight for silver coins was the karshapana of 3.5 grams weight in Magadha, while the solitary Kosalan hoard known is of 3/4-karshạpana standard. The weight goes back to the Indus valley culture, which had, in fact, produced accurately cut stone weights of just this magnitude. Taxilan currency belonged to a foreign weight standard just above 11 grams, which would approximate to the Indian rupee in historic times. The karshapana was of 32 units weight, whereas the frontier coin, shaped like a bent bar, was 100.

Originally the coins were issued as silver blanks by the traders themselves, and the weights checked regularly by their guilds during the period of circulation. The checking was shown by tiny marks punched on one side, which guaranteed weight and purity to all who knew the code of guild marks. These punch marks extended beyond the uttarapatha into Afghanistan and Iran; sometimes they are found even on a few Achaemenid darics, presumably such as had circulated in Gandhara. Some of the punch marks themselves derived from Indus characters, probably from the descendants of the Panis whom we have named and noted in passing. The other side of the silver piece was originally blank at the time of issue.

By the sixth century the kings had stepped in to put their own issuing marks on the coins, on the side that had once remained blank. This was a regular system of four marks for Kosala and five for Magadha and the rest. Because of the marks, we can distinguish between dynasties and say approximately how many kings there were in each, but giving the individual king's name is still not simple, and generally remains a matter of conjecture. Violent changes of dynasty are revealed by counterstruck coins; the new king restruck coins of the displaced ruler found in the treasury with his own marks before issuing them again for circulation.

The weights are as accurately adjusted as for modern machine-minted coins, with very low tolerance. This type of coinage, even the very existence of regular coinage so carefully weighed, implies highly developed commodity production. We read about whole villages (especially near Banaras) settled by basket-makers, potters, smiths, weavers, and the like. These artisans, though kinship groups, generally formed guilds (sreni) naturally with a tribe-like organisation inherited from their own past. This process is still visible in semi-tribal areas, e.g. Assam. The guild as a unit often had considerable wealth at its disposal which was not the private property of any member, but might be disbursed at need by the headman or guild council either to any member of the guild or to some external individual or organisation.

This happens to be the present-day custom in the poorer Indian professional castes, the prototypes of which are clearly to be traced back to this period or earlier; the late-Vedic craftsman had normally been a member, presumably of the vaisya caste, of the grama on the move. Not all the production of the artisans was consumed in the nearest town, for cities in the seventh or sixth centuries were still very small. A good deal, like cloth and metal articles, travelled over very long distances. Of natural products, salt could not be as handily mined in Bihar as in the Panjab salt range, hence needed exploration (even down to the sea) and long hauls. Bamboo was special forest produce that had become an indispensable commodity for baskets, construction work, and the like. Sandalwood rubbed into wet paste was one of many coolants and cleansers in great demand for the bath (a necessity rather than a luxury in the hot climate), especially as soap had not yet been invented. All these materials and trade articles were carted by caravans of 500 or more ox-wagons at a time. The carts had spoked wheels and rawhide tyres, which would suffice for the soft soil of the uttarapatha.

The dakshinapatha country was hilly, with difficult passes, broken and stony ground, and without broad, clear tracks comparable to the northern; there, pack trains of animals and on occasion porters with head-loads had to be employed. To exchange for the commodities, there had to be a considerable local surplus of grain, hides and so on, which could best be guaranteed by private property (in land, cattle, etc.) and the use of organised labour, generally the labour of sudras, whether hired workers or the occasional slaves. In wild country the trading had to be through the tribal chief, who could gather the surplus for the trader; either such chiefs or the groups that had advanced from a 'trade friends' position would eventually become independent of the rest of the tribe because of the new property thus acquired, so that the progressive dissolution of the more accessible tribes was to follow.

The horse was a valuable article of trade, being now mounted for riding; it had reached the Deccan before the sixth century. The elephant was much more valuable, but reserved for royal and army use and not a common trade object. The society of the day was still very far from being the caste-ridden, helpless, apathetic village-covered aggregate into which it would evolve within a dozen centuries, with a corresponding worn-out landscape. Nevertheless, the fruits of aggression were already considerable enough to be tempting. Furthermore, some authority backed by irresistible force was increasingly necessary to ensure an unhindered flow and exchange of commodities, which naturally involved regulation by law of intercourse between groups.

Let us digress a little to consider the theoretical position. The essential tool for the new state which was becoming necessary had to be a powerful, well-trained and properly organised professional standing army, whose recruitment and action would not be fettered by tribal prerogative, tribal law, or tribal loyalties, but which would serve society beyond the tribe-a society that exclusive tribal life does not recognise. Such an army could not be a tribal levy called up at need by the chief for a seasonal campaign. It had to be carefully disciplined, constantly drilled, regularly paid, well equipped at state expense, and suitably lodged in strategic garrison. All that was impossible without regular taxes to which tribal oligarchs normally would not submit. Neither the Licchavis nor the Mallas ever managed to create such a free standing army. whose soldiers lived entirely on their pay.

Only an absolute monarch unhampered by law could break through the barriers between various coherent groups which would not always regard themselves as adherent members of a wider society based solely upon property rights. This course was suggested by Machiavelli in a different context; his book Il Principe was advice to the prince to ride roughshod over wrangling Italian cities and unite them into a nation. But there Machiavelli stopped. Neither he nor his favoured candidate Cesare Borgia nor any other Italian saw the need to change the productive basis of late feudal

Italy-even though the Renaissance had already passed into the Baroque. Magadhan theoreticians proposed a relentless conduct which might have caused any Borgia to blench; but their openly declared principal aim was to change the face of the land.

The main task of their king and source of profit for the state was to clear the heavy jungle, to bring all wasteland under the plough, aided by a state monopoly of mining and metals. This sort of kingship had to burst all barriers of tribal privilege, property-sharing, and exclusiveness; later despotisms merely ruled over a passive substratum already in the fully developed agrarian stage. To round out the discussion, modern analogies of a kind may be shown. In certain east European countries, China, newly liberated portions of Africa, and the Arab world, some leaders assert that dictatorship is necessary to bring the country to a new stage, whether socialist or bourgeois-democratic. Latin-FIG. Silver punch-marks on the coins of Pascnadi, emperor of Kosala, contemporary of the Buddha.

The marks themselves have to be, restored from comparison of many different specimens, for they overlap and are often incomplete. Note that the Kosalan system was of four marks, and the weight 3/4 karshapana standard. American republics, until the latest Cuban revolution, generally followed the other type of dictatorship which never changed the class position but at best regulated the greed of the ruling class-as did the better Roman emperors.

The sixth-century kings of Magadha and Kosala met most of the requirements. Both were of low birth, without tribe or tribal assembly to restrain them. The Magadhan Bimbisara's lineage is not given in Pali records, but the Sanskrit Puranas ascribe him to the Sisunaga line. Certainly, the royal house and dynasty ended as Sisunagas about ten generations later. The termination naga for the name would be impossible in Vedic usage; here, it should indicate aboriginal blood, or at least aboriginal cults. The brahmin records speak of the dynasty with contempt as the lowest of kshatriyas, kshatra-bandhu, which means at any rate that they paid scant attention to Vedic customs, except an occasionally yajna for victory. Indeed, the most prominent pre-Buddhist shrine at Rajgir (Maniar Math) was dedicated to some Naga cults and maintained its character through the centuries till the place was deserted.

Bimbisara of Magadha had the special epithet Seniya 'with an army'. This indicates that he was the earliest king to have a regular standing army unconnected with any tribe. The Kosalan Pasenadi claimed descent from King Ikshvaku of Vedic fame; but the claim was not admitted in his own time and place. When he asked for a Sakyan girl in marriage, the demand embarrassed the Sakyans, though he held powers of life and death over them and they, too, claimed descent from the same King Ikshvaku. Ultimately, they cheated the monarch by sending the lovely Vasabha-khattiya, daughter of Mahanama Sakya by a slave woman Nạgamunda. The mother's name again shows aboriginal birth. The deceit was later exposed, but the son of this union, Vidudabha, remained heir-apparent. Pasenadi's chief queen Mallika was daughter of a flower gardenei, hence technically of low caste; but even the eastern caste system was not very rigid at the time, except for some brahmins.

Pasenadi went a step beyond Bimbisara in creating a new office of commander-in-chief, senapati, for his son and heir, who is always referred to as Vidudabha-senapati. No senapati ('Lord of the army') is known before him. The king had, like the earlier tribal chiefs, personally to lead and manage the army. However, the Malla Bandhula had virtually held supreme command over the Kosalan army and was treacherously murdered at Pasenadi's orders under suspicion of wanting to usurp royal power. This was an error of judgement, especially as Bandhula's nephew Digha-Karayana was allowed to retain the senior ministerial office. This minister is undoubtedly the master of statecraft referred to as Dirgha ('long') Carayana in Sanskrit.

(Not only is such change of pronunciation attested in other cases, e.g. Asoka's queen Kaluvaki for Caruvici, but the Kashmirian Kshemendra actually gives the name as Carayana in his Buddhist narrative poem Avaddnakalpalatd.) For the time being, however, neither Kosala nor Magadha provoked a war. Both kings were of relatively unaggressive temperament; both patronised the new religious philosophers with pleasure. They are reported as being close friends and admirers of the Buddha, but also as generous supporters of all major sects of the time, including a few Vedic brahmins. There was even a marriage alliance, for Pasenadi's sister was Bimbisara's chief queen and some accounts make his daughter wife to Bimbisara's son. However, both armies were in constant action against forest savages and perhaps small Aryan tribes; both kings performed costly yajnas for victory' in battle. That they gave away entire villages in priestly fee has been mentioned. Vivid descriptions remain of the misery and dismay of the peasantry when innumerable beasts were requisitioned-without payment, of course-for the royal fire sacrifices. Thus, the leading kings were not yet entirely free of the Vedic malpractice's which no longer suited the new class society.

The first step towards the inevitable conflict was taken by Ajatasatru, son of Bimbisara. This prince, undoubtedly with some unreported theoretician of statecraft behind him, imprisoned his own father and eventually had the aged and good-natured Bimbisara starved to death in the dungeon. Even the Buddhists, though shuddering at the parricide, admit that Ajatasatru was a just and able ruler; we have noted that he appears as a philosopher-king in a major Upanishad. Pasenadi's reaction was to rescind the gift of a village in the Kasi janapada which had formed part of his sister's dowry.

This was too valuable to be surrendered, a bridgehead for Magadha across the river from which both the Ganges and a branch trade route could be blockaded. The Magadhan hold upon the janapada was retained in a series of battles, all won by Ajatasatru. The Kosalan side was not slow in countermoves. Silver punch-marked coins of Magadhan type, probably of Ajatasatru, circa 480 B.C. The system is of five marks, and the weight when new was about fifty-four grains of silver, the full karshapana based on a weight system going back to the Indus valley, but not known outside India.

over the royal insignia in his keeping to Vidudabha, who already controlled the army and was promptly installed as king. The aged Pasenadi, deserted by all except one servant woman, fled for refuge to his nephew. The gates of Rajgir were closed for the night when the royal fugitive arrived; before they opened the next morning, Pasenadi had died of exhaustion outside the walls of the Magadhan capital. Ajatasatru gave a sumptuous funeral to his uncle's corpse and had a claim thereafter to the throne of Kosala. The claim could not be pressed for the moment. Not only Vidudabha but powerful free tribes like the Mallas and Licchavis had to be crushed. Such tribes were relatively the more dangerous to any monarch's progress, both as survivals of democracy and as formidable military obstacles.

Vidudabha moved along parallel lines by a massacre of the Sakyans, ostensibly to avenge the insult of his ancestry, but actually as part of a general move to end tribal freedom on the uttarapatha. The Licchavis had by this time extended their control to the Ganges from the north and levied tolls from all trade on the great river. The traders complained bitterly of the double imposts collected by these tribesmen and by the Magadhan king, who also claimed full control over the stream: So a fortified stockade was set up on the Ganges at Pataliputra (Patna) by the tri-junction with the Gandak and the Son (which flowed into the Ganges at this point till the fifteenth century A.D.). The Buddha traversed the still incomplete project on his final journey.

The brilliant future he is supposed to have prophesied for the place began a hundred years later, when Patna became the capital of Magadha, Rajgir being no longer conveniently situated for changed administrative needs. The Licchavis countered Ajatasatru's manoeuvre by a working agreement with the Mallas. The Licchavi tribe and the confederacy were broken up from within by a technique carefully described in the great book of Magadhan statecraft. A brahmin minister of Ajatasatru went over to the Licchavis in simulated disgrace (like Zopyrus, minister of Darius I to the Babylonians).

Though the Licchavis and Mallas had no brahmins within the tribe and followed no known Vedic practices, the guest's status, prestige, and supposed knowledge of the Magadhan king's intentions made him welcome. He utilised this trust to set one oligarch against another, to encourage each Licchavi to claim more than his allotted share; and to make the tribe neglect tribal meetings, collective army drill, and the tribe's judicial assembly. Such 'boring from within' would not have been possible unless inner decay of the tribe had advanced far, under the influence of wealth collected as tribute and taxes, but retained as private property of the oligarchs.

That internal disruption had preceded Ajatasatru's emissary is proved by the rise of an outstanding religious teacher like Mahavira among the Licchavis; and by the Mallas Bandhula and Carayana taking service outside the tribe. Life even among the best of the free tribes no longer offered full satisfaction to the ablest of the tribesmen. Eventually the rot progressed so far that the Licchavis would not meet regularly for the tribal council and tribal affairs. Then the secret agent sent word to Ajatasatru, who marched in suddenly to easy victory over his disorganised opponents. No details are known of the final defeat of the Mallas, but their ruin soon afterwards is not to be doubted. It was so thorough that the word Malla came to mean only 'wrestler' or pancratiast, from the original tribe's fondness for exercise.

A western Malla tribe, whether related to the Gangetic Mallas or not, was slaughtered about 150 years later on the middle Indus by Alexander's army. Some Licchavis, however, did survive Ajatasatru's campaign, so that the war was not to wipe out the tribesmen but to extinguish the sort of tribal life they led. The cunning Magadhan brahmin minister is referred to only by his nickname Vassakara, 'he who subdues', derived from this spectacular intrigue. He was undoubtedly one of the great past masters of statecraft whose opinions and policies must have been cited in the Arthasastra under his unknown official name.

The Kosalan question was settled by an unexpected bit of luck for Magadha. Vidudabha had been so careless as to pitch his army camp in the dry, sandy bed of the Rapti river. A sudden cloudburst upstream swept away the whole Kosalan encampment and was regarded as retribution for the massacre of the Sakyans. There remained neither king nor armed force thereafter to contest Ajatasatru's claim to the vacant throne of Kosala. It must not be imagined from all these episodes that the extant sources present a connected historical narrative. The pieces have first to be sorted out from the many different stories and legends and then fitted into some plausible sequence. No description of the countryside, no account of any battle or campaign survives.

We do not even know how far Ajatasatru extended his rule; it is certain that his successors had a great deal left to do. There is passing mention that the Pradyota king of Avanti was about to invade Magadha, for which reason Ajatasatru's liigh ministers Vassakara and Sunidha refortified the capital Rajgir. The Avanti kingdom was rich and powerful, one of the sixteen 'great janapada' in fact, with the capital Ujjain on the southern trade route. It fell eventually to Magadha, but how and to what particular Magadhan king is not known. The Vatsa (Vamsa) kingdom of Kosambi on the Yarauna was also in the list of sixteen.

Their king, Udayana, is known for his standing quarrel with Ujjain and famous as hero of a charming cycle of romance which involves his enchanting queen, Vasavadatta. But all this does not say how long the kingdom lasted, or when Magadha took it over at last. The Kurus, Surasenas, Matsyas (perhaps descended from the Rigvedic tribe of the Ten Kings battle), were all tribal states in the list of sixteen; they did not last beyond the fourth century, though the Surasenas of Mathura were known by repute to the Greeks.

At a date which cannot be later than 470 B.C. and not more than sixty years earlier (which is wonderful accuracy for ancient Indian chronology!), Magadha had become the major dominant though not yet paramount power in the Gangetic basin. An absolute monarchy, with complete control over the richest deposits of ore and over the north-eastern ends of the two main trade routes, it was still faced with a massive task: that of pushing back the great forest and bringing more land under regular cultivation with the plough. There was no significant military rival left, but numerous small tribes remained unsubdued.

The process of aggression could not be stopped till the 'whole earth'-which to Indians meant only the whole country-from the snowy mountains of the north to 'the four oceans', was brought under one rule. This fulfilment of the 'manifest destiny' took another two centuries. Then came a totally new problem: how long could the state continue ruthlessly to violate all law and ethics while its citizens had begun to live by an exceptionally decent moral code? The economic reality underlying this formal contradiction was a conflict of interest between state and trader, private enterprise and production under the government's direct supervision. The older problem of transition to an agricultural society had then been so completely solved that people forgot it had ever existed in history.

Bibliography

Adikaram, E. W.: *Early History of Buddhism in Ceylon,* D. S. Puswella, Migoda, 1946.

Agrawala, V. S.: *Shiva Mahadeva: The Great God,* Veda Academy, Varanasi, 1966.

Ahmad, Imtiaz: *State and Foreign Policy: India's Role in South Asia,* Vikas, New Delhi, 1993.

Ahmad, Jamil-ud-din: *Some Recent Speeches and Writings of Mr. Jinnah,* Lahore, Ashraf, 1952.

Aiyar, R. Krishnaswami: *Outlines of Vedaanta,* Chetana, Bombay, 1978.

Archer, W. G.: *The Kama Sutra,* Unwin Hyman, London, 1990.

Ashton, S.R. : *British Policy Towards the Indian States, 1905-1939,* London, Curzon, 1982.

Aurobindo, Sri: *Vyasa and Valmiki,* Acharya Press, Pondicherry, 1956.

Avalon, Arthur and Ellen: *Hymns to the Goddess,* Ganesh and Co., Madras, 1964.

Aziz, Ashraf: *Light of the Universe: Essays on Hindustani Film Music,* Three Essays Collective, New Delhi, 2003.

Bagchi, P. C.: *Studies in Dharmashastra,* University of Calcutta Press, Calcutta, 1939.

Bahadur, K.P.: *The Wisdom of Vedaanta,* Sterling Publishers Private Limited, New Delhi, 1996.

Banerjea, J. N.: *Pauranic and Vedanta Religion,* University of Calcutta, Calcutta, 1996.

Bankimchandra, C.: *Essentials of Dharma,* Sanskrit Book Depot, Calcutta 1979.

Basu, Manoranjan: *Dharmashastra: A General Study,* Shrimati Mira Basu, Calcutta, 1976.

Beaumont, Roger : *Sword of the Raj: The British Army in India, 1747-1947*, Indianapolis, Bobbs-Merrill, 1977.

Benjamin, Joseph : *Scheduled Castes in Indian Politics and Society*, New Delhi, Ess Ess Publications, 1989.

Bhattacharyya, B.: *Nispannayogavali of Mahapandita Abhyakara Gupta*, Oriental Institute, Baroda, 1949.

Borchert, Bruno: *Mysticism: Its History and Challenge*, Samuel Wiser, York Beach, 1994.

Bose, D. N.: *Dharmashastra: Their Philosophy and Occult Secrets*, Kali Press, Calcutta, 1965.

Bowle, John: *The Imperial Achievement: The Rise and Transformation of the British Empire*, Little, Brown, 1974.

Brockington, J. L.: *Righteous Rama: The Evolution of an Epic*, Oxford, London, 1984.

Bromley, D.: *Krishna Consciousness in the West*, Bucknell University Press, Lewisburg, 1989.

Brooks, E.: *The Original Analects: Sayings of Confucius and His Successors*. Columbia University Press, New York, 1988.

Bruhn, Klaus: *The Jina-Images of Deogarh*, MacMillan, Leiden, 1969.

Burke, Mary Louise: *Swami Vivekananda in America: New Discoveries*, Advaita Ashrama, Calcutta, 1966.

Chaudhary, M.: *Partition and the Curse of Rehabilitation*, Calcutta, Bengal Rehabilitation Organization, 1964.

Chaudhuri, Nirad: *Thy Hand, Great Anarch! India: 1921-1952*, London, Chatto & Windus, 1987.

Coomeraswamy, Ananda K.: *Buddha and the Gospel of Buddhism*, MacMillan, London, 1928.

Crawford, Cromwell S.: *Ram Mohan Roy: His Era and Ethics*, Acharya Press, New Delhi, 1984.

Dalton, Dennis : *Gandhi's Power : Nonviolence in Action*, New Delhi, OUP, 2001.

Danielou, Alain: *The Complete Kama Sutra*, Park Street Press, Rochester, 2000.

Dasgupta, Shahana: *Rani Lakshmibai: The Indian Heroine*, Rupa & Company, Calcutta, 2002.

Datta, V.N.: *Sati: Widow Burning in India*, Manohar, New Delhi, 1990.

David, M. D.: *John Wilson and his Institutions*, Mumbai, 1957.

De Bary: *Self and Society in Ming Thought*, Columbia University Press, New York, 1970.

De, Sushil Kumar: *Ancient Indian Erotics and Erotic Literature*, Firma K. L. Mukhopadhyay, Calcutta, 1959.

Deak, Istvan: *The Lawful Revolution: Louis Kossuth and the Hungarians 1848-1849*, Columbia University Press, 1979.

Dhar, Niranjan: *Vedanta and Bengal Renaissance*, Minerva Associates, Calcutta, 1977.

Dikshit, D.P. *Political History of the Chalukyas of Badami*. New Delhi: Abhinav, 1980.

Donat, K.: *Meditate the Tantric Yoga Way*, George Allen and Unwin, London, 1973.

Doniger, W.: *The Rig Veda: An Anthology*, Penguin, New York, 1981.

Duboi, Abbe: *Hindu Manners, Customs and Ceremonies*, Fifth Indian Impression, CUP, 1985.

Dwivedi, M.: *The Principal Upanishads*, Adyar Library, Madras, 1931.

Eaton, Richard M.: *Sufis of Bijapur, 1300-1700: Social Roles of Sufis in Medieval India*, Princeton University Press, Princeton, 1978.

Edwardes, Michael: *Battles of the Indian Mutiny*, London; B. T. Batsford Ltd., 1963.

Erickson, Erik H.: *Gandhi's Truth: On the Origins of Militant Nonviolence*, Norton, New York, 1970.

Farquhar, J.N.: *Modern Religious Movements in India*, Munshiram, New Delhi, 1967.

Fay, Peter Ward: *The Opium War, 1840-42*, University of North Carolina Press, 1975.

Fisher, Michael H.: *The Politics of British Annexation of India - 1757-1857*, Oxford, 1996.

Frauwallner, E..: *History of Indian Philosophy*, Motilal, Delhi, 1973.

Gambhirananda, S.: *Brahma Sutra Shamkar Bhasya*, Adavita Ashrama, Calcutta, 1977.

Gambhirananda, Swami: *Brahma Sutra Shamkar Bhasya*, Adavita Ashrama, Calcutta, 1977.

Gandhi, M. K.: *The Story of My Experiment With Trust*, Washington, Public Affairs Press, 1948.

Garbe, R.: *The Philosophy of Ancient India*, Chicago University Press, Chicago, 1899.

Goradia, Nayana: *Lord Curzon: The Last of the British Moghuls*, New Delhi, Oxford University Press, 1993.

Goudriaan, T.: *Ritual and Speculation in Early Tantrism*, State University of New York Press, New York, 1992.

Gough, A.E.: *The Philosophy of the Upanisads and Ancient Indian Metaphysics*, MacMillan, London, 1882.

Grant, G. P.: *Philosophy in the Mass Age*, Copp Clark, Toronto, 1959.

Grisenold, H.D.: *Insights into Modern Hinduism*, Oxford, New York, 1934.

Growse, F. S.: *The Ramayana of Tulasidasa*, Motilal Banarsidass, Delhi, 1995.

Gurumurthy, S. : *Hindu Heritage, Assimilative, Not Divisive*, Vigil, Madras 1993.

Haich, E.: *Sexual Energy and Yoga*, Aurora Press, New York, 1982.

Hasan, Murhirul: *Legacy of a Divided Nation: India's Muslims Since Independence*, New Delhi, Oxford, 1997.

Hasan, Mushirul: *India's Partition: Process, Strategy and Mobilization*, New Delhi, Oxford UP, 1993.

Heifetz, Hank: *The Origin of the Young God: Kalidasa's Kumara-sambhava*, University of California Press, Berkeley, 1985.

Heimann, Betty: *Facets of Indian Thought*, Geroge Allen & Unwin, London, 1964.

Heinsath, Charles: *Indian Nationalism and Hindu Social Reform*, Princeton University Press, Princeton, 1964.

Heschel, J.: *God in Search of Man: A Philosophy of Judaism*, Noonday Press, New York, 1997.

Hirschman, Edwin: *White Mutiny: The Ilbert Bill Crisis in India and the Genesis of the Indian National Congress*, New Delhi, Heritage, 1980.

Hixon, L.: *Mother of the Universe: Visions of the Goddess, Tantric Hymns of Enlightenment*, Quest Books, Wheaton, 1994.

Hopkins, J.: *Kalachakra Tantra Rite of Initiation*, Wisdom Publications, Boston, 1982.

Hopkirk, Peter: *The Great Game: The Struggle for Empire in Central Asia*, Kodansha, 1992.

Hume, R.E.: *The Thirteen Principle Upanishads*, Oxford University Press, London, 1971.

Hutchins, Francis: *Spontaneous Revolution: The Quit India Movement*, New Delhi, Manohar, 1971.

Irene, S.: *Vedic Heritage Teaching Program*. Arsha Vidya Gurukulam, Coimbatore, 1994.

Iyar, K.: *Vedanta: The Science of Reality*, Ganesh and Co., Mardas, 1930.

Iyengar, B.K.S.: *Light on the Yoga Sutras of Patanjali*, Aquarian Press, London 1993.

Jacob, K.: *Religion and Ethics in Advaita*, C.M.S. Press, Kottayam, 1982.

Jafar, Malik Muhammad: *Jinnah as a Parliamentarian*, Lahore, Afzar Publications, 1977.

Jain, Kailash Chand, *Lord Mahavira and His Times*, Saraswati Press, Delhi, 1974.

James, Lawrence: *The Rise and Fall of the British Empire*, St. Martin's, 1997.

James, Robert Rhodes: *The British Revolution, 1880-1939*, New York, Knopf, 1976.

Jean, M.: *Tantrik Yoga*, The Aquarian Press, Wellingborough, 1970.

John, B.: *Mantras: Sacred Words of Power*, George Allen and Unwin, London, 1977.

John, Elsner: *Pilgrimage: Past and Present in the World Religions*, Harvard University Press, Cambridge, 1995.

John, K.: *The Origin and Development of the State Cult of Confucius*, Paragon Book, New York, 1966.

Karmarkar, D.: *Sankara's Advaita*, Karnatak University, Dharwar, 1976.

Kaushik, Asha : *Globalization, Democracy and Culture : Situating Gandhian Alternatives*, Jaipur, Pointer, 2002.

Kaviraj, G.: *Aspects of Indian Thought*, University of Burdwan, Calcutta, 1966.

Kavlekar, K.K. : *Non-Brahmin Movement in Southern India, 1873-1949*, Kolhapur, Shivaji University, 19790

Keith, A.B. : *Rigveda Brahmanas*, Harvard University Press, Cambridge, 1920.

Keith, Arthur Berriedale: *The Religion and Philosophy of the Veda and Upanishads*, MacMillan, Delhi, 1925.

Kishwar, Madhu : *Religion at the Service of Nationalism, and Other Essays*, OUP, Delhi, 1998.

Klaus, K.: *A Survey of Hinduism*, State University of New York Press, Albany, 1989.

Knipe, M.: *Hinduism: Experiments in the Sacred*, Harper, San Francisco, 1991.

Knott, K.: *Hinduism, A Very Short Introduction*, Oxford University Press, New York, 1998.

Kosambi, D. D. : *The Culture and Civilisation of Ancient India in Historical Outline*, London, Routledge and Kegan Paul, 1956.

Kottackal, Jacob: *Religion and Ethics in Advaita*, C.M.S. Press, Kottayam, 1982.

Kuiper, F.B.J. : *Aryans in the Rigveda*, Rodopi, Amsterdam, 1991.

Kuppuswamy, Sastri S.: *Compromises in the History of Advaitic Thought*, Kalyani Press, Madras, 1940.

Louis, Fischer: *Essential Gandhi: An Anthology of His Writings*, Vintage, New York, 1983.

Low, D. A. and Brasted, Howard: *Freedom, Trauma, Continuities: Northern India and Independence*, New Delhi, Sage Publications, 1998.

Maheshwari, Shriram: *Rural Development in India: A Public Policy Approach*, New Delhi, Sage, 1995.

Makhan, L.: *The Ramayana of Valmiki*, Munshiram Manoharlal, New Delhi, 1978.

Mathew, Arnold: *Culture and Anarchy*, The University Press, Cambridge, 1935.

Mayer, A. : *Caste in an Indian Village: Change and Continuity 1954-1992*, Delhi, OUP, 1996.

Mazumder, Sukhendu : *Politico-Economic Ideas of Mahatma Gandhi: Their Relevance in the Present Day*, New Delhi, Concept Pub., 2004.

Mearns, David J.: *Shiva's Other Children: Religion and Social Identity amongst Overseas Indians*, Sage, Walnut Creek, 1995.

Mearns, J.: *Shiva's Other Children: Religion and Social Identity amongst Overseas Indians*, Sage, Walnut Creek, 1995.

Mehra, Parshotam: *A Dictionary of Modern Indian History, 1707-1947*, New Delhi, Oxford University Press, 1985.

Metcalf, Thomas R.: *The Aftermath of the Revolt: India, 1857-1870*, Princeton, Princeton University, 1964.

Mohan, K.: *The Mahabharata*, Munshiram Manoharlal, Delhi 1997.

Mookerjee, Ajit: *Kali The Feminine Force*, Thames and Hudson, London, 1988.

Mookerji, Satkari: *Modern Polity and Vedanta*, Sanskrit College, Calcutta, 1972.

Moon, Penderel: *The British Conquest and Dominion of India*, London, Duckworth, 1989.

Morris-Jones, W.H.: *The Government and Politics of India*, London, Hutchinson, 1971.

Nanda, B. R. : *Gandhi and His Critics*, Oxford University Press, Delhi, 1993.

Neale, Walter C.: *Economic Change in Rural India: Land Tenure and Reform in the United Provinces, 1800-1955*, New Haven, 1962.

Nevile, P.: *Lahore: A Sentimental Journey*, New Delhi, Penguin, 1993.

Oddie, G.A. : *Hindu and Christian in South-East India*, London, Curzon Press, 1991.

Pathak, Dr S.P.: *Jhansi during the British Rule*, Ramanand Vidya Bhawan, Delhi, 1987.

Preston, Diana: *The Boxer Rebellion*, Berkley Books, 2000.

Raimundo Panikkar: *The Vedic Experience: Mantramanjari*, Longman Todd, London, 1977.

Raja, C. Kunhan : *The Taittiriya Sarvanukramani of Yaska*, Madras, 1931.

Ramamurti, A.: *Advaitic Mysticism of Sankara*, Visvabharati, Santiniketan, 1974.

Ranajit Guha: *A Construction of Humanism in Colonial India*, CASA, Amsterdam, 1993.

Renou, Louis: *The Nature of Dharmashastra*, Walker and Co., New York, 1997.

Robson, Brian: *Sir Hugh Rose and the Central India Campaign*, Sutton Publishing Ltd for the Army Records Society, UK, 2000.

Satyapal Verma: *Role of Reason in Sankara Vedanta*, Parimal Publication, Delhi, 1992.

Savarkar, Vinayak Damodar : *The Indian War of Independence* 1857 Rajdhani Granthagar, Delhi, 1988.

Scheftelowitz, Isidor : *Die Kasmirische Rezension von Katyayanas Sarvanukramani,* Zeitschrift fur Indologie und Iranistik, 1922.

Shukla, D. N.: *Vastu-Shastra,* Motilal Banarsidass, Delhi, 1966.

Singh, Birendra Kumar: *Early Chalukyas of Vatapi, circa A.D. 500 to 757*, Delhi, Eastern Book Linkers, 1991.

Smith, Col. J. T. : *Silver and the India Exchanges,* Effingham Wilson, London, 1876.

Strauss, L.: *Political Philosophy,* The Bobbs Merrill Co., New York, 1975.

Swami Vishnu Tirtha: *Devatma Shakti,* Swami Shivom Tirth, Rishikesh, 1962.

Talageri, Shrikant : *Aryan Invasion Theory and Indian Nationalism,* Voice of India, Delhi, 1993.

Tejomayananda, Swami: *Hindu Culture: An Introduction,* Chinmaya Publications, Piercy, 1993.

Thapar, Romila : *Ashoka and the Decline of the Mauryas,* London, Oxford University Press, 1961.

Thompson, Edward: *The Making of the Indian Princes,* Oxford University Press, London, 1943.

Trautmann, Thomas R.: *Kautilya and the Arthasastra: A Statistical Study,* Leiden, Brill, 1971.

Trimingham, J.: *Sufi Orders in Islam,* Oxford University Press, New York, 1998.

Utpat, V.N.: *Riddles of Buddha and Ambedkar,* Itihas Patrika Prakashan, Thane 1988.

Vable, D.: *The Arya Samaj. Hindu without Hinduism.* Vikas Publ., Delhi, 1983.

Vedalankar, Pandit Nardev : *Basic Teachings of Hinduism,* Veda Niketan, Durban, 1978.

Visvantha, K.: *Essentials of Hinduism,* Narosa Pub. House, New Delhi, 1989.

Wendy Doniger: *Siva: The Erotic Ascetic,* Oxford University Press, Delhi, 1998.

Zaidi, A. Moin: *Evolution of Muslim political Thought in India,* New Delhi: S. Chand, 1975-79

Index

A

Abhinandannath, 38.
Acaranga Sutra, 86, 123, 171.
Administration, 29, 99, 201, 229, 230, 271.
Agamas, 92, 99, 100, 114, 170, 171, 175, 176, 177, 178, 179, 180, 182.
Ajita Kesakambali, 2, 190, 191, 192, 193.
Ajitnath, 35, 36, 37.
Ajivika, 5, 185, 186, 187, 188, 189, 190.
Anantnath, 50.
Anekantavada, 72, 75, 79, 80, 81, 82, 83, 84, 85, 86, 87, 88, 108.
Anga, 24, 29, 34, 37, 38, 40, 45, 48, 83, 86, 92, 99, 100, 101, 102, 118, 123, 153, 154, 159, 163, 164, 165, 166, 167, 171, 172, 173, 174, 175, 178, 179, 183, 188, 206, 207, 209, 210, 212, 215, 216, 217, 220, 224, 225, 226, 227, 228, 229, 231, 233, 234, 235, 238, 240, 243, 246, 247, 250, 270.
Antakrddaauah, 176.
Anuttaraupapatikadauah, 176.
Aranath, 43, 56.
Arthashastra, 195, 241, 247, 248, 252.
Ascetic Life, 11, 33, 171.
Atharvaveda, 240, 250.
Avanti, 70, 162, 205, 206, 209, 221, 223, 234, 239, 240, 248, 249, 250, 271, 283.

B

Barabar Caves, 185.
Bhagavati Sutra, 175, 186, 188, 189, 190, 216, 228.
Bindusara, 186, 250.
Biography, 97, 153, 182.
Bodhisattva, 124.
Brahmana, 1, 2, 6, 7, 8, 182, 201, 224, 228, 234, 252, 253, 254, 255, 256, 261, 277.
Buddhism, 1, 2, 3, 4, 5, 8, 11, 12, 79, 80, 116, 119, 122, 123, 148, 173, 228, 232, 239, 240, 244, 247, 248, 268, 271, 278, 284.
Buddhist Logic, 88.

C

Carvaka, 10, 194, 195, 196, 197, 198, 199, 200, 201.
Chanakya, 186, 187.
Chandragupta Maurya, 100, 225, 250, 258, 266.
Chandraprabha, 44, 45.
Chedi or Cheti, 234.
Contributions, 29, 77, 85, 160.

D

Description, 25, 61, 64, 82, 92, 167, 169, 172, 175, 256, 258, 281, 283.
Dharmanath, 51.
Digambar, 15, 21, 22, 57, 70, 73, 74, 75, 96, 100, 101, 102, 103, 107, 108, 109, 110, 113, 135, 136, 149, 150, 151, 152, 153, 154, 155, 158, 159, 163, 165, 167, 171.
Drstivada, 167, 169, 174, 177, 178.

E

Edicts of Ashoka, 252.

F

First Buddhist Council, 228.
Formation of States, 203.

G

Gandhara, 68, 161, 171, 174, 206, 209, 210, 217, 234, 250, 251, 252, 253, 276.
Gautama Buddha, 230, 231, 232, 233, 249.
Guru-Shishya Parampara, 147.

H

Heterodox Ideas, 185.

J

Jain Contribution, 160, 161.
Jain Doctrines, 77.
Jain Texts, 68, 76, 81, 84, 88, 92, 115, 116, 118, 119, 120, 121, 125, 127, 128, 180, 227.
Jain Tirthankar, 22, 24, 35, 36, 37, 39, 42, 43, 44, 45, 46, 47, 48, 49, 50, 51, 52, 55, 56, 57, 63, 64, 65, 66, 101, 138, 140, 149, 157, 158, 160, 162, 180.
Jainism, 1, 2, 3, 5, 15, 16, 17, 19, 20, 21, 22, 37, 64, 66, 67, 68, 70, 71, 73, 75, 76, 79, 80, 83, 85, 86, 87, 88, 89, 90, 100, 101, 105, 106, 107, 108, 110, 111, 115, 116, 117, 119, 120, 122, 123, 124, 132, 133, 135, 140, 142, 147, 148, 149, 151, 152, 153, 154, 156, 157, 158, 160, 161, 162, 163, 164, 165, 170, 171, 177, 180, 181, 182, 183, 184, 186, 188, 194, 200, 205, 216, 228, 233, 266.
Jnatrdharmakathah, 176.

K

Kalpasutra, 155, 180, 181.
Kamboja, 206, 209, 213, 237, 244, 245, 251, 252, 253.
Karma Theory, 115, 122.
Kashi Kings, 210.
Kashtha Sangh, 152, 154.
Kasi, 8, 205, 206, 207, 208, 209, 210, 211, 212, 213, 214, 215, 218, 219, 224, 233, 234, 236, 237, 238, 253, 274, 281.
Kosala, 188, 205, 206, 207, 209, 210, 212, 215, 216, 217, 218, 219, 220, 221, 222, 223, 224, 225, 228, 232, 234, 238, 253, 270, 271, 273, 274, 275, 276, 279, 280, 281, 283.
Kosala and Magadha, 271, 273.
Kosala Kingdom, 216, 217, 218, 219, 220, 221.

Kunthunath, 55, 56.
Kuru, 5, 206, 207, 209, 212, 213, 218, 219, 220, 222, 234, 235, 236, 237, 238, 239, 240, 241, 242, 243, 244, 245, 246, 248, 250, 251, 253, 270, 284.
Kurukshetra War, 213, 218, 219, 222, 234, 236, 237, 243.

L

Licchavi, 10, 229, 230, 231, 233, 239, 259, 261, 263, 265, 272, 278, 281, 282, 283.

M

Machcha or Matsya, 248.
Magadha, 10, 148, 161, 205, 206, 207, 208, 210, 216, 218, 220, 225, 226, 227, 228, 230, 231, 233, 234, 235, 239, 247, 248, 249, 250, 251, 252, 253, 264, 270, 271, 273, 274, 275, 276, 279, 280, 281, 282, 283, 284.
Mahajanpadas, 203.
Mahavamsa, 231, 232.
Mahavira, 1, 2, 3, 5, 10, 15, 22, 23, 68, 70, 71, 72, 73, 74, 76, 78, 79, 82, 83, 85, 86, 97, 98, 99, 102, 113, 118, 132, 145, 148, 149, 150, 151, 154, 165, 167, 169, 170, 171, 172, 173, 174, 175, 176, 177, 178, 180, 186, 188, 189, 190, 191, 192, 194, 216, 229, 230, 233, 249, 282.
Mahayana, 124.
Makkhali Gosala, 5, 10, 186, 188, 189, 192.
Malla, 59, 163, 165, 203, 206, 221, 228, 229, 230, 233, 234, 270, 272, 278, 280, 281, 282, 283.
Mallinath, 21, 57, 150, 155, 176.
Mantras, 144.
Mauryan Period, 225, 247.
Mauryan Rule, 224.
Military Campaigns, 209.
Munisuvrata, 22, 63, 70.
Murtipujaka, 157, 158.

N

Nami Natha, 65.
Neminath, 22, 66, 67, 180.
New Religious Ideas, 1, 2, 201, 202.
New Religious Movements, 201.
Nomenclature, 275.

P

Padmaprabha, 42.
Pakudha Kaccayana, 194.
Panchala, 203, 206, 212, 214, 220, 234, 237, 238, 240, 241, 242, 245, 246, 247, 248, 253, 270.
Parshva, 15, 43, 44, 67, 68, 69, 70, 73, 101, 147, 148, 180.
Period of Mahajanpadas, 203.
Praunavyakaranani, 177.
Purana Kassapa, 7, 186, 187, 190, 191.
Purvas, 100, 101, 167, 168, 169, 170, 178.
Pushpadanta, 45.

Q

Quotations, 8, 187, 199.

R

Rajgir, 228, 274, 279, 281, 282, 283.

References in Mahabharata, 207, 218, 219, 224.
Relativity, 72, 77, 82.
Religious Ideas, 1, 2, 201, 202.
Republics, 204, 205, 252, 253, 254, 256, 257, 258, 259, 260, 263, 265, 266, 268, 269, 270, 271, 279.
Rigveda, 227, 242, 250.
Rishabha, 22, 23, 24, 34, 73, 221.

S

Samantabhadra, 83, 87, 151, 164.
Samavayanga, 167, 174, 175, 178.
Sambhavanath, 37.
Samhita, 66, 229, 251, 253.
Sanchi, 165.
Sanjaya Belatthaputta, 191.
Sarnath, 47.
Shakya, 203, 231.
Shantinath, 52, 54, 55.
Shatapatha Brahmana, 242, 244.
Sheetalnath, 46, 47.
Shreyansanath, 47.
Shvetambar Accounts, 58.
Speculations on Origins, 242.
Sravasti, 162, 217, 218.
Sthananga, 172, 173, 174, 175.
Sumatinath, 39, 40, 42.
Suparshvanath, 43, 44.
Surasena, 206, 212, 214, 217, 220, 234, 248, 284.
Sutrakrtanga, 86, 171.
Svetambara, 21, 22, 68, 74, 102, 103, 106, 107, 110, 111, 134, 135, 141, 150, 151, 152, 154, 155, 156, 158, 159, 163, 167, 171, 172, 174.

T

Tapa Gachchha, 155, 156, 157, 158.
Taran Panth, 152, 159.
Tattvartha Sutra, 74, 181.
Terapanth, 80, 96, 141, 151, 152, 153, 155, 156, 157, 158, 159.
The Atharvaveda, 240, 250.
The Rigveda, 250.
The Yajurveda, 7, 36, 67.
Tristutik, 155, 157, 158.
Tristutik Gachchha, 155, 158.

U

Upanishad, 8, 10, 14, 67, 79, 97, 284.
Upasakadauah, 176.

V

Vaishali, 228, 229.
Vamsa or Vatsa, 238.
Vasishtha, 233.
Vasupujya, 22, 48, 49.
Vimalnath, 49, 50.
Vinaya Pitaka, 233.
Vipakauruta, 177.
Vyakhyaprajnapti, 175.

Y

Yajurveda, 7, 36, 73.
Yapaniya, 151, 159, 161, 163.

□□□